Matisse

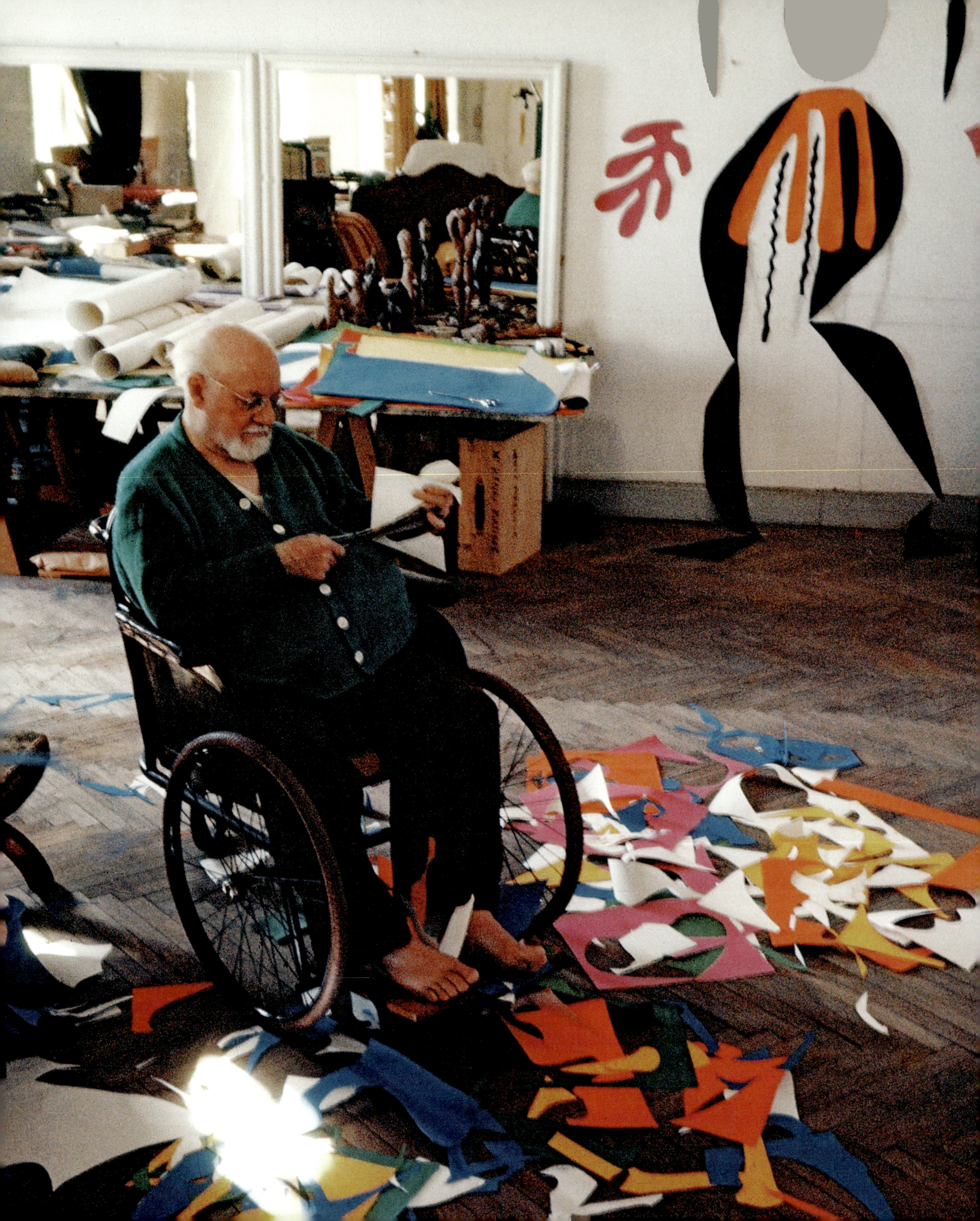

Gilles Néret

Henri Matisse

1869–1954

Cut-outs

TASCHEN

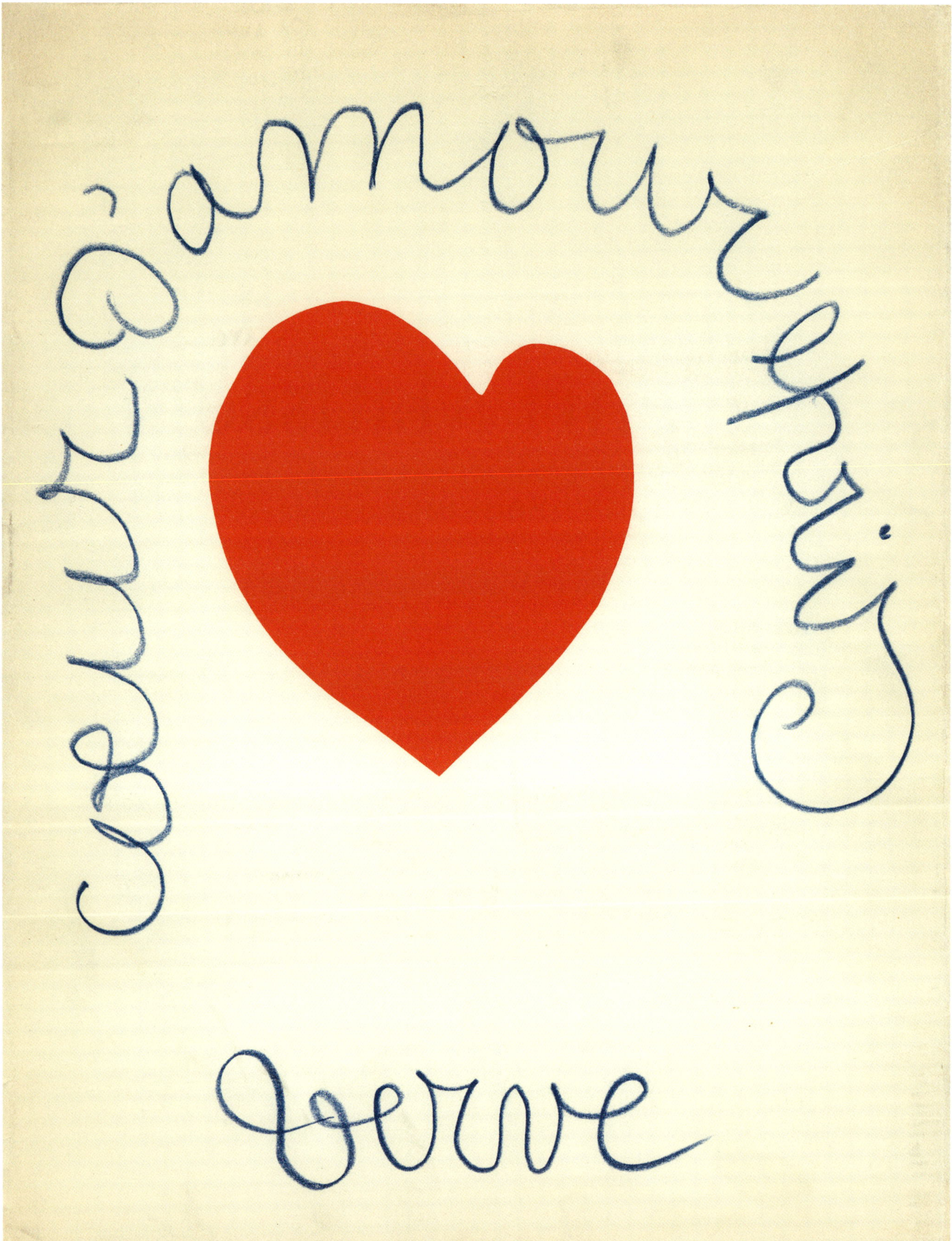
cœur d'amour épris
verve

Contents

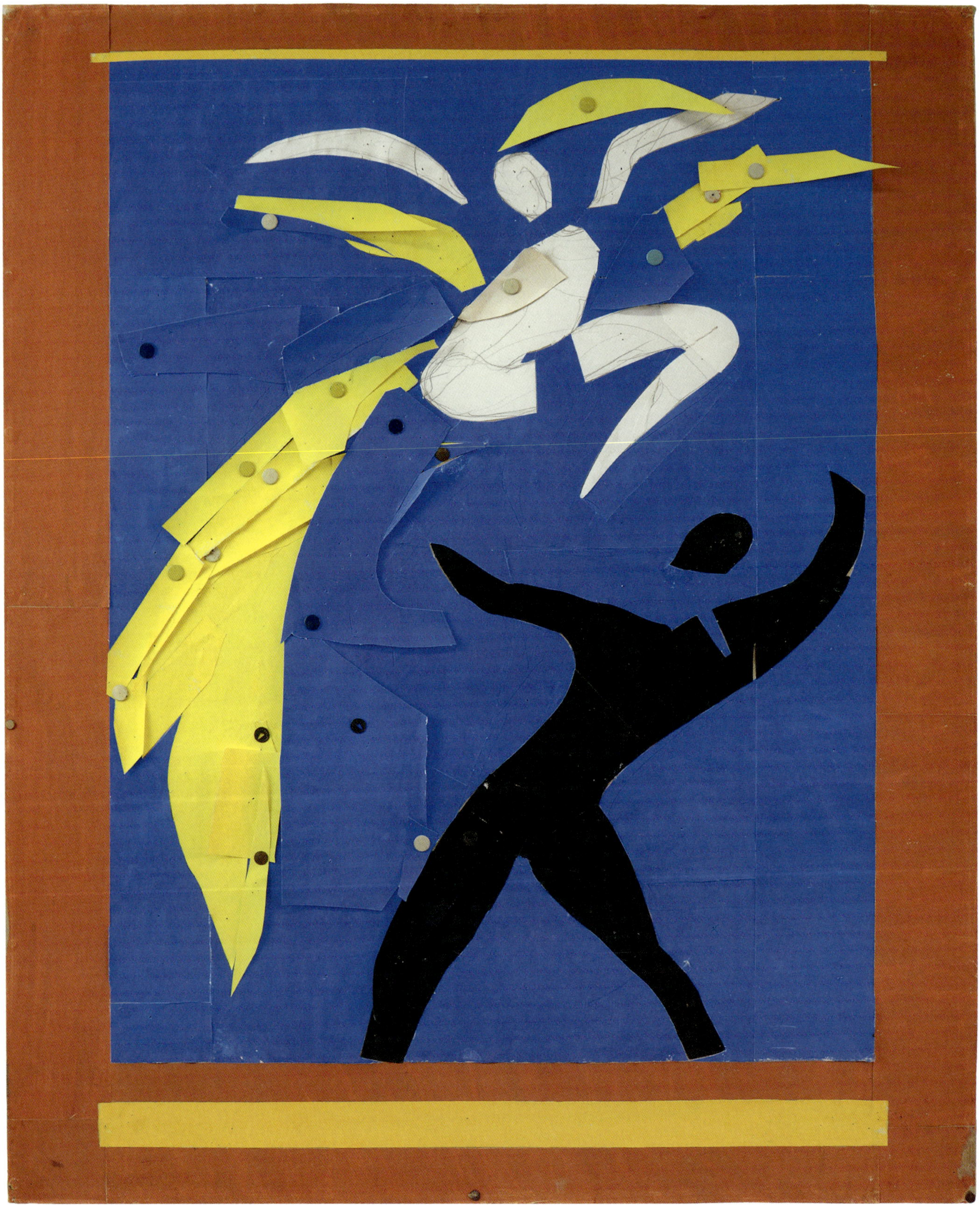

"You have to know how to preserve that freshness and innocence a child has when it approaches things"

"South Pole, North Pole": thus Picasso is said to have defined the century's two most illustrious painters, those who played the greatest role in 20th-century painting. Matisse and Picasso were indeed great rivals, their relations over half a century founded on discreet friendship, if not complicity. The poet of colour found his counterpart in the breaker of forms. "I feel through colour", said Matisse, "so my pictures will always be organised by it. Yet this requires that the sensations be condensed and that the means employed be brought to their utmost expressivity."

One of the hallmarks of a truly great artistic œuvre is that it never stops at the discoveries it has made but immediately sets out in new directions. Furthermore, when an artist uses all the forms of expression – painting, drawing, and sculpture – simultaneously, this can lead to disorientation. For Matisse, in his quest to refine form and exalt colour, the end justified the means, and he offered revolutionary solutions under the guise of classical appearances in the best tradition of French painting. It is this apparently innocuous revolutionary aspect that some still fail to perceive: this poised art, full of purity and calm mastery, this "joy in painting the beauty of the universe" that stand out so clearly in an epoch when the absurd, the unquiet, the "convulsive" reigned supreme. The gouache cut-outs from the end of his life have also been misunderstood. They have been taken for the last hobby of a crippled old man, whereas they are, like Matisse's *Chapelle du Rosaire at Vence* (pp. 56–63), "the end-product of an entire life of work and the flowering of an enormous, sincere, and difficult effort", of a life devoted to exalting colour and evoking the happiness of living and painting, which were, for him, inseparable. For the gouache cut-outs are continuous with a purpose from which the artist never departed after he had found himself as a fauve: the work is born of the untrammeled confrontation of colours.

Around 1943, in Cimiez and later at Vence, in the sunlit South of France, Matisse felt that he had said all he had to say in painting. And he found colour difficult to manipulate because of his illness. It was then that he first had recourse to sheets of paper precoloured with gouache which he could cut to the shapes he desired. The result: the extraordinary *Jazz* album (published in 1947), "improvisations in colour and rhythm" – like those of a Louis Armstrong or a Charlie Parker – in which Matisse's memories of the circus, of popular stories and of his travels took form in vivid, violent images. To link them and to

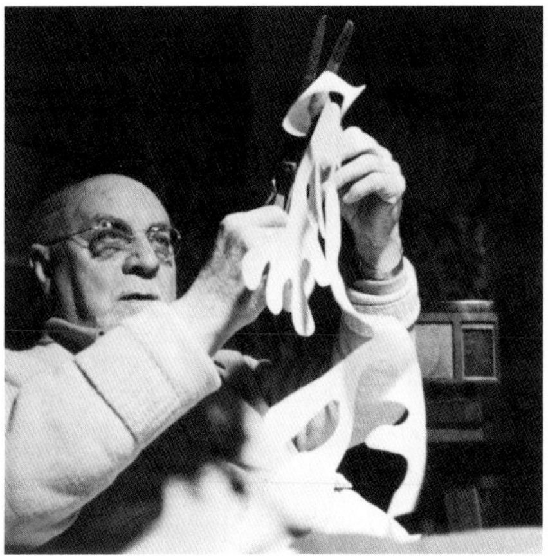

Henri Matisse working on his cut-outs, Vence, 1948

Two Dancers, 1937–38
Study for the curtain of the ballet *L'Étrange Farandole*
Pencil, gouache on paper, cut and pasted on cardboard, 80 x 64.4 cm (31½ x 25¼ in.)
Paris, Musée national d'art moderne, Centre Pompidou

The Dance, 1931–33
Oil on canvas, 3 plates
Left: 340 x 387 cm (134 x 152¼ in.)
Centre: 355 x 498 cm (139¾ x 196 in.)
Right: 333 x 391 cm (131 x 154 in.)
Musée d'art moderne de la Ville de Paris

To solve the problem presented by the composition of the enormous work for Dr Barnes, Matisse for the first time had the idea of cutting out pieces of coloured paper, which he could then move around at will, like a stage director, till he had found the right positions for them. Unfortunately, as there was an error in the dimensions specified, Matisse had to make a second version. There was a silver lining to this cloud for the Musée d'art moderne de la Ville de Paris, which possesses the first version.

mitigate the contrasts between them, Matisse wrote an accompanying text, in a large, harmonious script (pp. 32 and 48 top right), full of striking phrases: "Sculpting the living colour reminds me of the direct carving of the sculptors … My curves are not mad …"

Incredible man! He was now confined to his rocking chair or his bed and was, it might be thought, lost to painting. Yet he again found a way to transcend the art of drawing, grasping the desired opportunity to work towards a perfect synthesis of everything he had learnt. With nothing more than a pair of scissors and paper precoloured to precisely the shades that he had requested, he solved the problems of form and space, outline and colour, structure and orchestration which he had always sought to harmonize. Moreover, this new enterprise at last allowed him to accord full importance to line rhythms and to forms, which he had often in the past had to sacrifice to colours and tonal relations.

Here, realism and abstraction were reconciled at the endpoint of a long process that grew out of its own logic and not, as some defenders of abstract art have impudently asserted, out of carelessness or the temptation to climb onto some contemporary bandwagon. Matisse laid all ambiguity to rest when he wrote that he "drew in colour", and when he stated to André Lejard, "I am currently focusing on material more matt and more immediate, and this leads me to seek

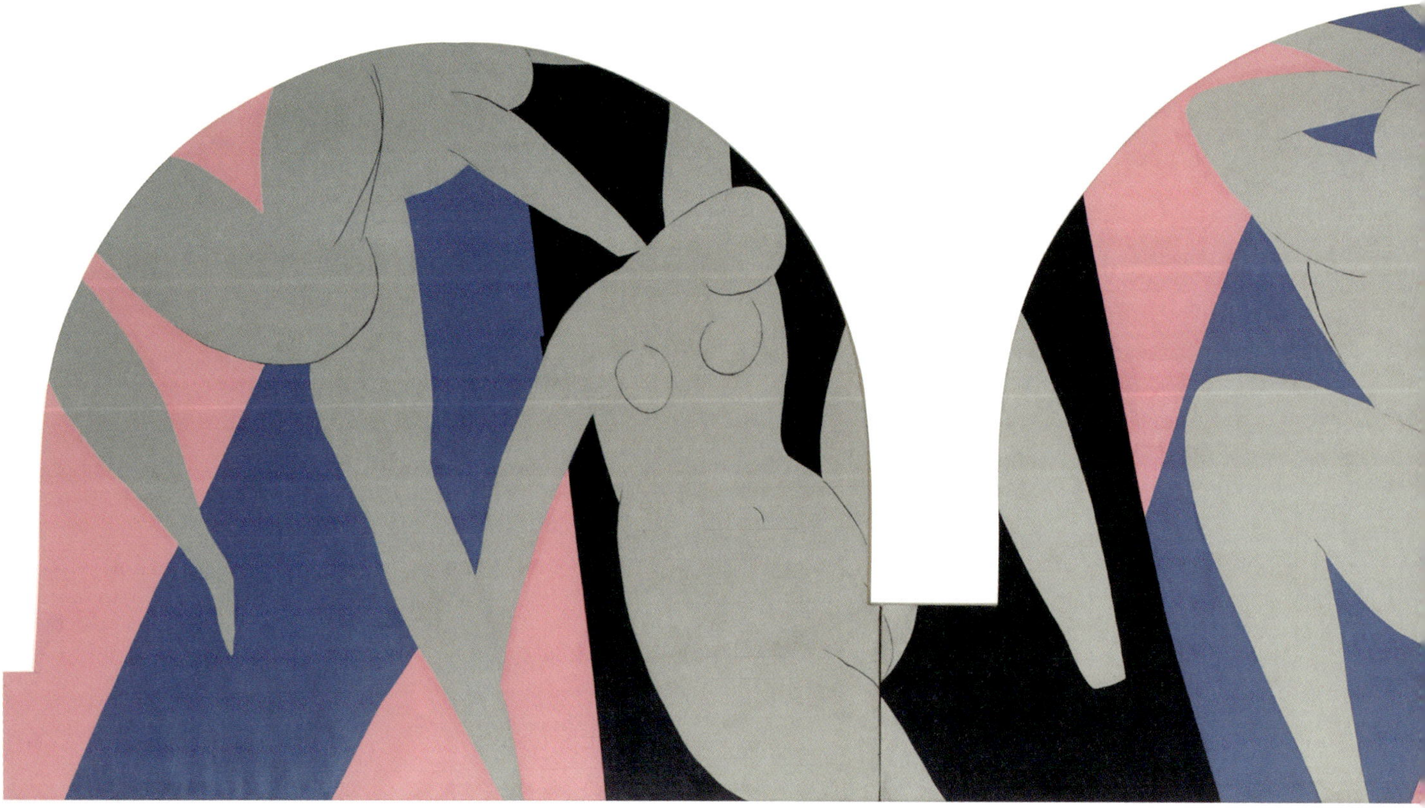

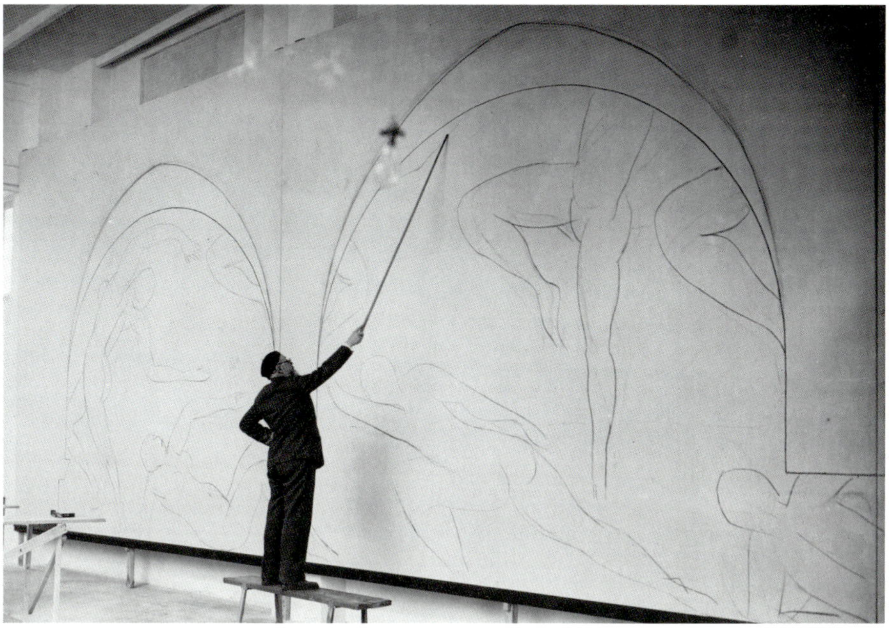

Matisse working on Dr Barnes' ***The Dance***,
Nice, 1931

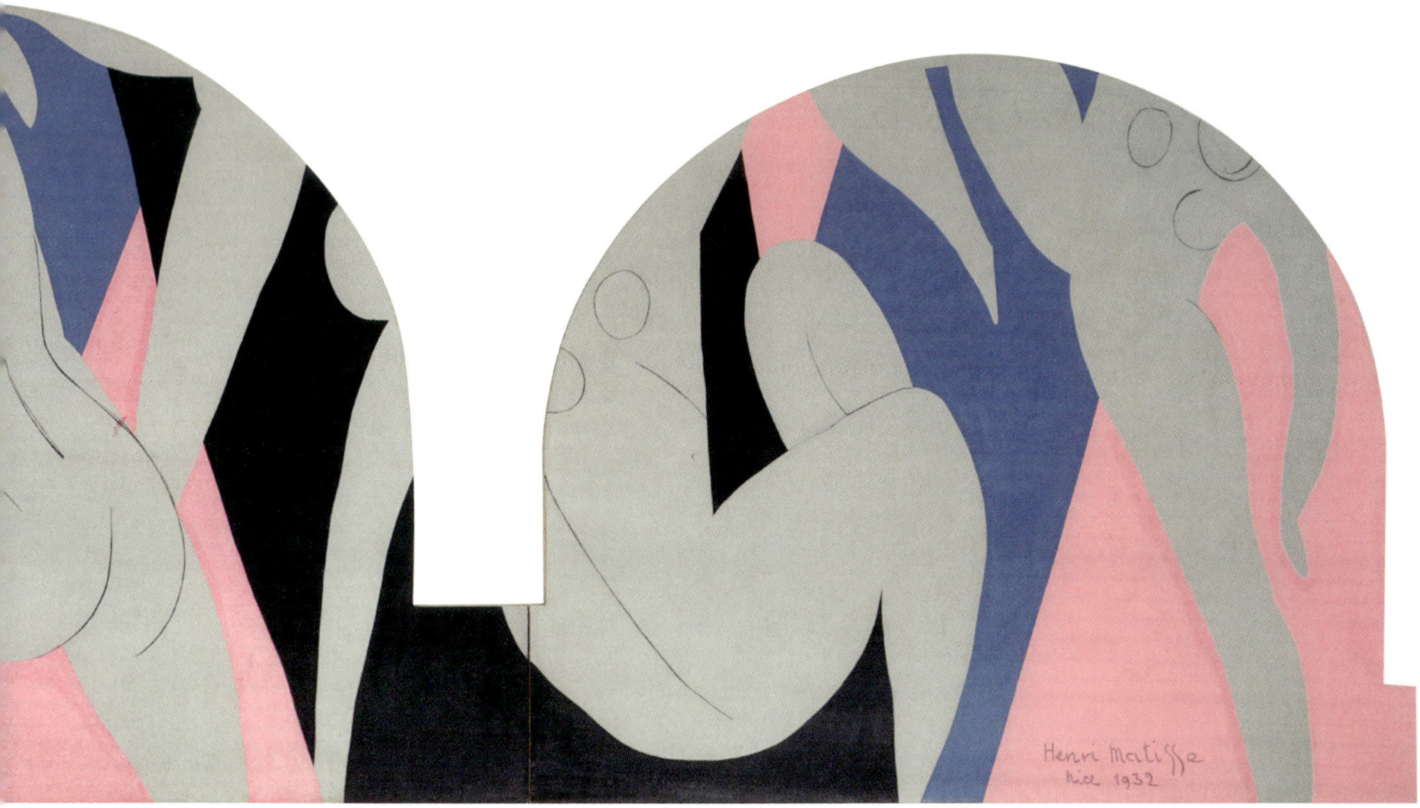

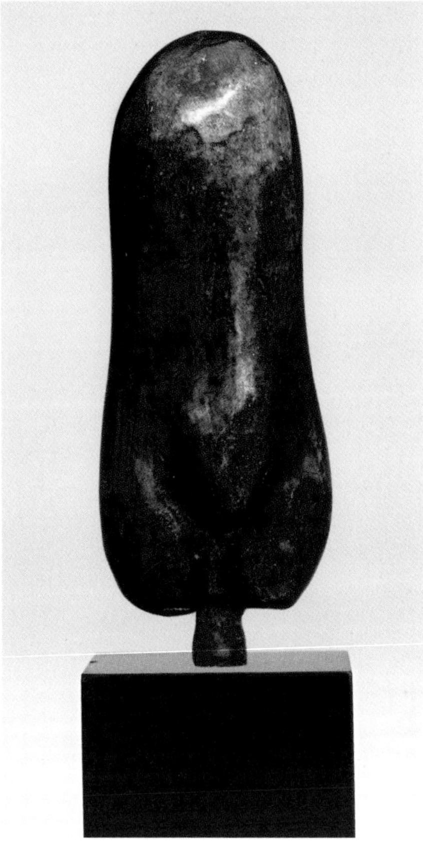

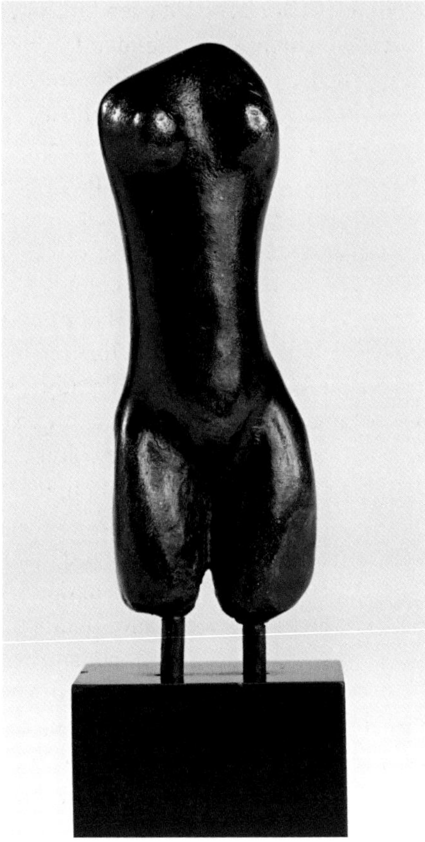

From modelling clay to carving directly into colour, Matisse's work is that of a sculptor …

LEFT
Small Torso, 1929
Bronze, height: 9.9 cm (4 in.)
San Antonio, McNay Art Museum

RIGHT
Small Thin Torso, 1929
Bronze, height: 8 cm (3¼ in.)
Nice, Musée Matisse

a new means of expression. Paper cut-outs allow me to draw in colour. For me it is a question of simplification. Instead of drawing the outline and establishing colour within it, I draw directly in the colour, which is more exact for not being transposed. This simplification guarantees precision; as I reconcile two means now become one … It is not a beginning, it is an endpoint."

Olympian amusement, twilight bedazzlement, the frivolity of the sage … hasty remarks and judgements about the painted paper cut-outs have proliferated. Indeed, Georges Duthuit acknowledges that there may be some truth in them, a truth "equally applicable to Goethe chatting with Eckermann or to the titanic author of *The Magic Mountain* leaving an unfinished picaresque novel". If there is, it is no less true to see in Matisse one of those "great artists grown old" of whom Barrès speaks, artists who, "hastening to explain themselves, contracting their means of expression as they shortened their signature", have attained "the concision of enigmas or epitaphs".

Despite the considerable international acclaim that greeted *Jazz*, Matisse was not at first satisfied. It was some time before he got used to the transposition by stencil printing to which his publisher Tériade subjected the cut-outs; they could not otherwise be reproduced. The technique is not perfectly accurate, but it has its use today, for some of the cut-outs have since faded, and we now look to Tériade's stencils for the truth of Matisse's colours. Matisse, in 1944, wrote to Tériade about *Jazz*, that "this twopenny ha'penny toy is wearing me out and my whole being revolts at its invasive growth!"

A grave difficulty faced the critics: this new way of painting could not be related to any that had come before. It was a new approach; it had never been used before. It could not even be compared to the Cubist collages (Picasso, p. 12 bottom), which were intended to present the spectacle of a geometry created from various and unexpected materials. Nor to the biomorphic signs of Arp or the abstract vocabulary of Kandinsky (p. 12 top). Yet it was enough to recall the early Matisse, the fauve who wanted a "work born of the untrammelled confrontation of colours". *The Dance* and *The Music* executed for Shchukin, and *The Dance* commissioned by Dr Barnes (pp. 8–9), the latter designed by pinning paper cut-outs, should have given the game away; all of these exhibited wide surfaces free of small-scale colour. As to sculpting in colour, we need only put the plate from *Jazz* entitled *White Torso and Blue Torso* (below) alongside the *Small Torso* and *Small Thin Torso* of 1929 (p. 10) to see how it is done.

Only a Matisse who had already mastered both sculpture and painting could be so daring as to apply the technique of the sculptor to the substance of painting, and carve a block of pure colour. It was all the more natural for him because drawing with a pair of scissors implied no real change in his aesthetic. "There is no discontinuity", he explained, "between my former paintings and my cut-outs; only with more absoluteness and more abstraction, I have attained a form filtered down to the essential, and, of the object that I formerly presented in the complexity of its space, I have retained the sign that is sufficient and necessary to make it exist in its own form and for the whole in which I have conceived it."

In a 1945 text for *Verve*, entitled "On Colour", Matisse wrote about Ingres and Delacroix: "Both express themselves by 'arabesques' and by 'colour'." He had discovered a point common to two very different painters. It was a point dear to his heart, and he detected it in others: "Gauguin and Van Gogh will later be

Forms. White Torso and Blue Torso,
Jazz, 1943
Stencil
Lille, Palais des Beaux-Arts

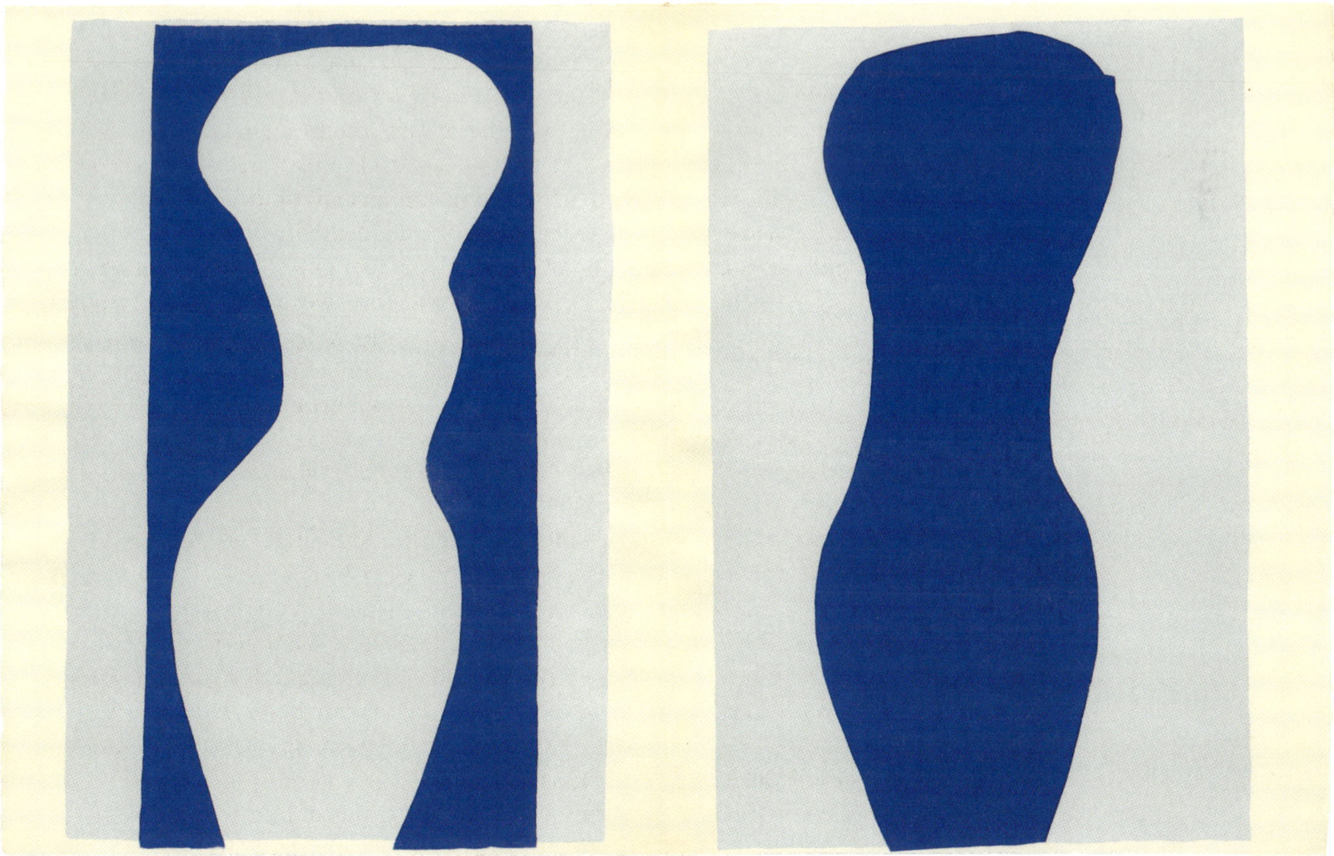

Wassily Kandinsky
Succession, 1935
Oil on canvas, 80.9 x 100 cm (32 x 39¼ in.)
Washington, D.C., The Phillips Collection

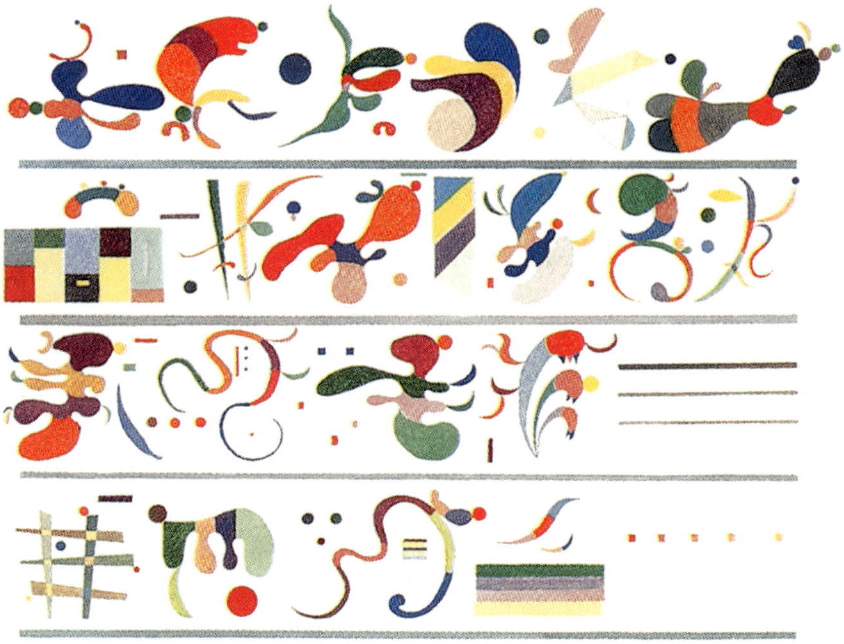

seen to have lived by the same rhythm: arabesques and colour!" But before Matisse, no-one had taken the association between colour and arabesques so far, to the point of reducing the canvas to these two modes of expression. Till then, the draughtsman and colourist had complemented each other in a more or less equal partnership; now they could work together on an equal footing, in an osmosis in which each maintained the autonomy of his vision. In this way, Matisse remade for himself Braque's dictum that "Form and colour do not merge; there is simultaneity".

The artist confided to Alfred Barr that, no longer able to move or swim, he had, thanks to his gouache cut-outs, surrounded himself with water and extraordinary gardens, pinning the maquettes of his works to the walls of his apartment and spending his days contemplating and transforming them. These are scenes and landscapes that go "beyond" any scene or landscape and even any "work". The "beyond" evoked by the last works took the form of that poignant and yet serene adieu *The Sorrows of the King* (pp. 82–83). This picture is the last great pictorial effort by Matisse to be made in pasted gouache cut-outs. It is the last salute by the artist – who is represented by the sombrely clad king, guitar in hand – to the world around him, to the themes he loved. Matisse has drawn them all around him, down to the last woman dancer, as if to have himself buried with them like an Ancient Egyptian Pharaoh. "You are going to simplify painting!" The prediction of his master, Gustave Moreau, had been fulfilled to the letter, in the brass fanfares of Fauvism and in the final sustained chord of the cut-outs. At the approach of death, Matisse was proud that he "could at last sing like a child following the impulses of his heart from the top of the mountain he has climbed". As Baudelaire had already stated: "Genius is just childhood to which one can return at will."

But let us leave the last word to Matisse himself, writing, at 83, to his dear friend Rouveyre: "My survival in my works … that I desire … I never think of it, for, having thrown the ball as best I could, I cannot be certain whether it will fall on land or sea or into that precipice from which nothing ever returns."

Pablo Picasso
Guitar, 1913
Glued paper, 66.4 x 49.6 cm (26¼ x 19½ in.)
New York, The Museum of Modern Art

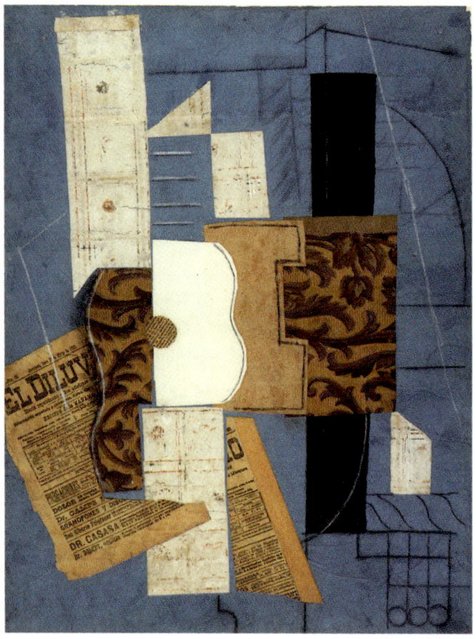

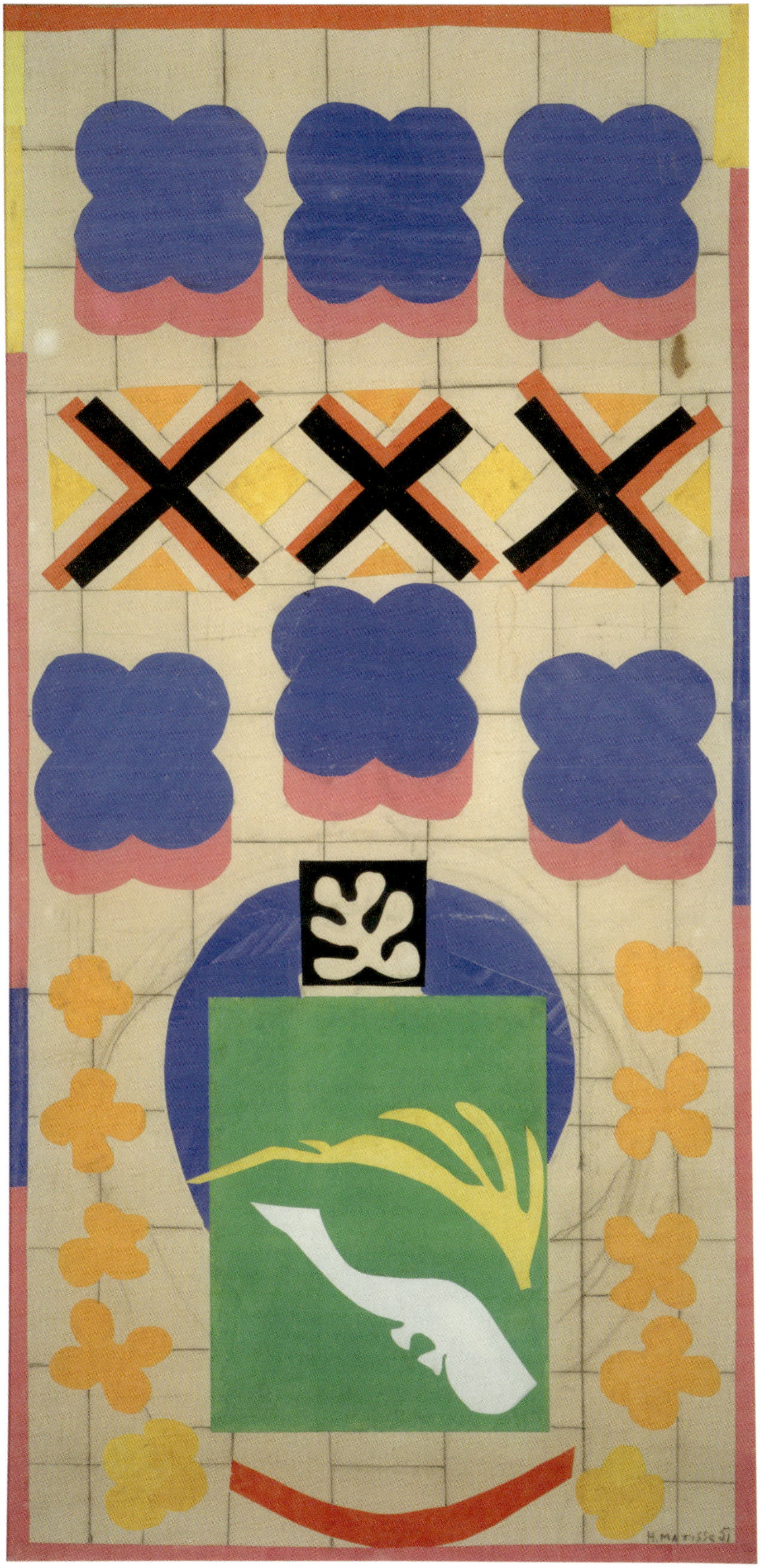

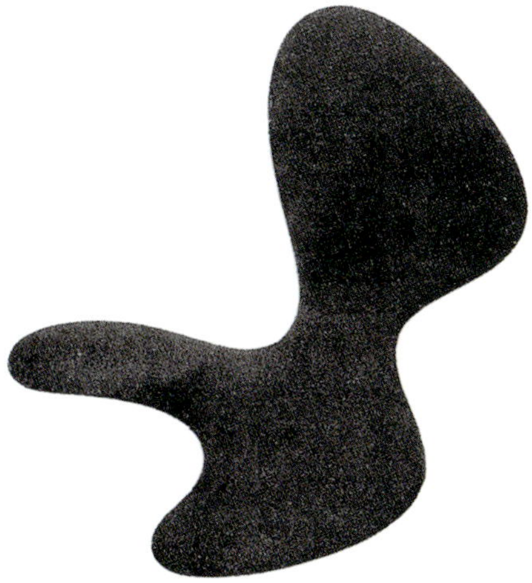

Jean Arp
Collage, 1941–42
Collage and oil, 18.5 x 24.6 cm (7¼ x 9¾ in.)
Kunstmuseum Basel

Chinese Fish, 1951
Maquette for the stained-glass window for Tériade's villa in Saint-Jean-Cap-Ferrat
Gouache on paper, cut and pasted on paper
192.2 x 91 cm (75¾ x 36 in.)
Private collection

Matisse's method was entirely new. It had never been used before. It cannot be categorized; it is neither Cubist (Picasso) nor abstract (Kandinsky) nor Dadaist (Arp).

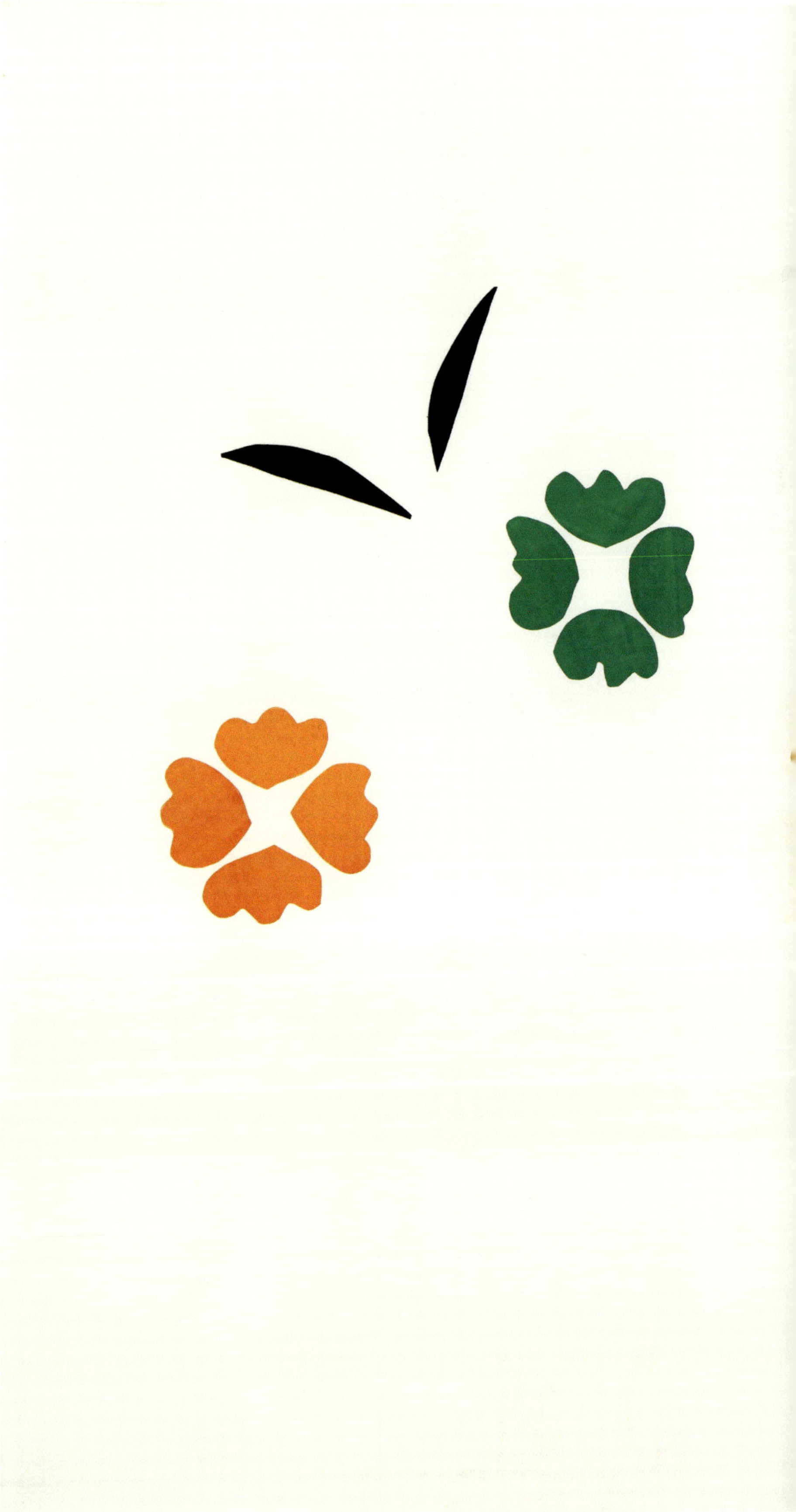

La Négresse, 1952
Paper collage on canvas, 453.9 x 623.3 cm
(178¾ x 245½ in.)
Washington, D.C., National Gallery of Art,
Ailsa Mellon Bruce Fund

This is the black dancer, Josephine Baker, queen of the Roaring Twenties and Thirties, famous for appearing on stage wearing nothing but a belt of bananas.

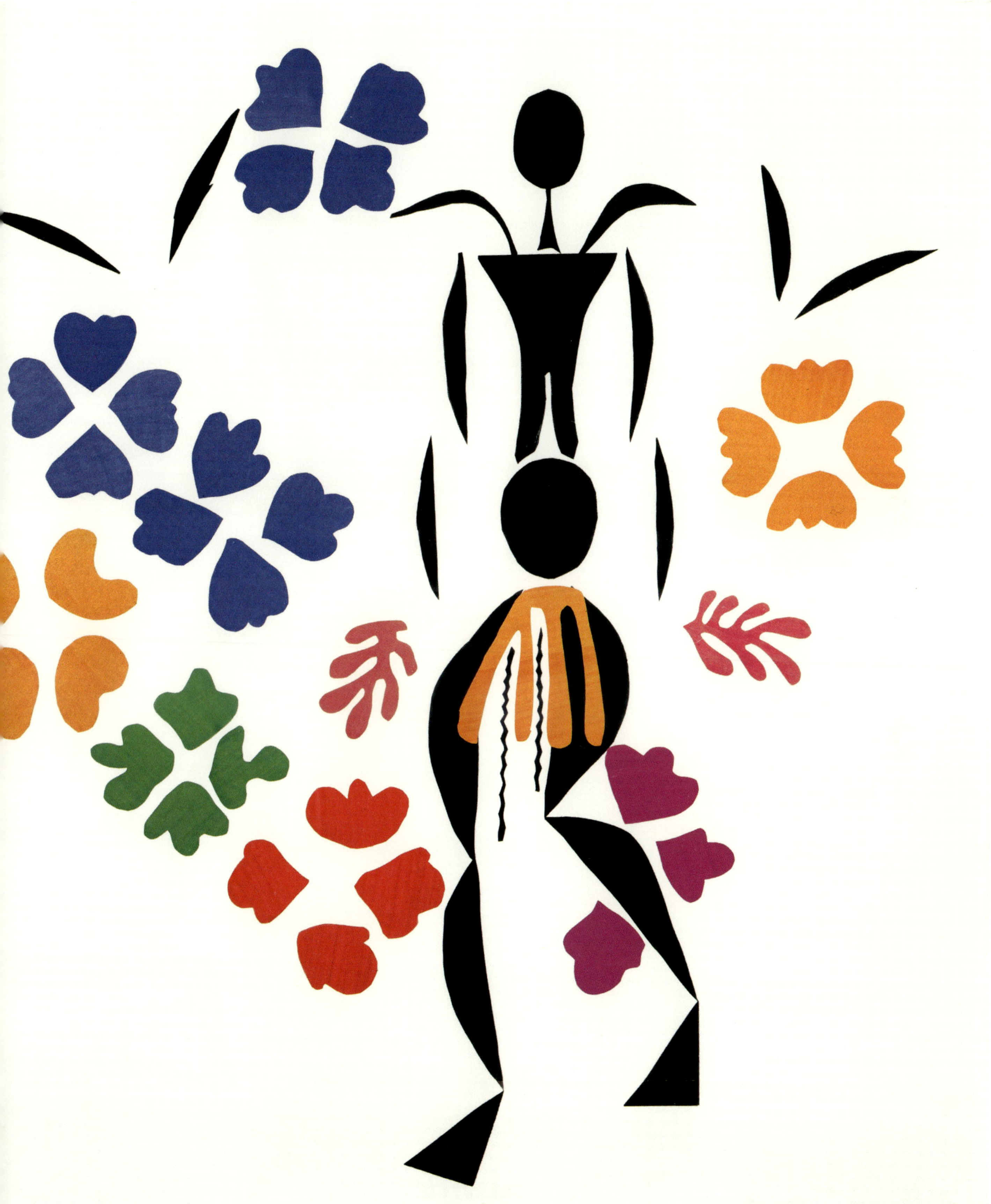

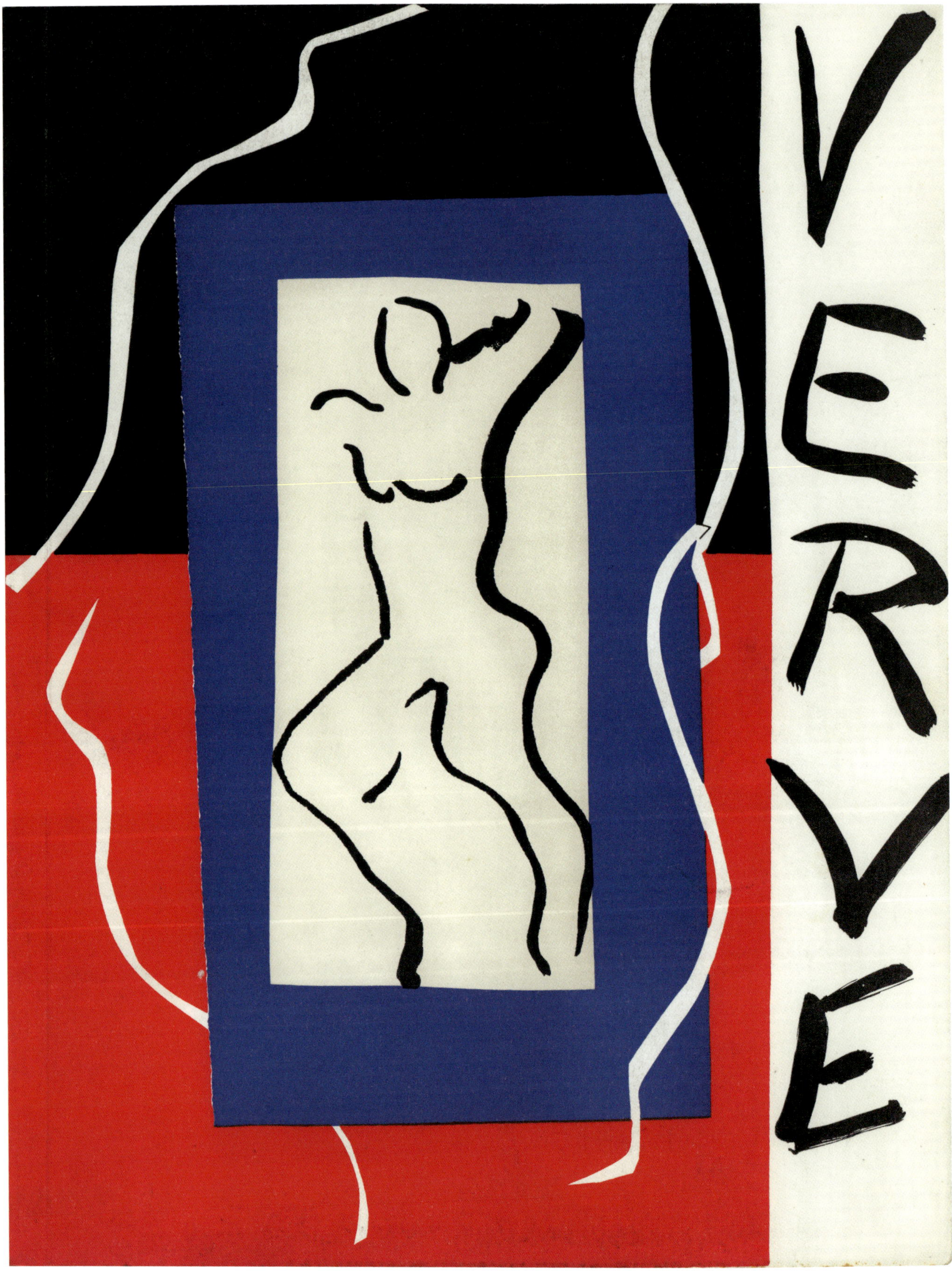
VERVE

An Ideal: Life Itself

Matisse, the famous painter, and Tériade, the as yet little known publisher of *Verve*, shared an ideal: for both, painting was life itself. Hence the enthusiasm with which Matisse created this cover (p. 16), cutting out its elements from printing-press samples. He himself executed the calligraphy with paintbrush and Indian ink. Tériade then lithographed the composition in the workshops of Fernand Mourlot.

Matisse's fear that his intentions would be betrayed by colour printing were assuaged by the success of the thirteenth number of *Verve* (pp. 18–19). Thus fortified, his collaboration with Tériade continued for over two years, during which the *Jazz* project was conceived, along with plans for illustrations to *The Portuguese Nun* and *Charles d'Orléans*.

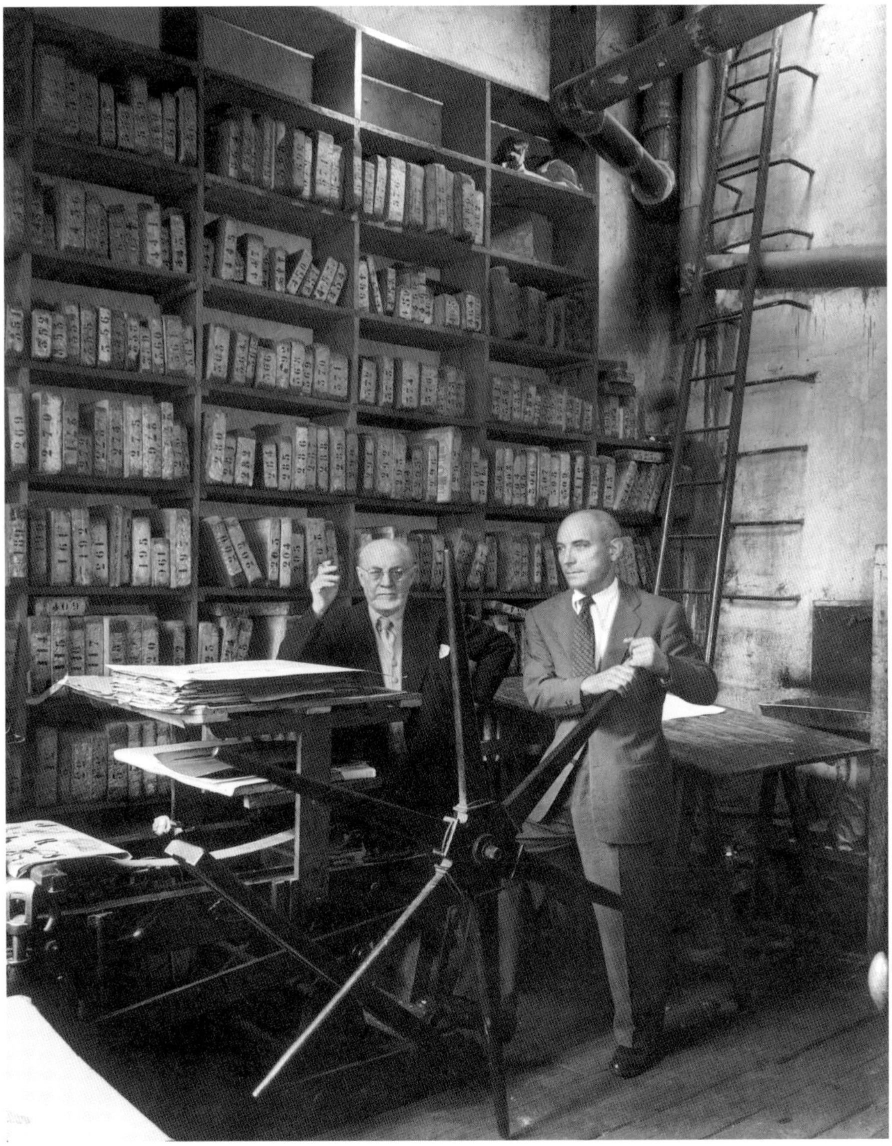

Henri Matisse at Mourlot's lithography workshop (with the director, Fernand Mourlot)
Photo: Hélène Adant

***Verve*, No. 1**, December 1937
Front cover

PAGES 18–19
***Verve*, No. 13**, November 1945
Front and back cover

PAGES 20–21
***Symphonie chromatique*,** cover maquette for the journal *Verve*, vol. II, no. 8 (1940), 1939
Coloured papers, cut and pasted
35.2 x 55.3 cm (14 x 21¾ in.)

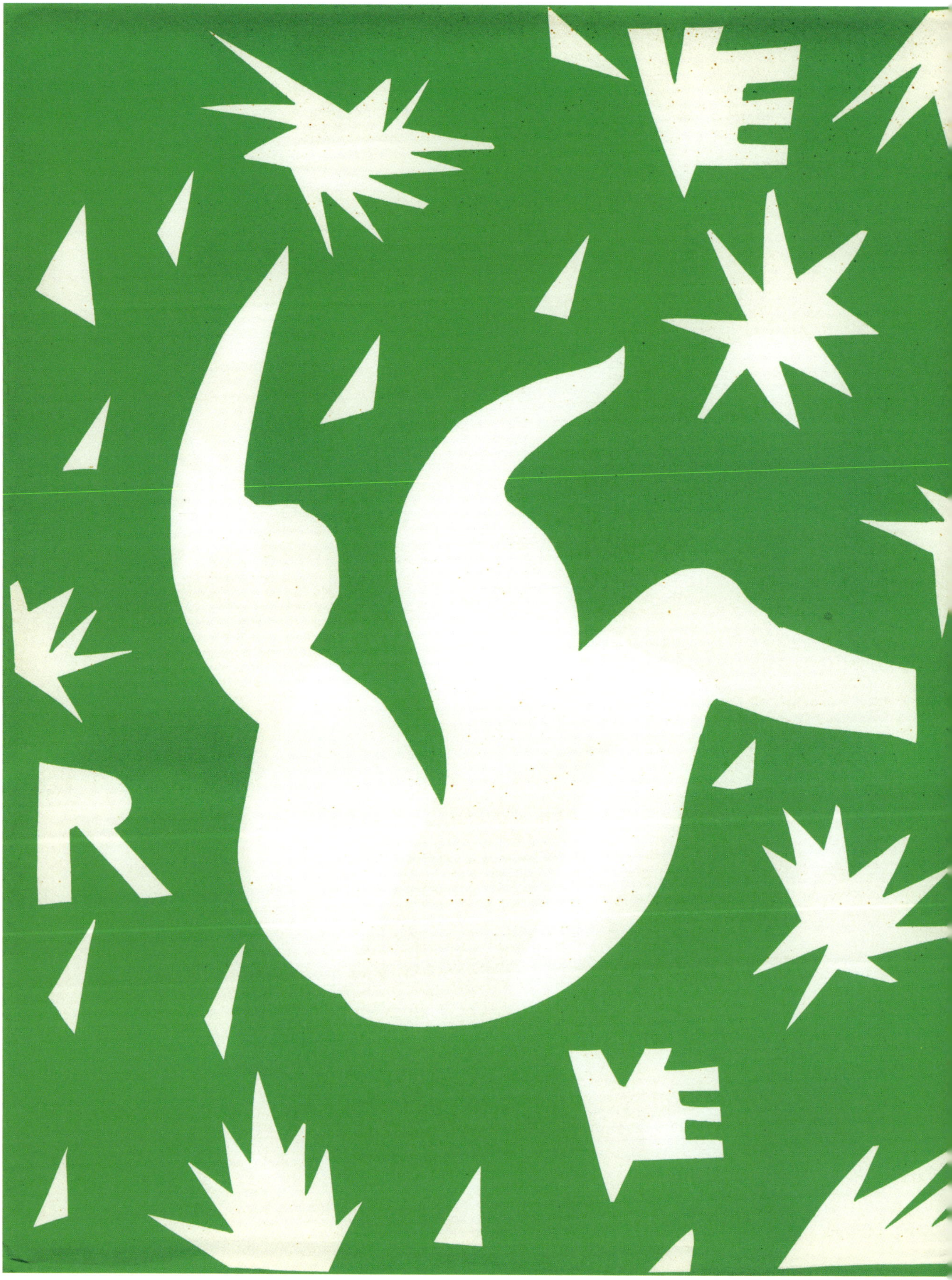

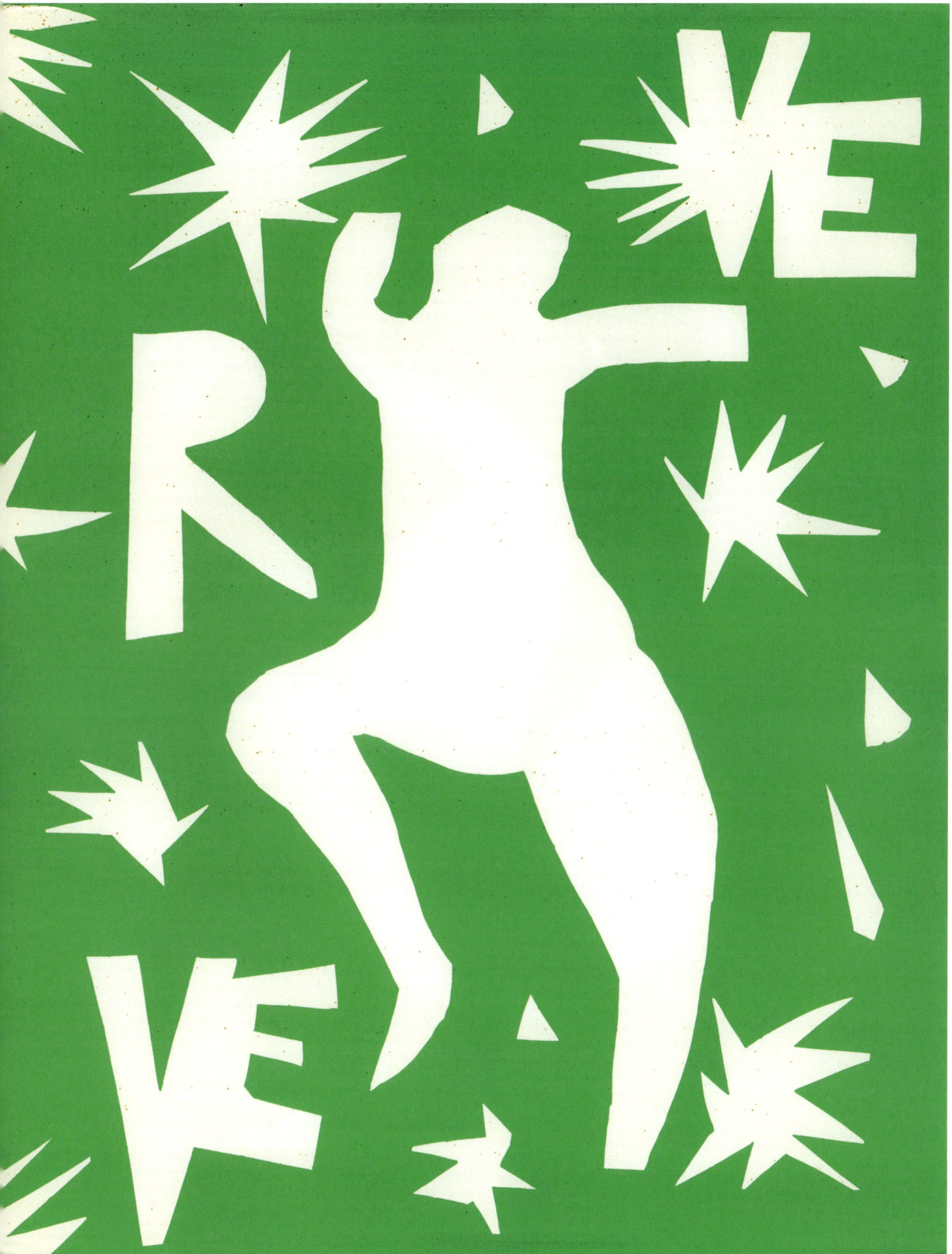
RÊVE
VE

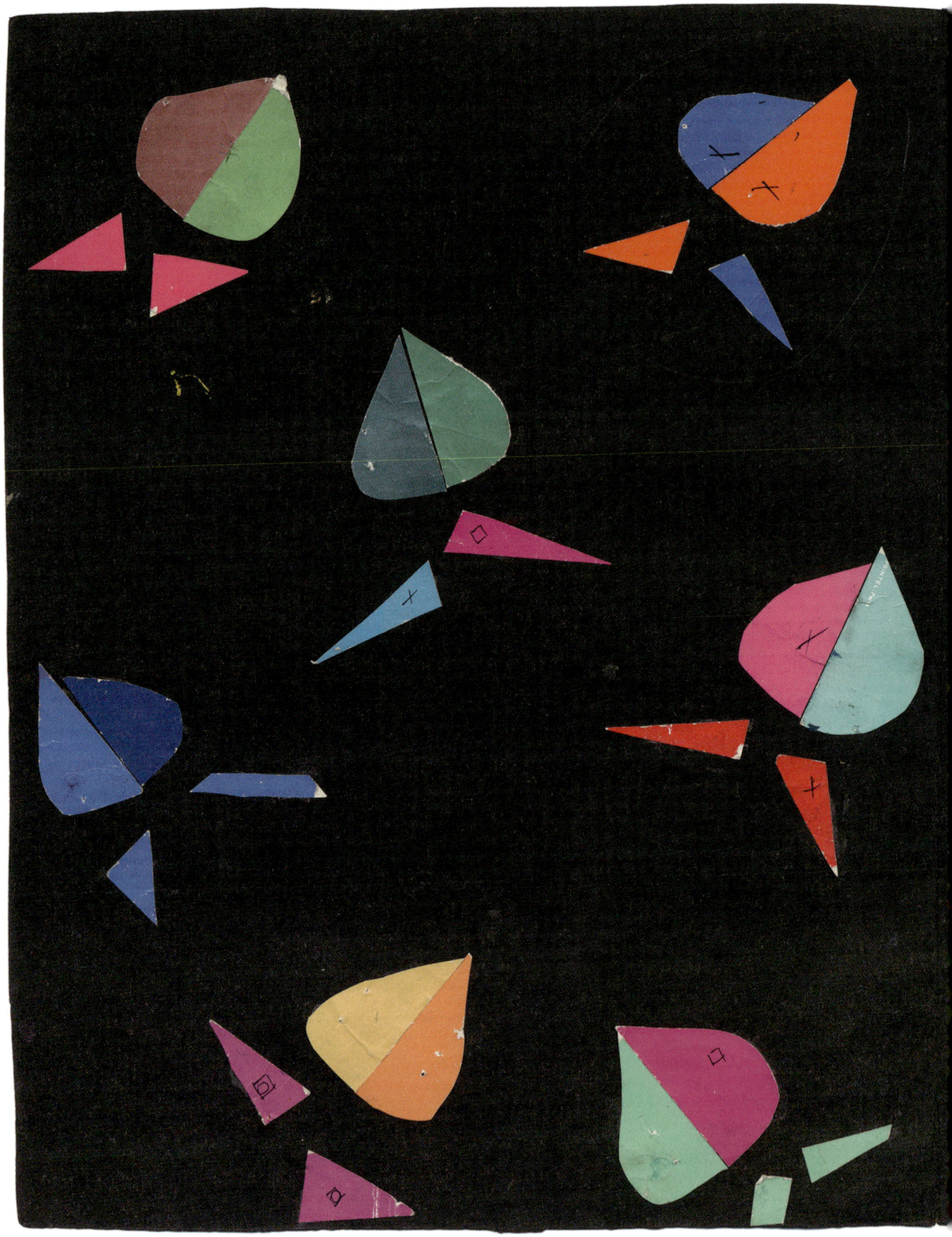

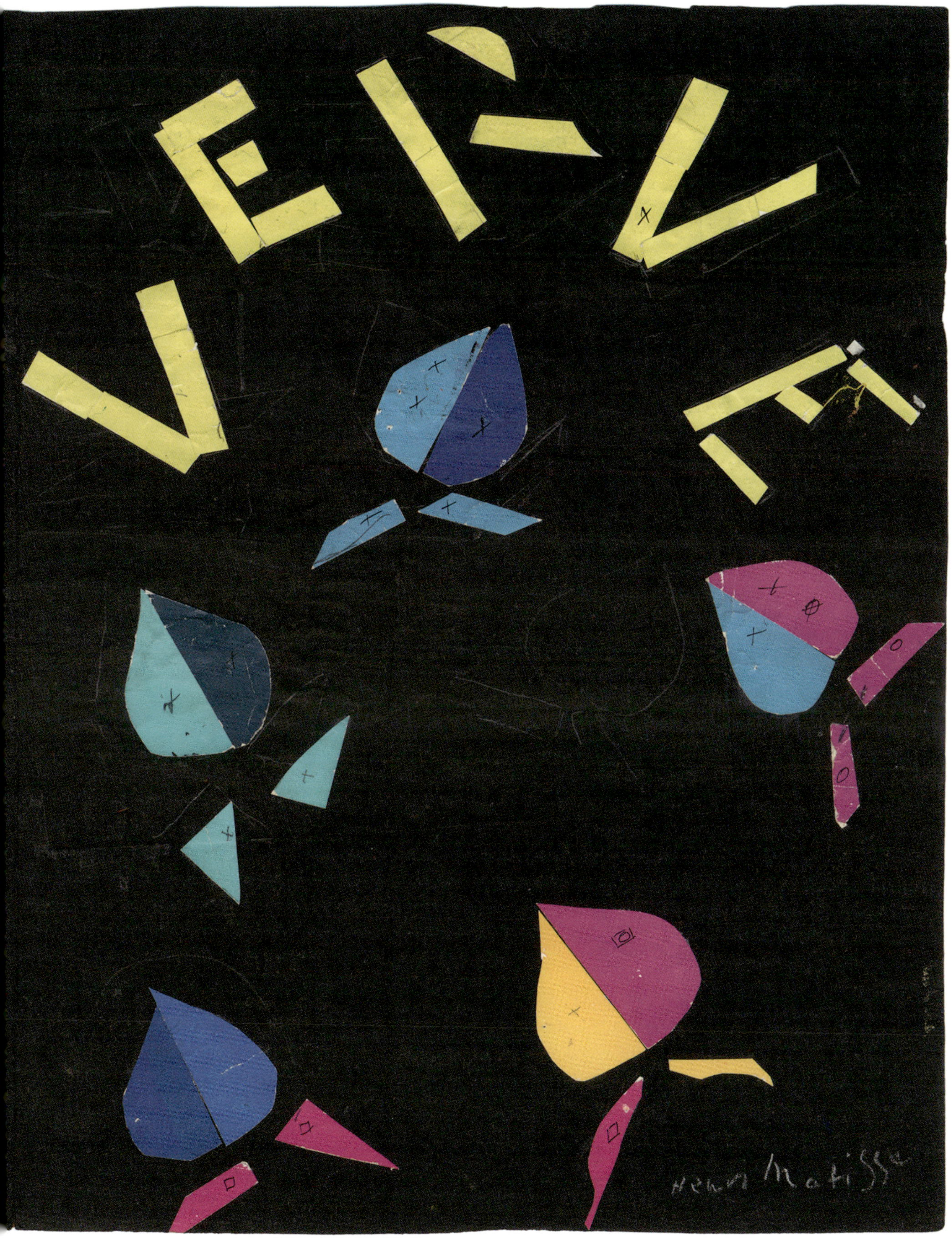
VERVE
Henri Matisse

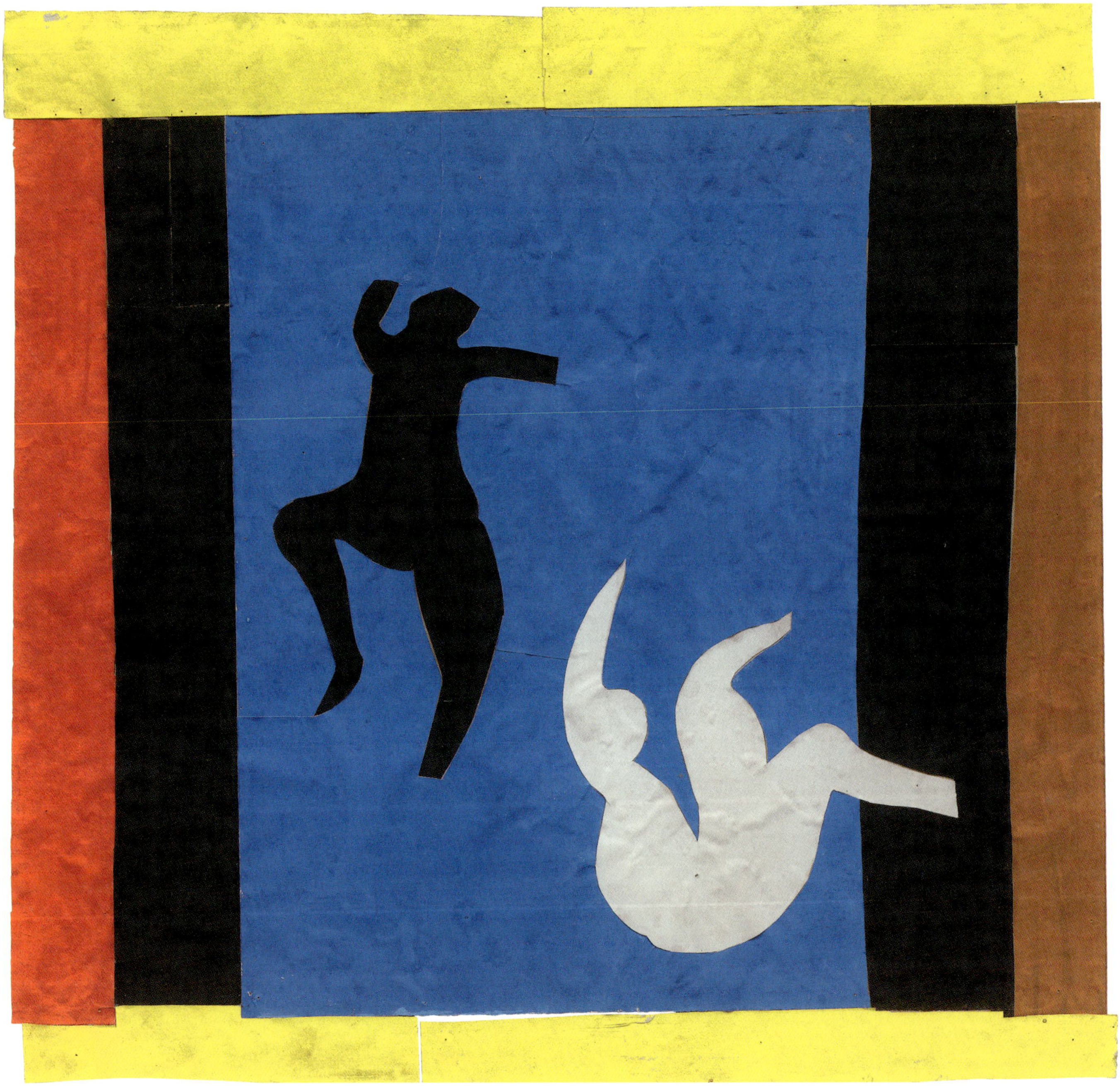

Two Dancers, 1937–38
Study for the curtain of the ballet
L'Étrange Farandole
Gouache on paper, cut and pasted on paper
61 x 62 cm (24 x 24½ in.)
Private collection

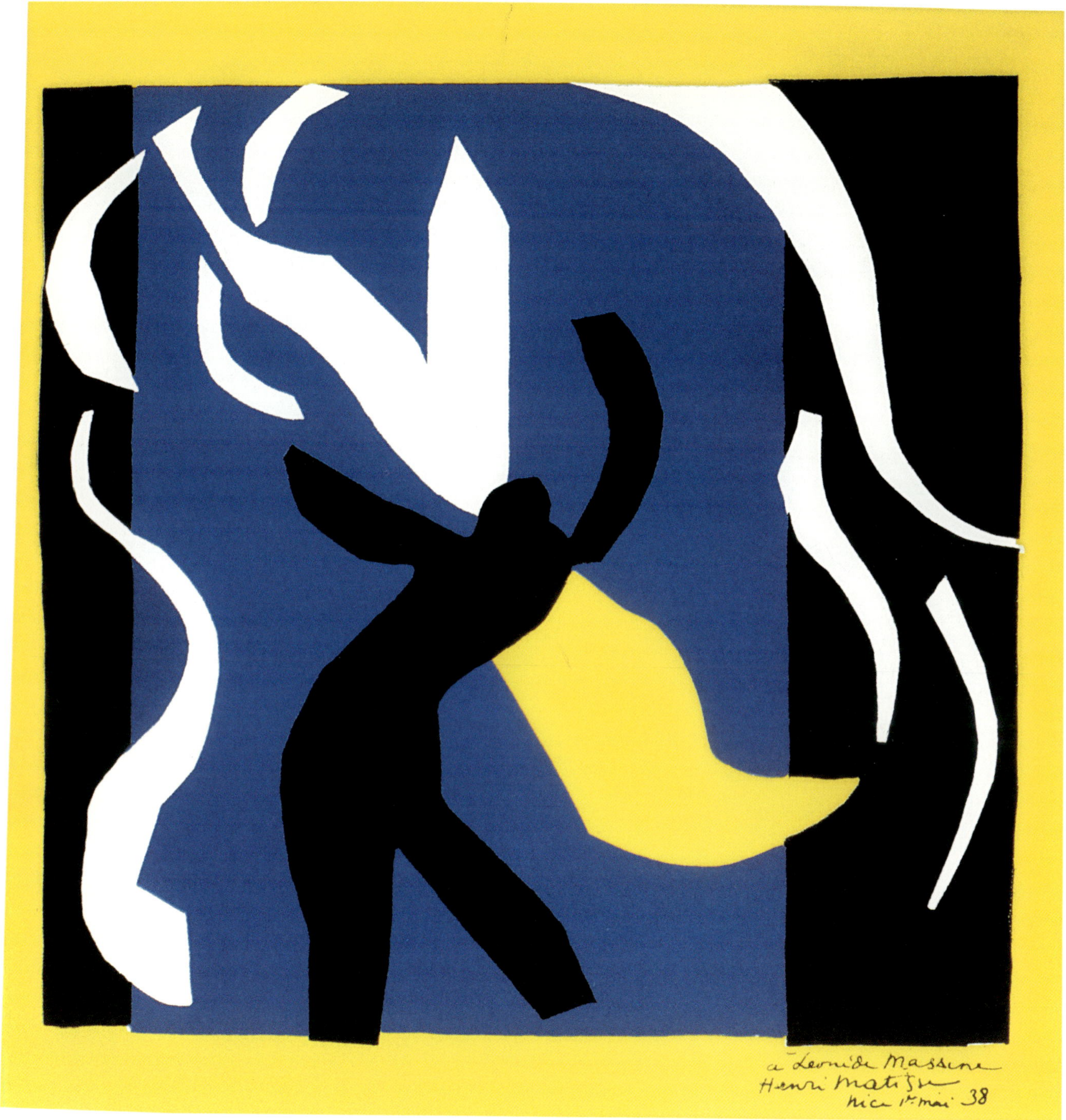

Dancer, 1937–38
Study for the curtain of the ballet
L'Étrange Farandole
Gouache on paper, cut and pasted on paper
61 x 61 cm (24 x 24 in.), private collection
Lithographic reproduction of the original
paper cut-out

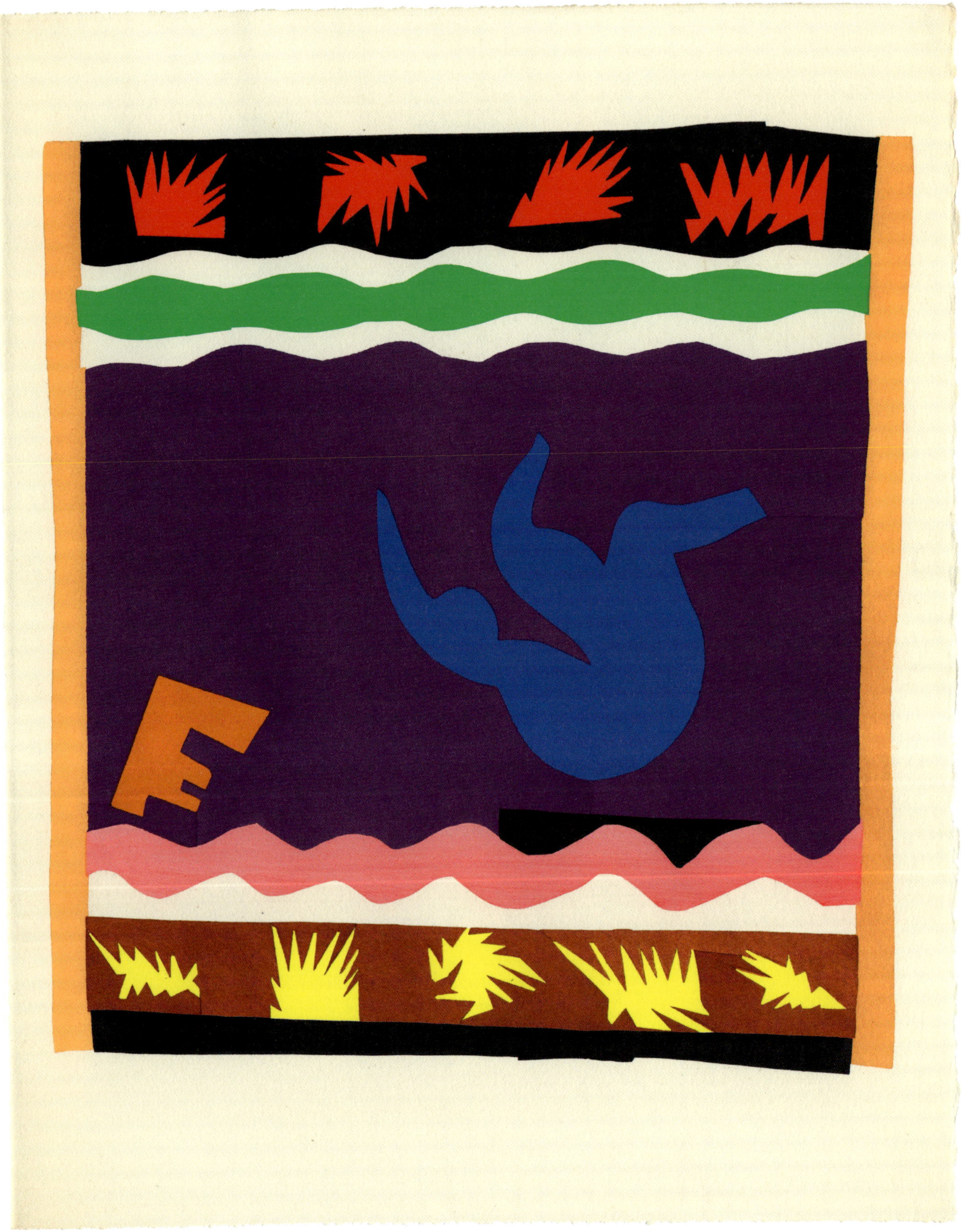

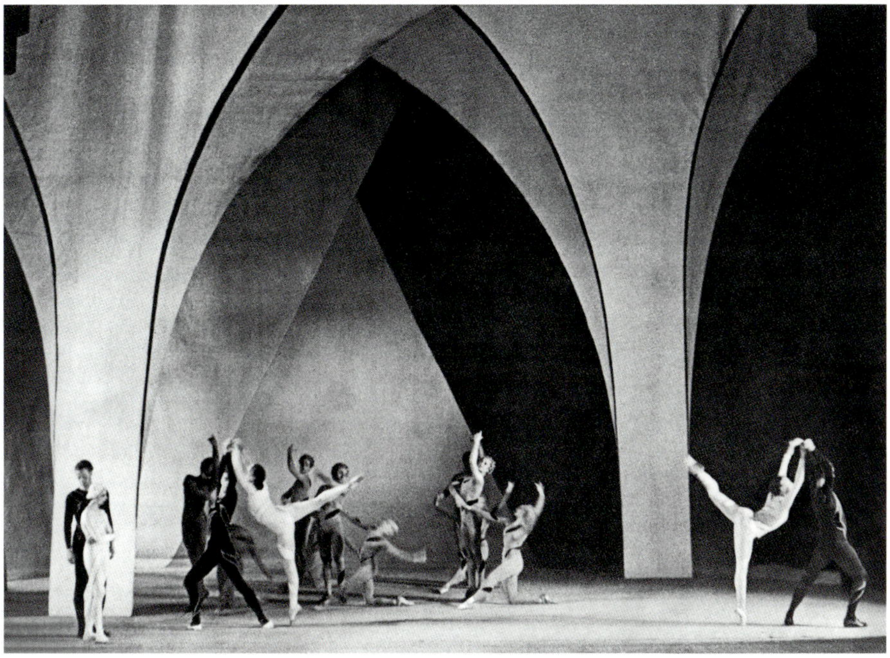

L'Étrange Farandole was premiered in Monte Carlo by the Ballets Russes. The score was the 2nd Symphony of Shostakovich, the choreography was by Léonide Massine and the costumes by Matisse. The ballet's subject was the eternal struggle between spirit and matter. A couple of dancers were clad in white by Matisse to symbolize the spirit of poetry resisting the attacks of black or red figures symbolizing brutal and evil forces. Man succeeds in dominating them temporarily before succumbing to his "Destiny".

Programme cover and drawing for the costumes for the ballet *L'Étrange Farandole*

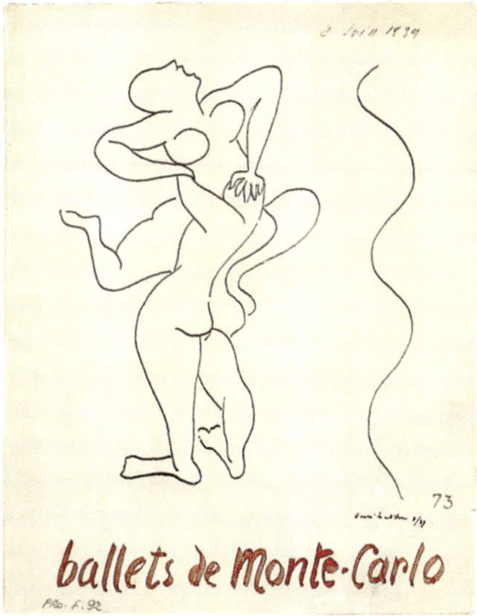

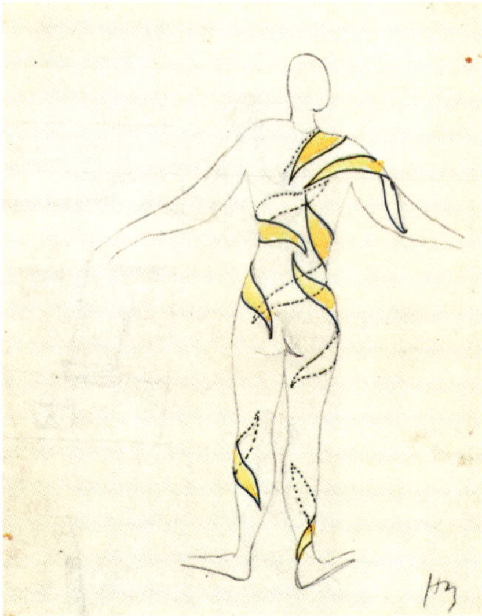

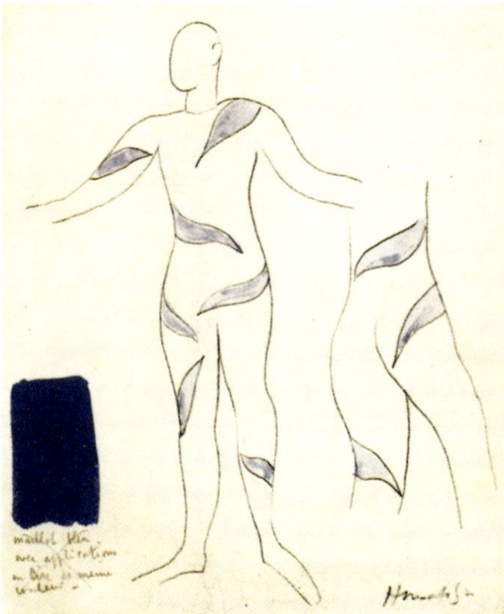

The Toboggan, *Jazz*, 1943
Stencil

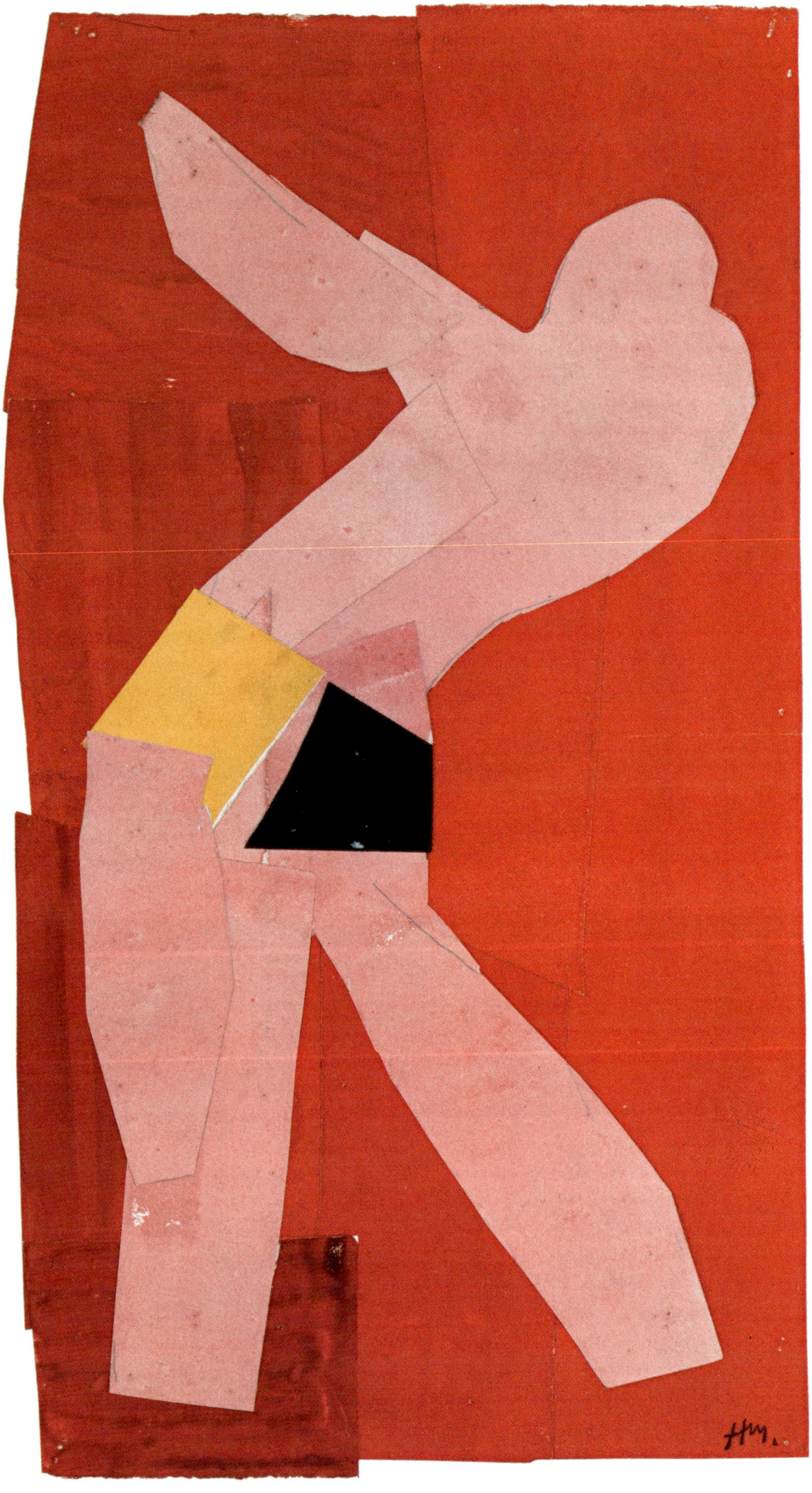

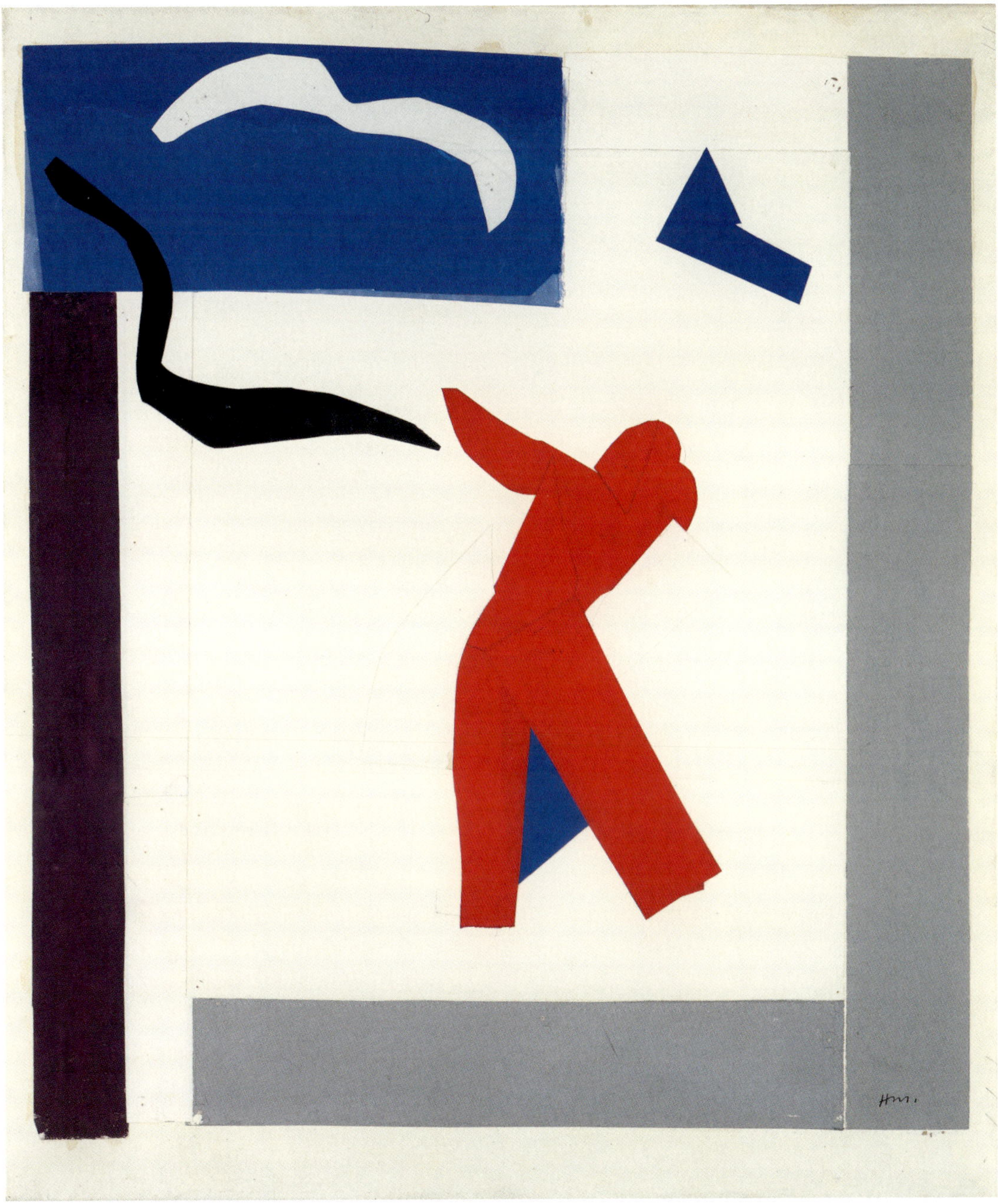

PAGE 26
Small Dancer on Red Background, 1937–38
Gouache on paper, cut and pasted on paper
37 x 19.5 cm (14½ x 7¾ in.), private collection

ABOVE
Red Dancer, 1938
Gouache on paper, cut and pasted on paper
75 x 62 cm (29½ x 24½ in.), private collection

PAGE 28
The Clown, *Jazz*, 1943, stencil

PAGE 29
Calligraphic title by Matisse for *Jazz*

PAGES 30–31
The Circus, *Jazz*, 1943, stencil

PAGE 32
Jazz, page 18

PAGE 33
Mr Loyal, *Jazz*, 1943, stencil

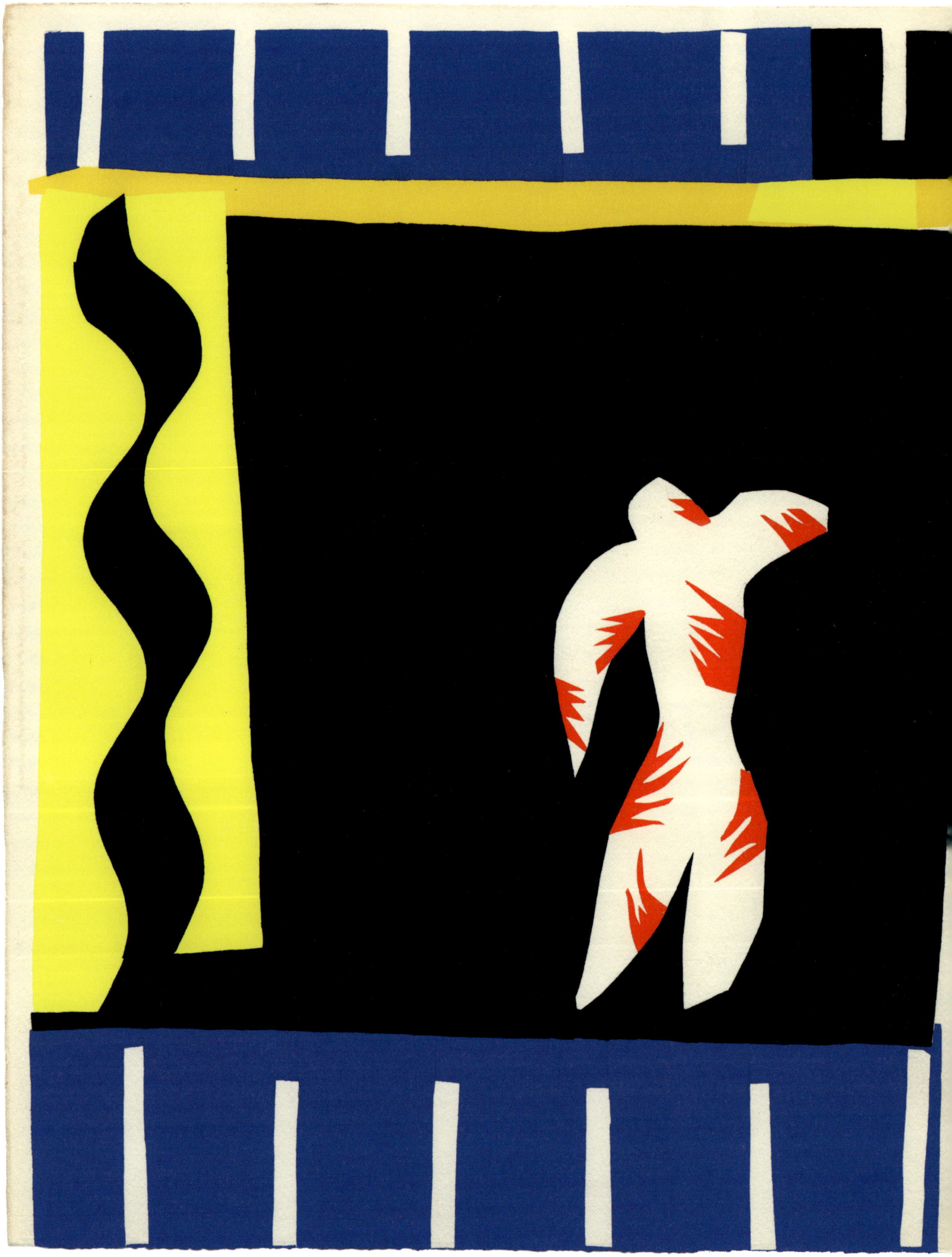

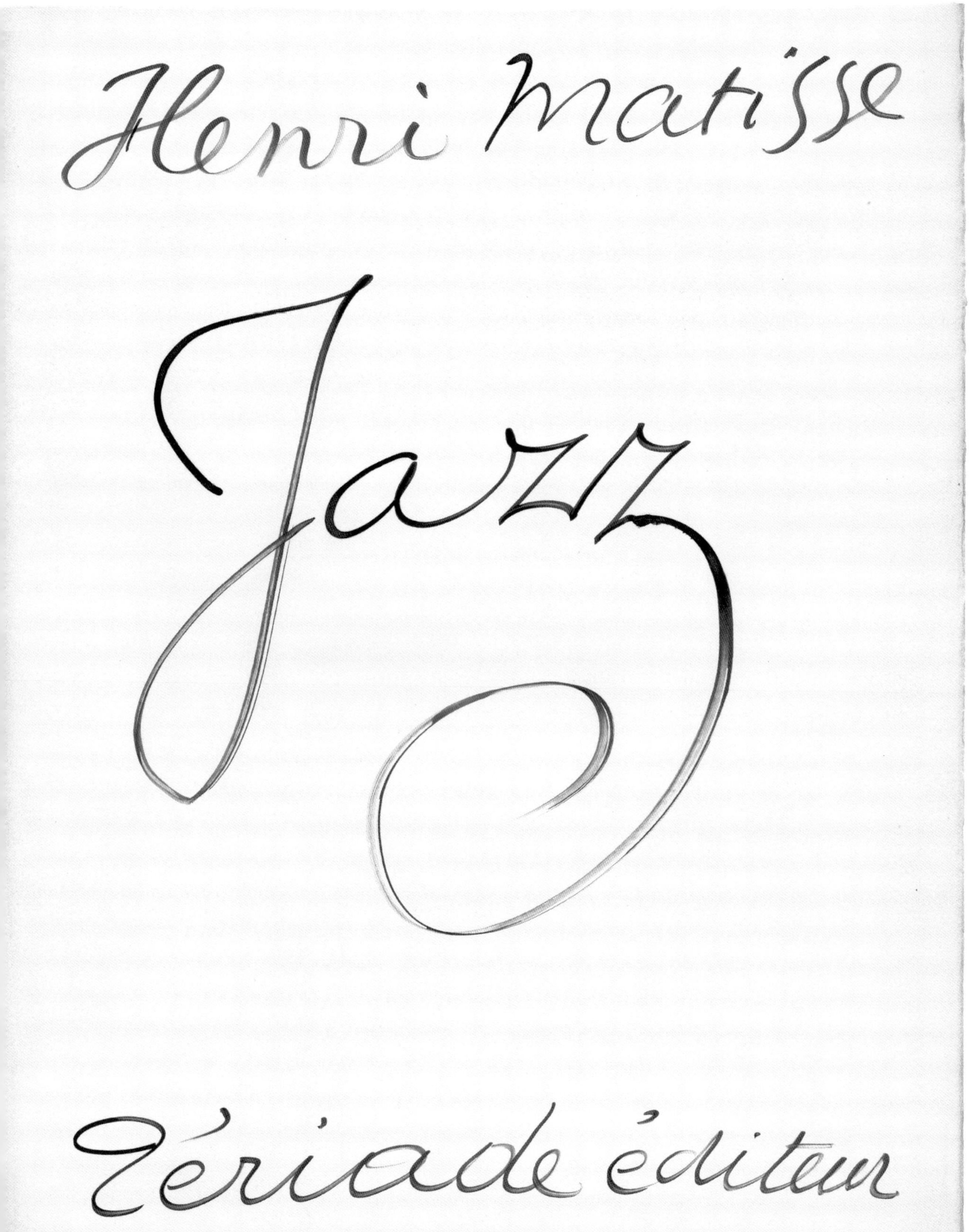

Henri Matisse

Jazz

Tériade éditeur

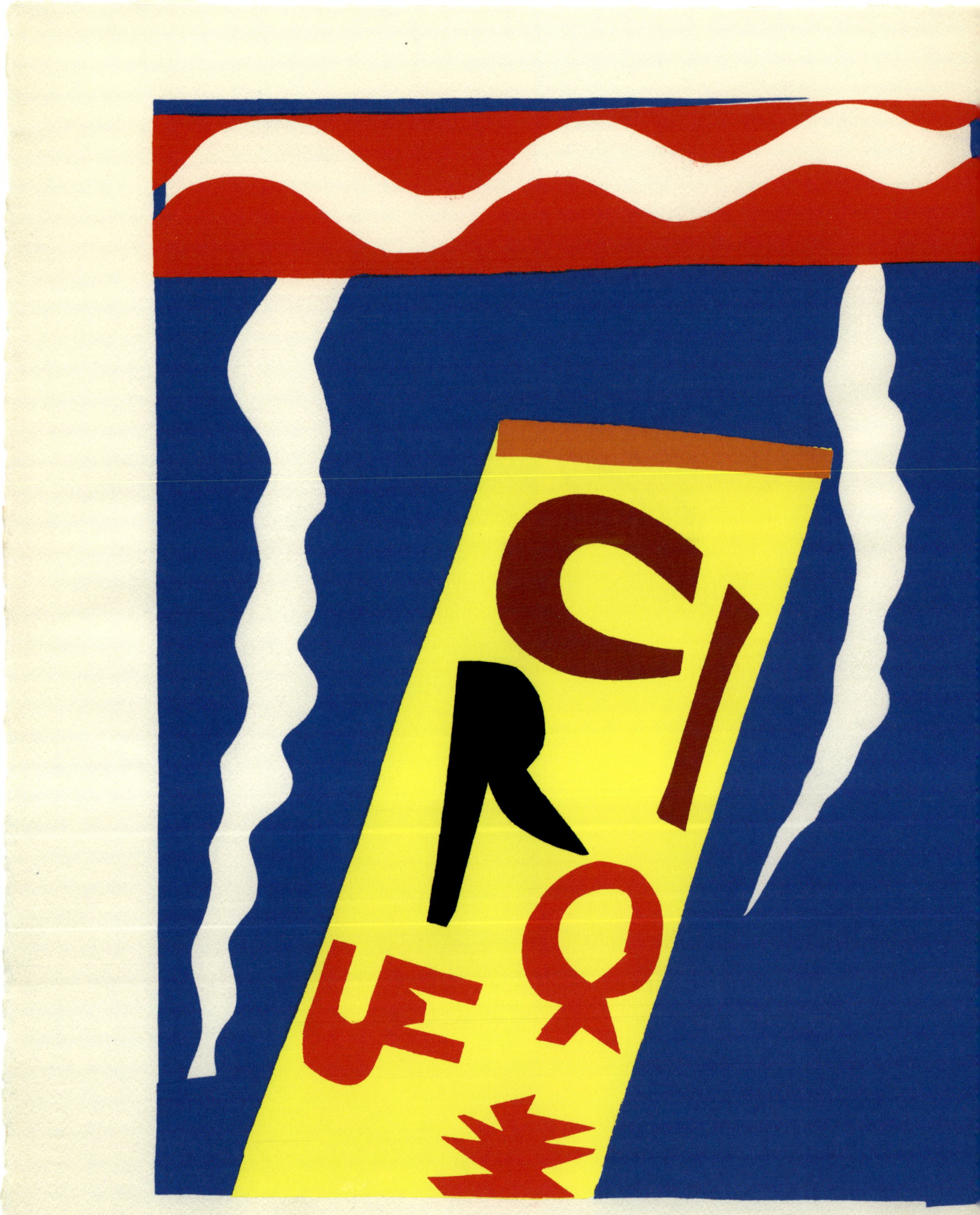
CIRQUE

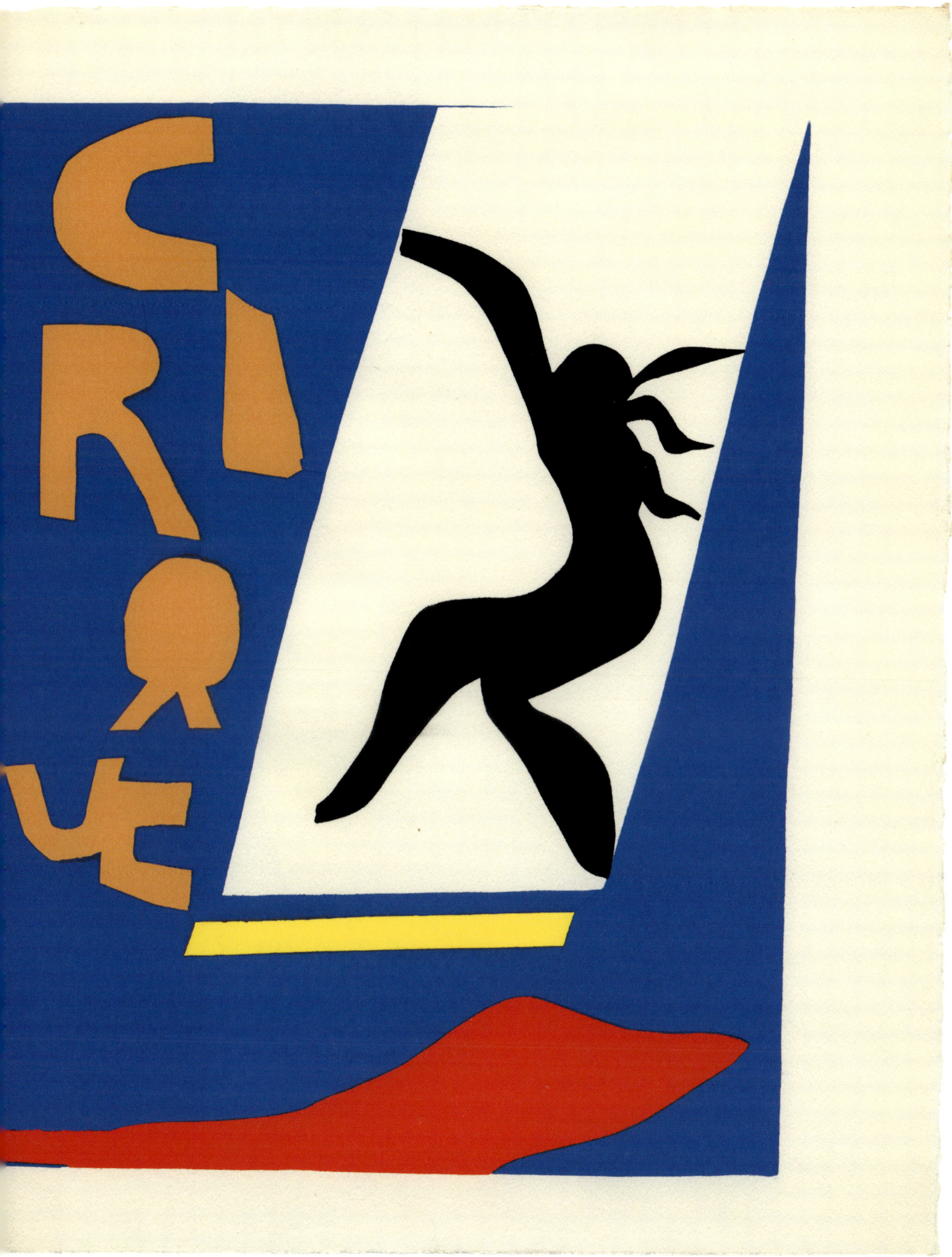
CIRQUE

Ces pages ne
servent donc
que d'accompa-
gnement à
mes couleurs,
comme des
asters aident
dans la compo-
sition d'un
bouquet de

18

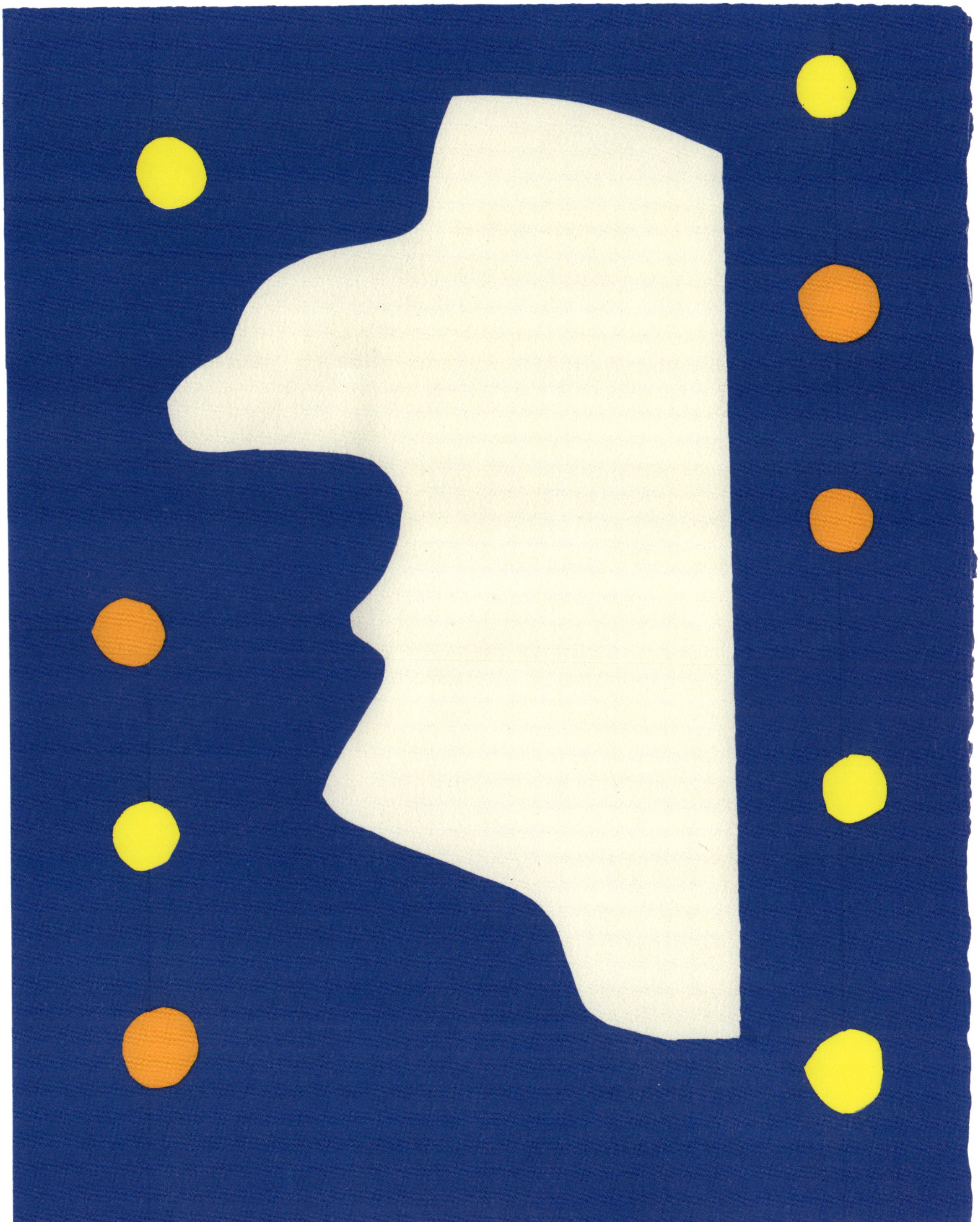

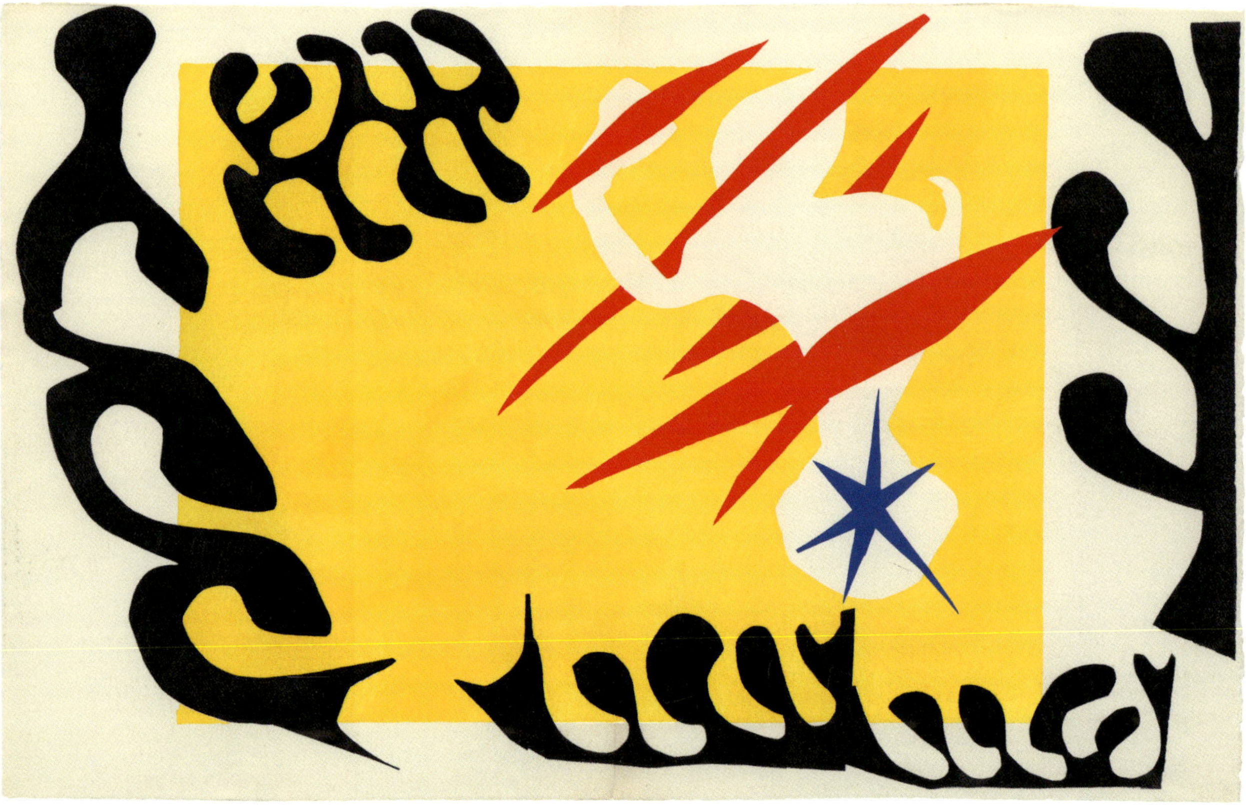

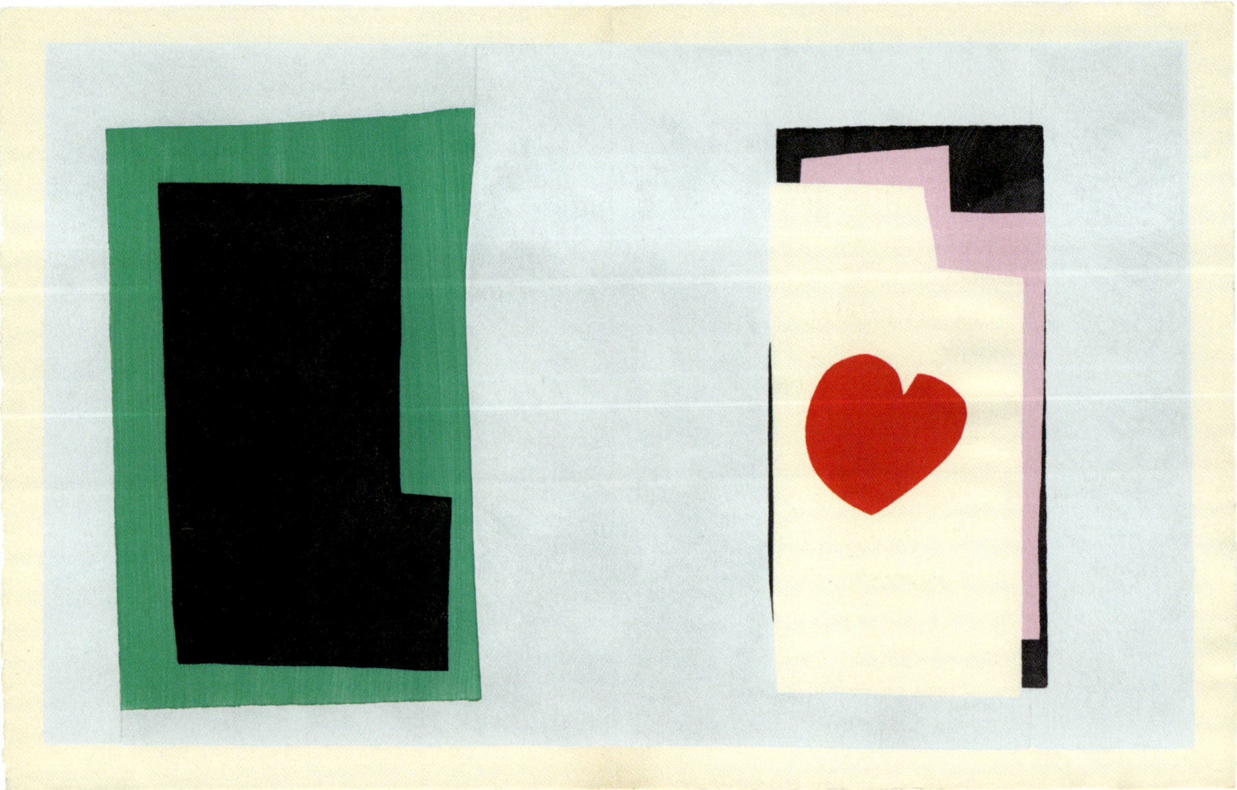

The Nightmare of the White Elephant, *Jazz*, 1943, stencil

The Heart, *Jazz*, 1943–44, Stencil

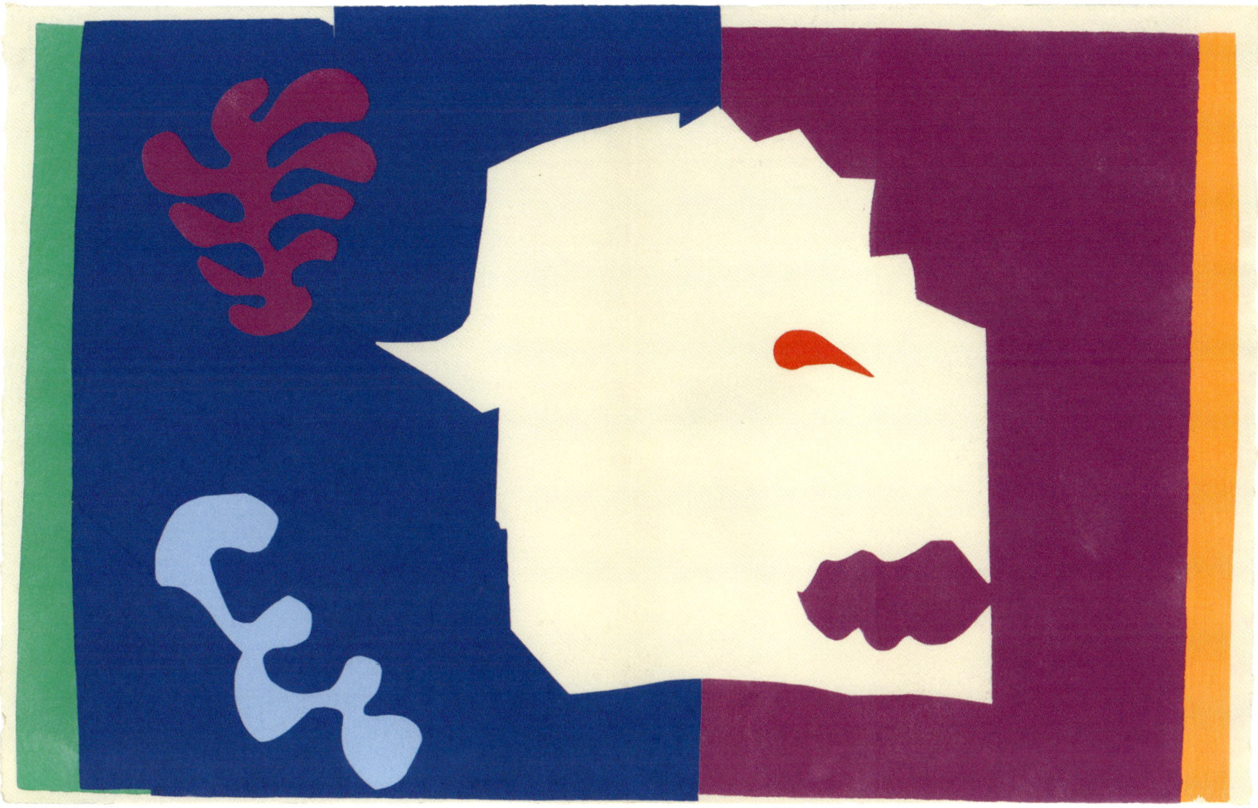

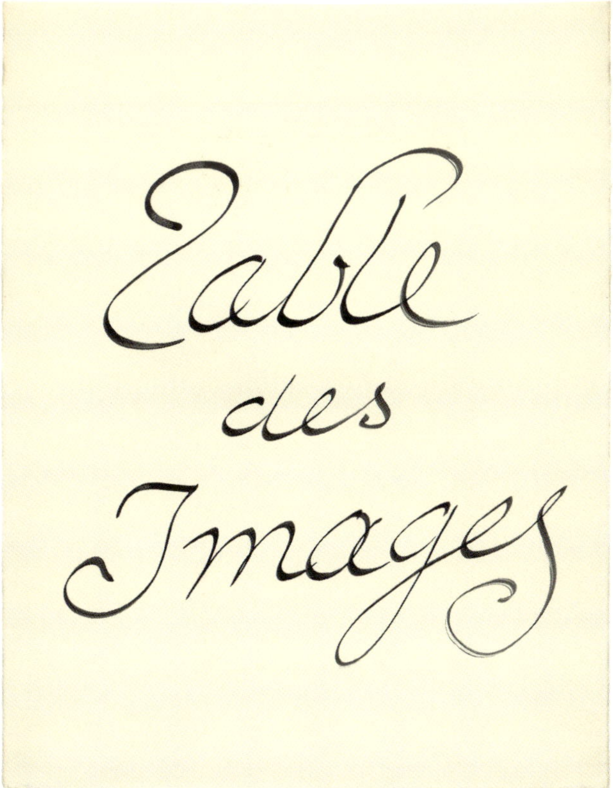

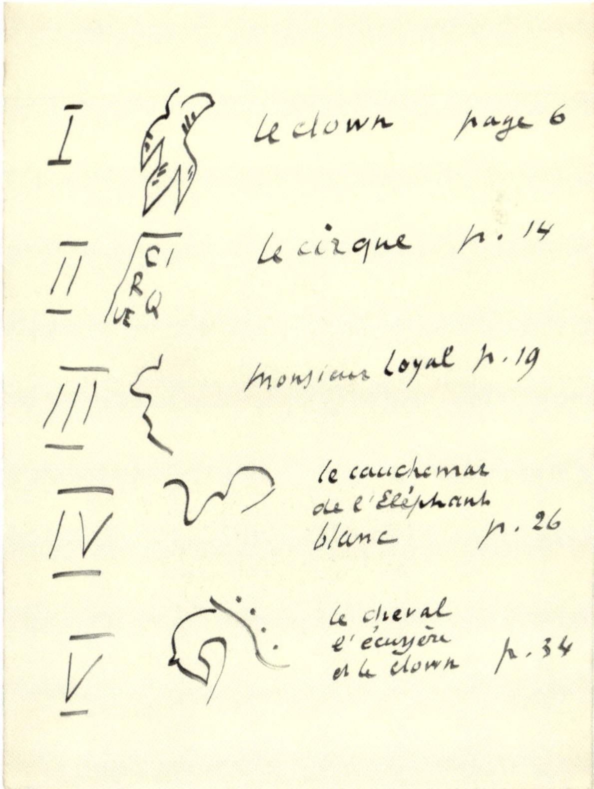

The Wolf, *Jazz*, 1944, stencil

Page 1 of "Picture Index" of *Jazz*

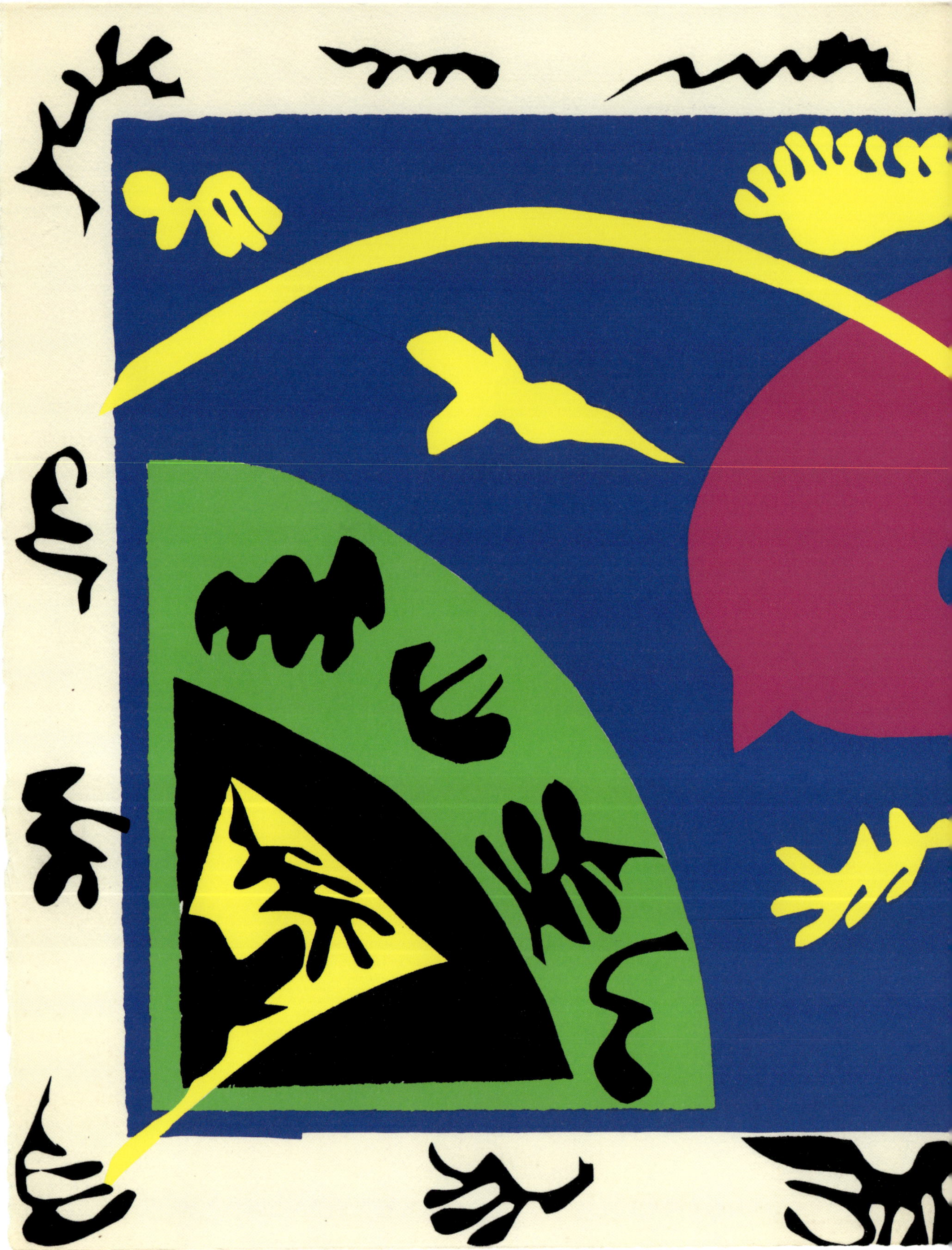

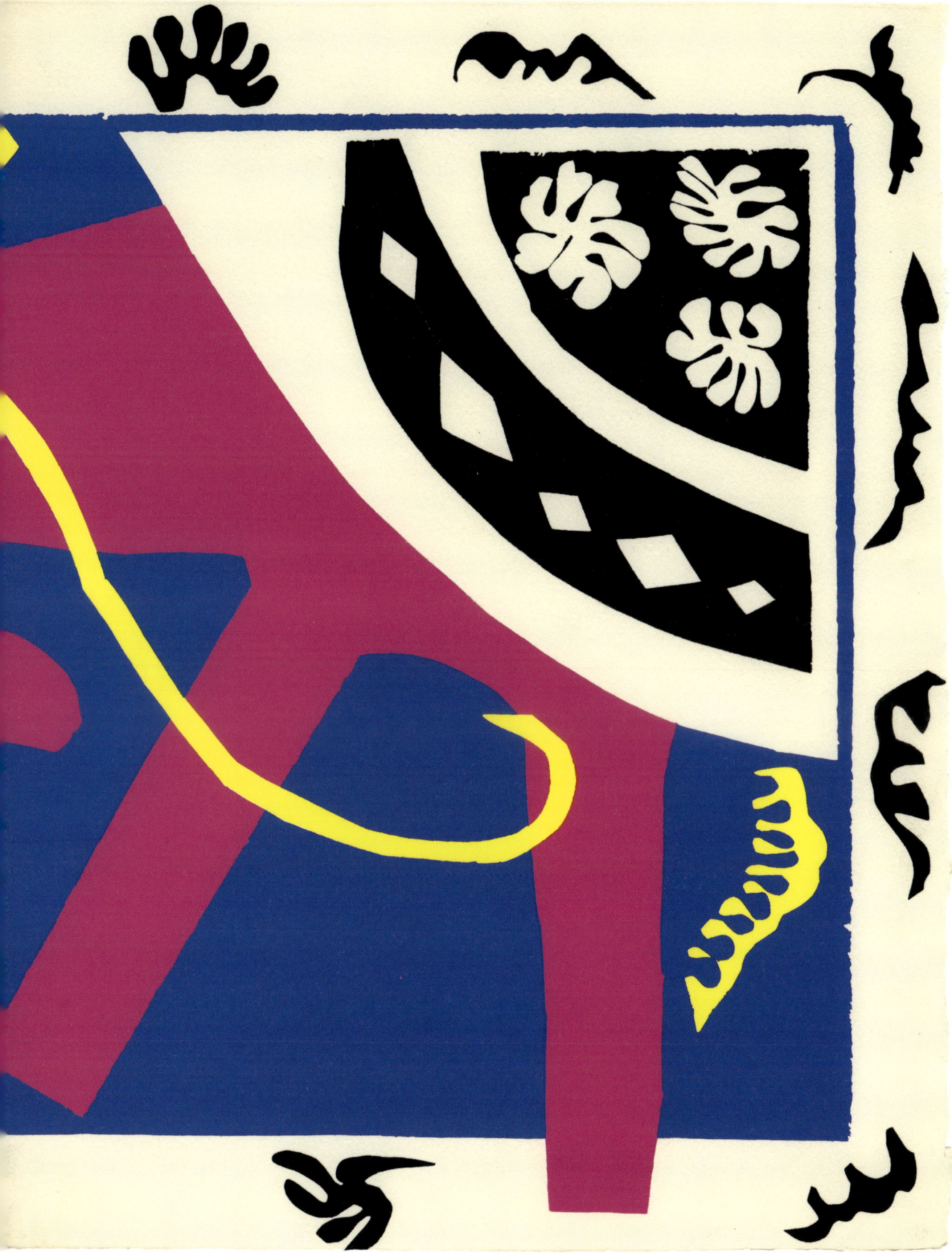

PAGES 36–37
The Horse, the Squire and the Clown
Jazz, 1943–44
Stencil

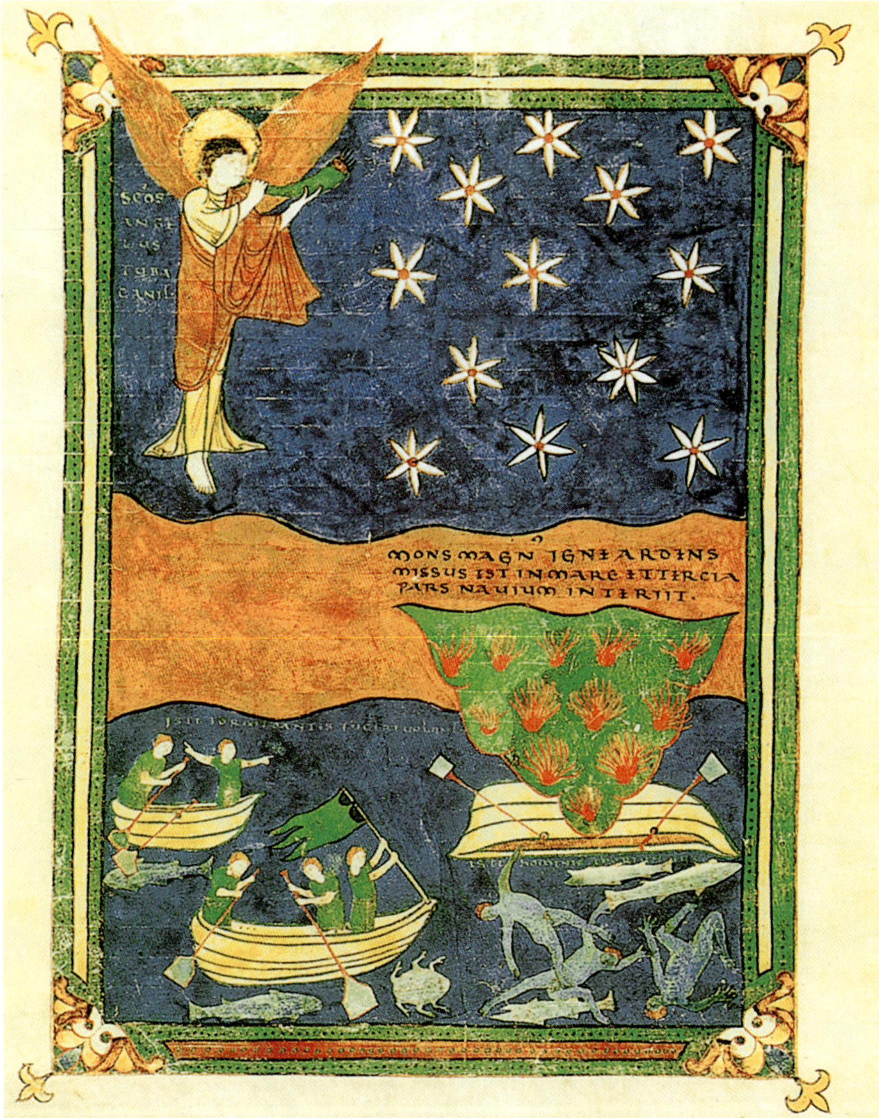

Apocalypse of Saint-Sever
12th century. Folio 139

Sculpting the Living Colour …

Jazz was published by Tériade Editeur in Paris, in 1947, in a big infolio volume measuring 42 x 32.5 cm (16½ x 12¾ in.). The twenty colour plates were stencil printed in 170 copies after the gouache cut-outs by Matisse, using the same Linel inks as the artist. *Jazz* offers a complete repertory of forms. The many-pointed stars, the leaves, and the seaweed with its deep undercuts: these recur throughout the plates like leitmotifs. Curiously enough, these same forms, or their ancestors, can be found in a 12th-century illuminated manuscript, the *Beatus of Saint-Sever.* We can be certain that Matisse knew the *Beatus*, which Mourlot, his engraver, had lithographed. There is no doubt that *Icarus* and other plates from *Jazz* owe a considerable debt to the *Beatus*, which was, in its time, one of the major sources of Romanesque sculpture. Had not Matisse claimed that he wanted to "sculpt the living colour"?

Icarus, *Jazz*, 1943
Stencil

PAGES 40–41
The Burial of Pierrot, *Jazz*, 1943
Stencil

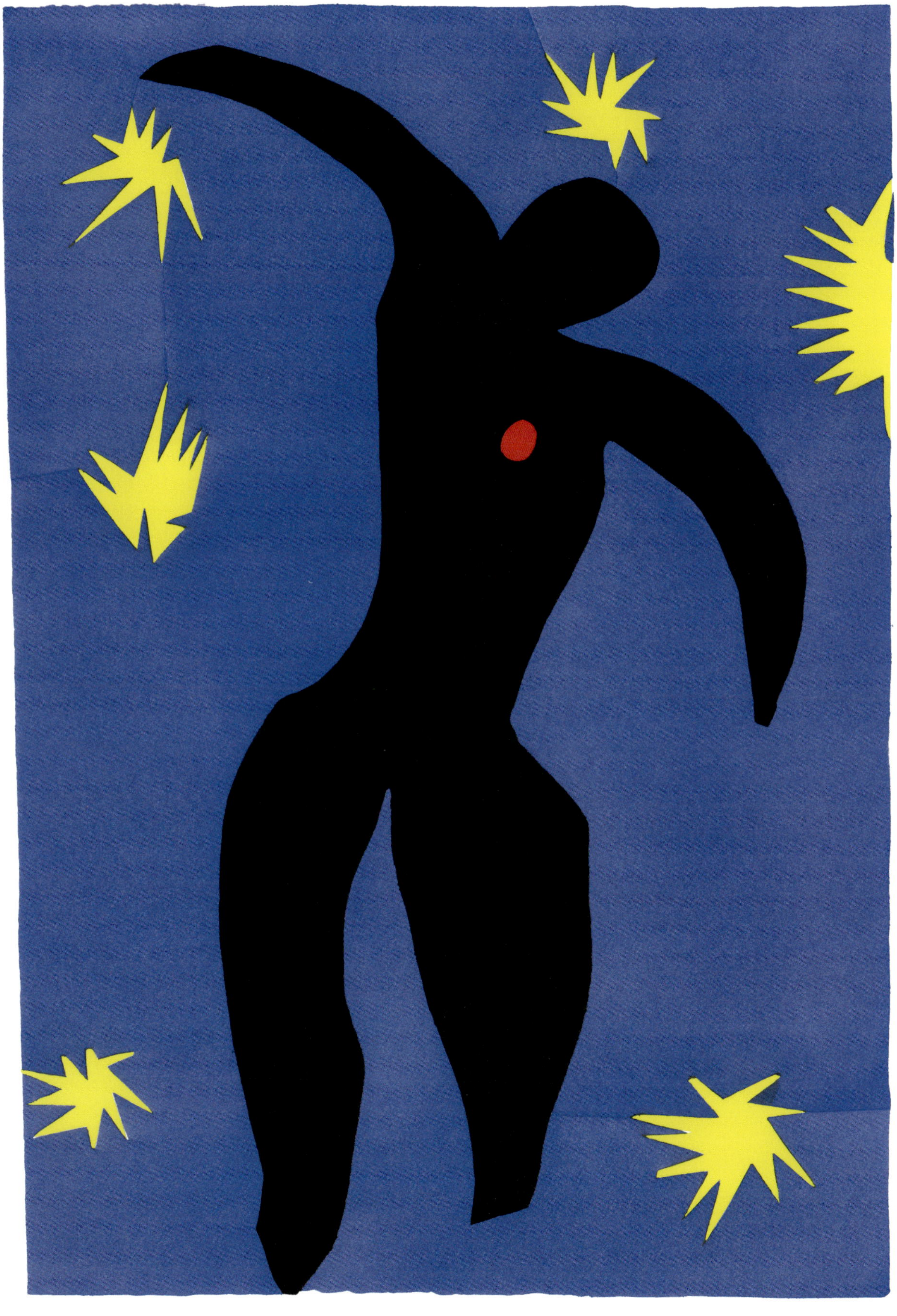

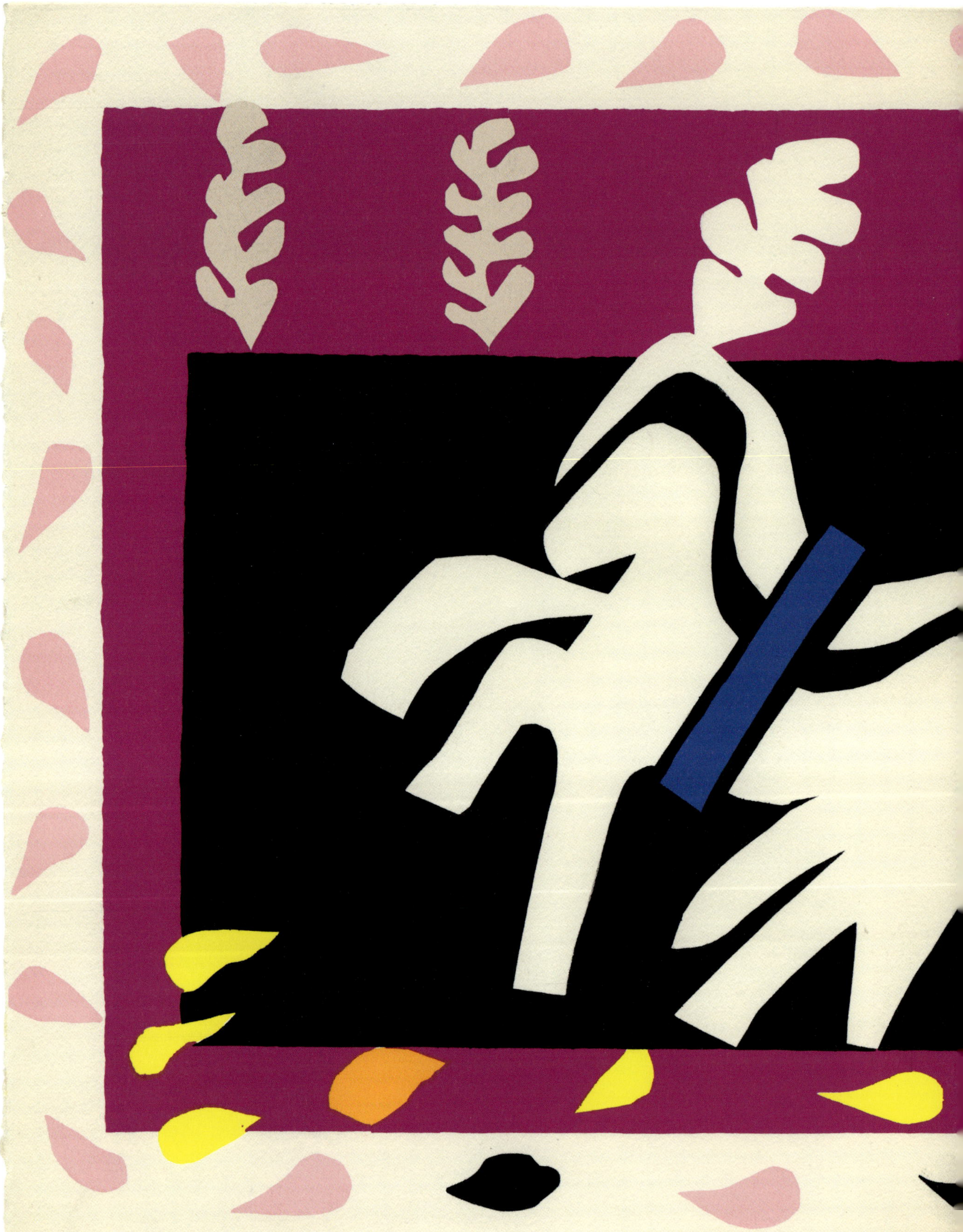

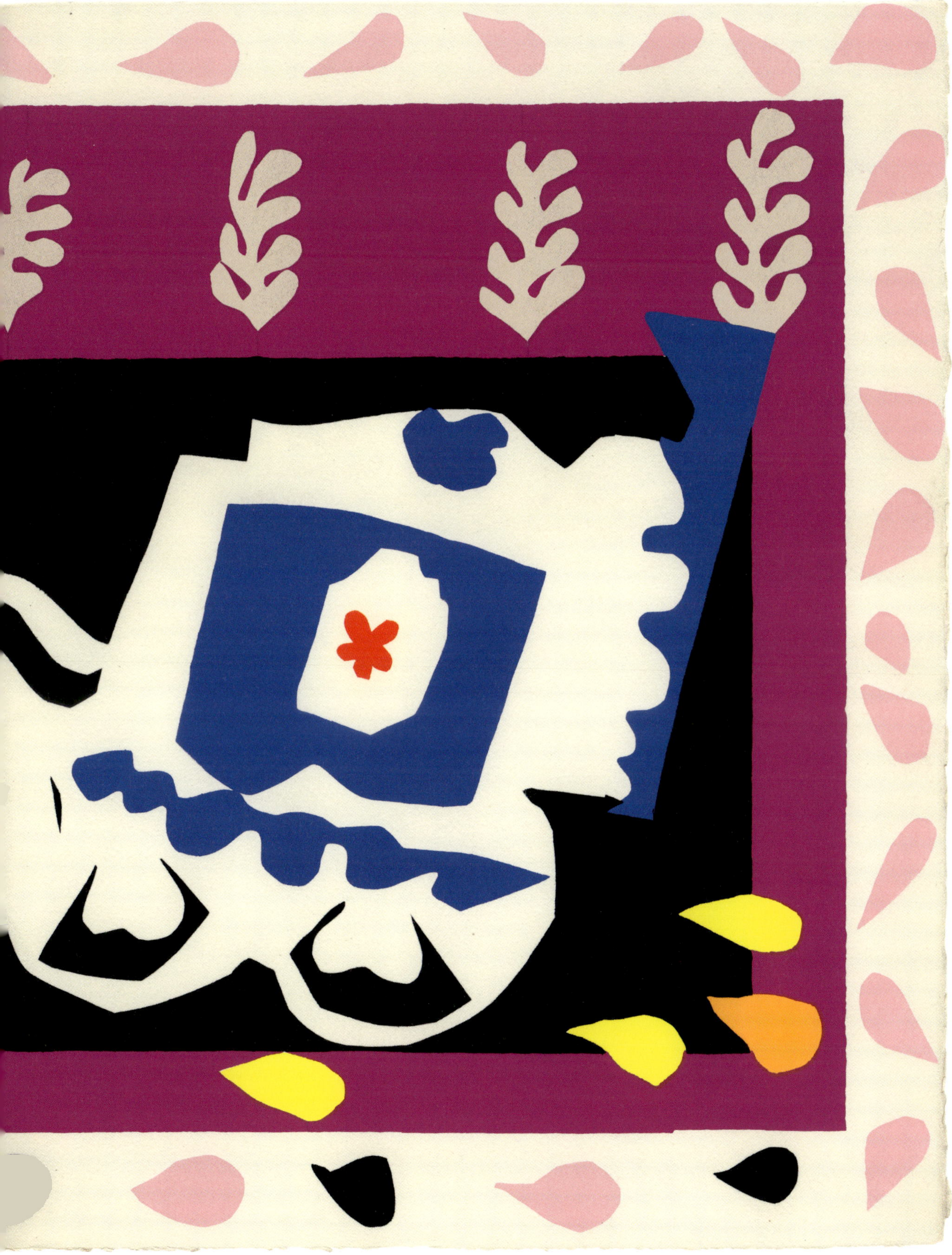

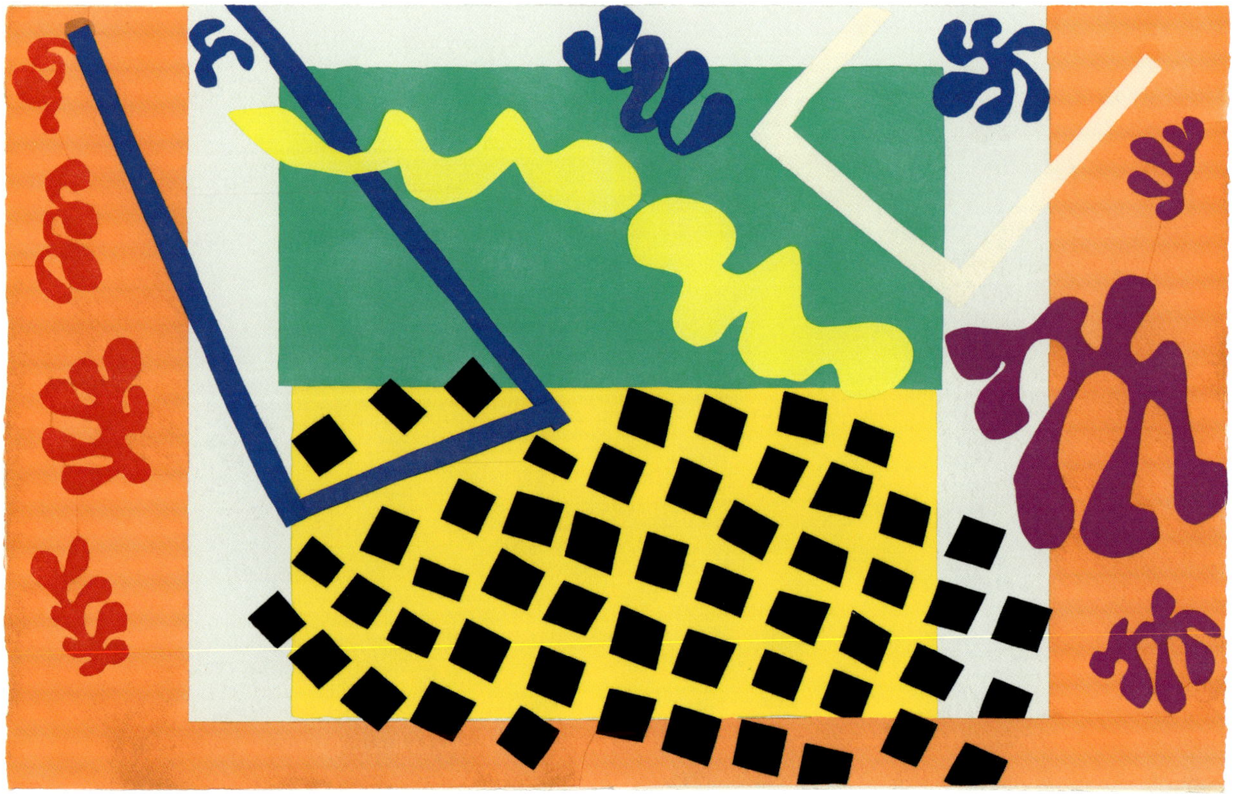

The Codomas, *Jazz*, 1943, stencil

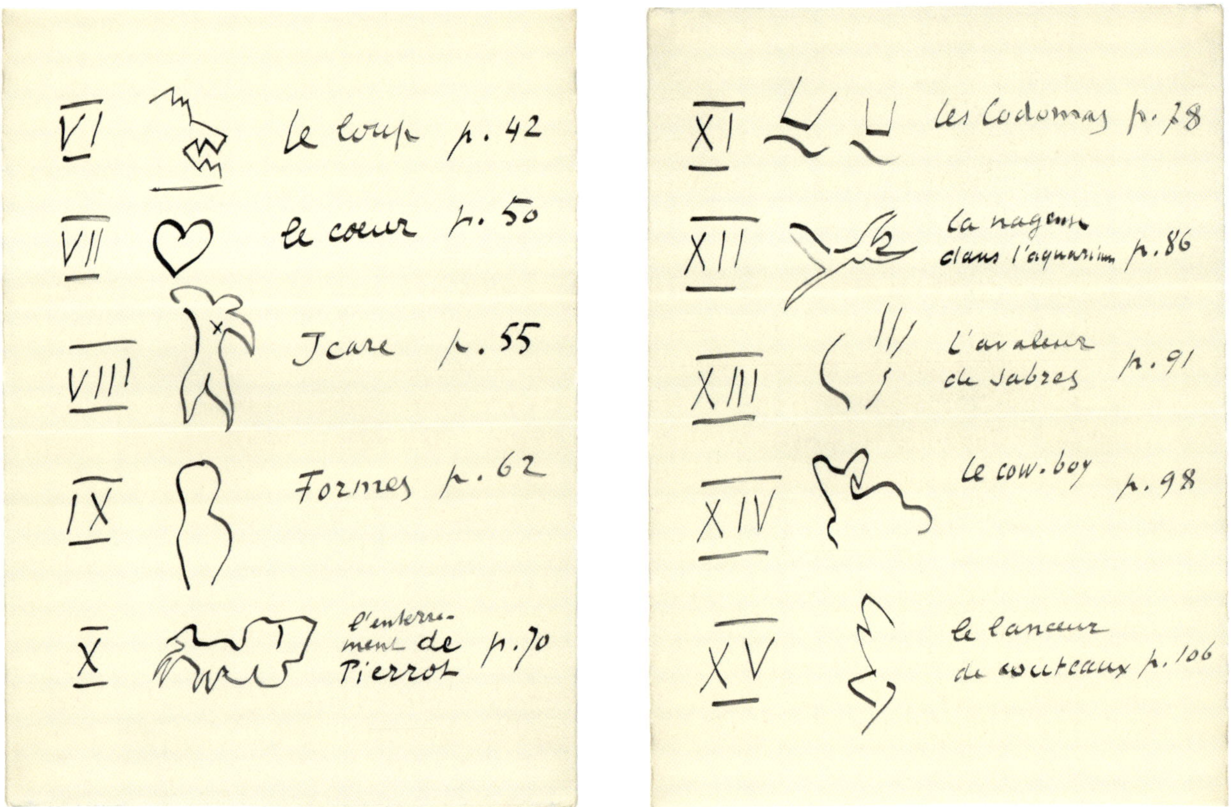

VI le loup p. 42
VII le coeur p. 50
VIII Icare p. 55
IX Formes p. 62
X l'enterrement de Pierrot p. 70

XI les Codomas p. 78
XII la nageuse dans l'aquarium p. 86
XIII l'avaleur de sabres p. 91
XIV le cow-boy p. 98
XV le lanceur de couteaux p. 106

Pages 2 and 3 of "Picture Index" of *Jazz*

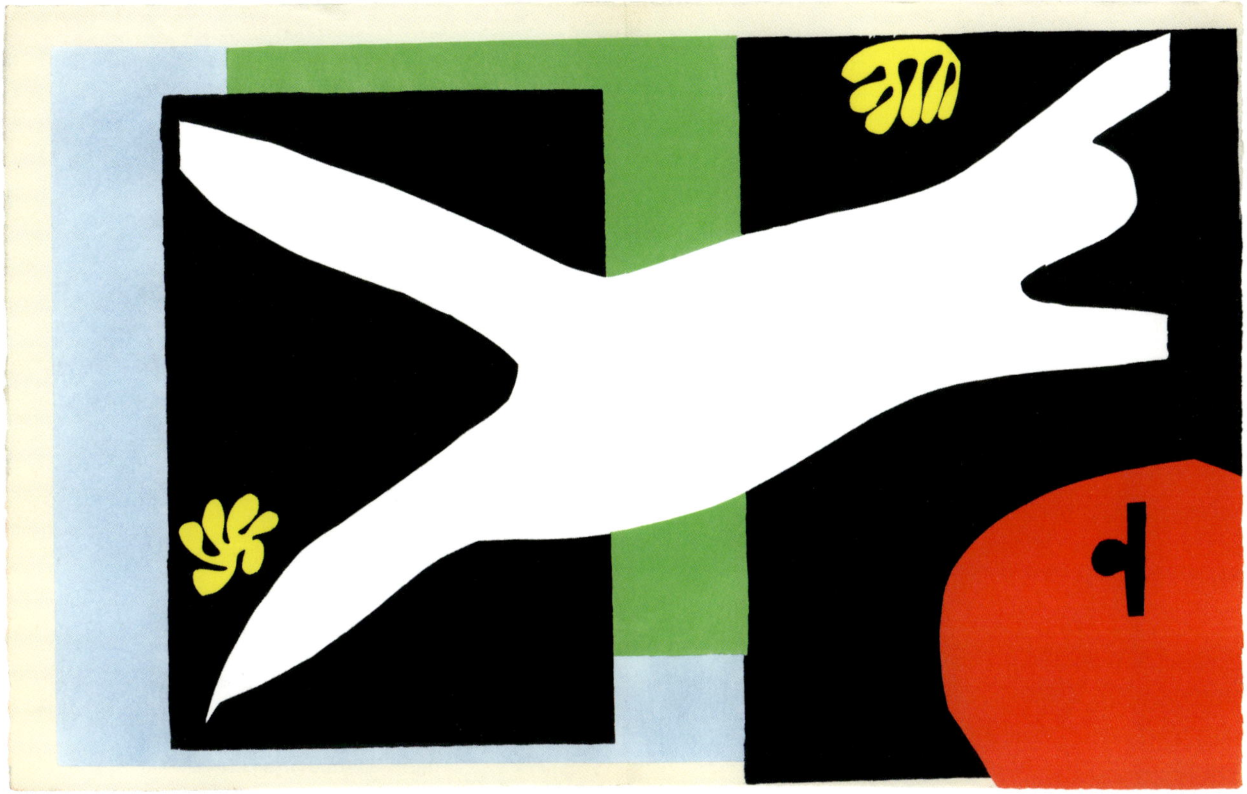

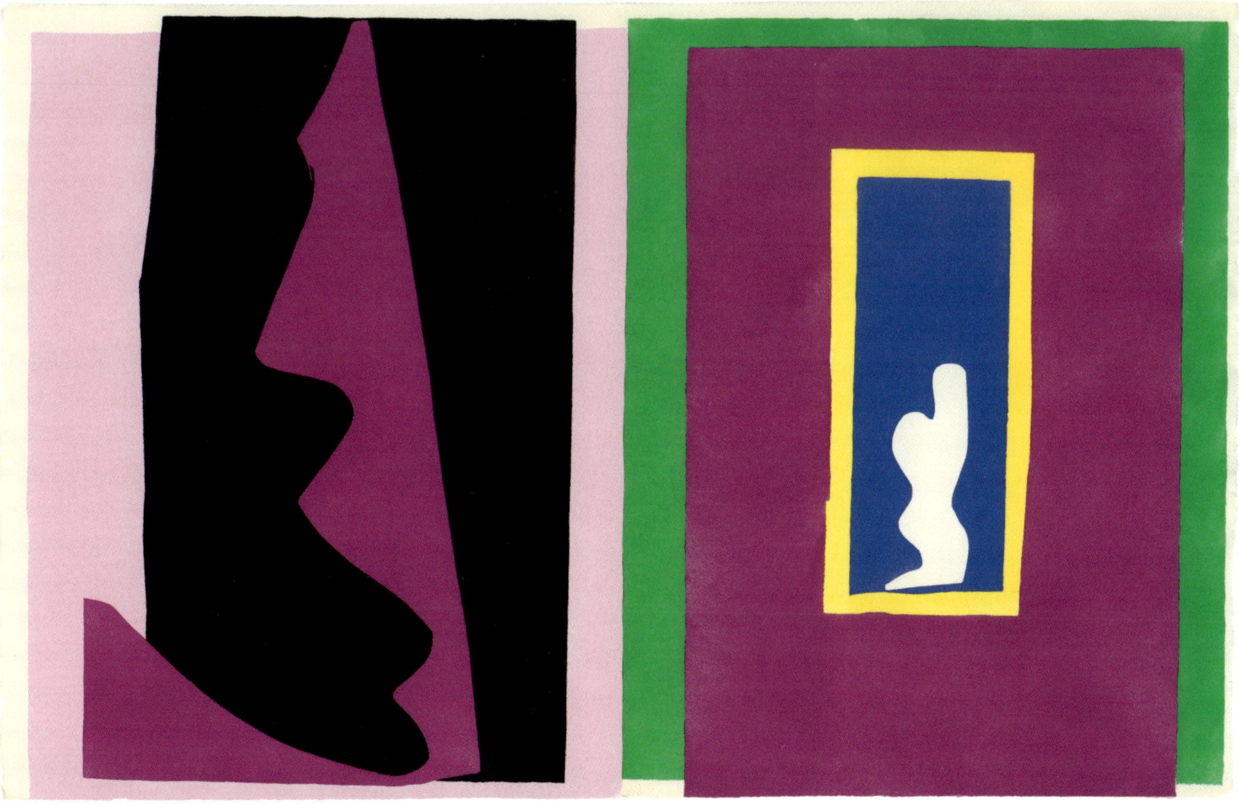

The Woman Swimming in the Aquarium,
Jazz, 1944–46, stencil

The Destiny, *Jazz*, 1943–46
Stencil

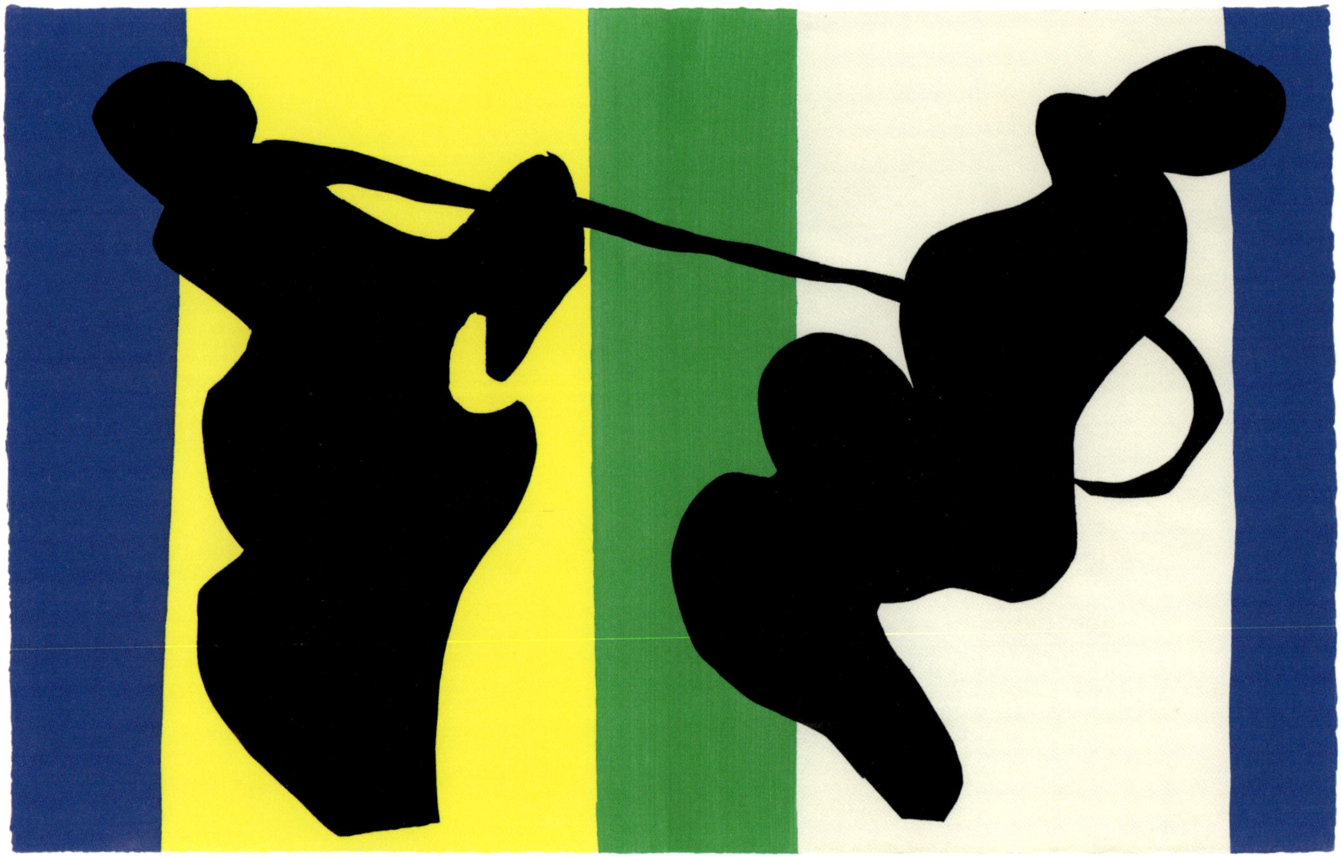

The Cowboy, *Jazz*, 1943–46
Stencil

Juggling with Forms

Concerning his illustrations to Mallarmé's poems, Matisse wrote: "I compare my two pages to the objects chosen by a juggler. Let us imagine, in relation to this question, a white ball and a black ball and on the other hand two pages, the light and shade so very different and yet side by side. Despite the difference between the two objects, the art of the juggler makes a harmonious whole in the eyes of the spectator." In the same way, Matisse explained that, undecided what to put between the works in *Jazz*, he chose handwritten texts as another form of "juggling".

The Sword Swallower, *Jazz*, 1943–46
Stencil

PAGES 46–47
The Knife-Thrower, *Jazz*, 1943–46
Stencil

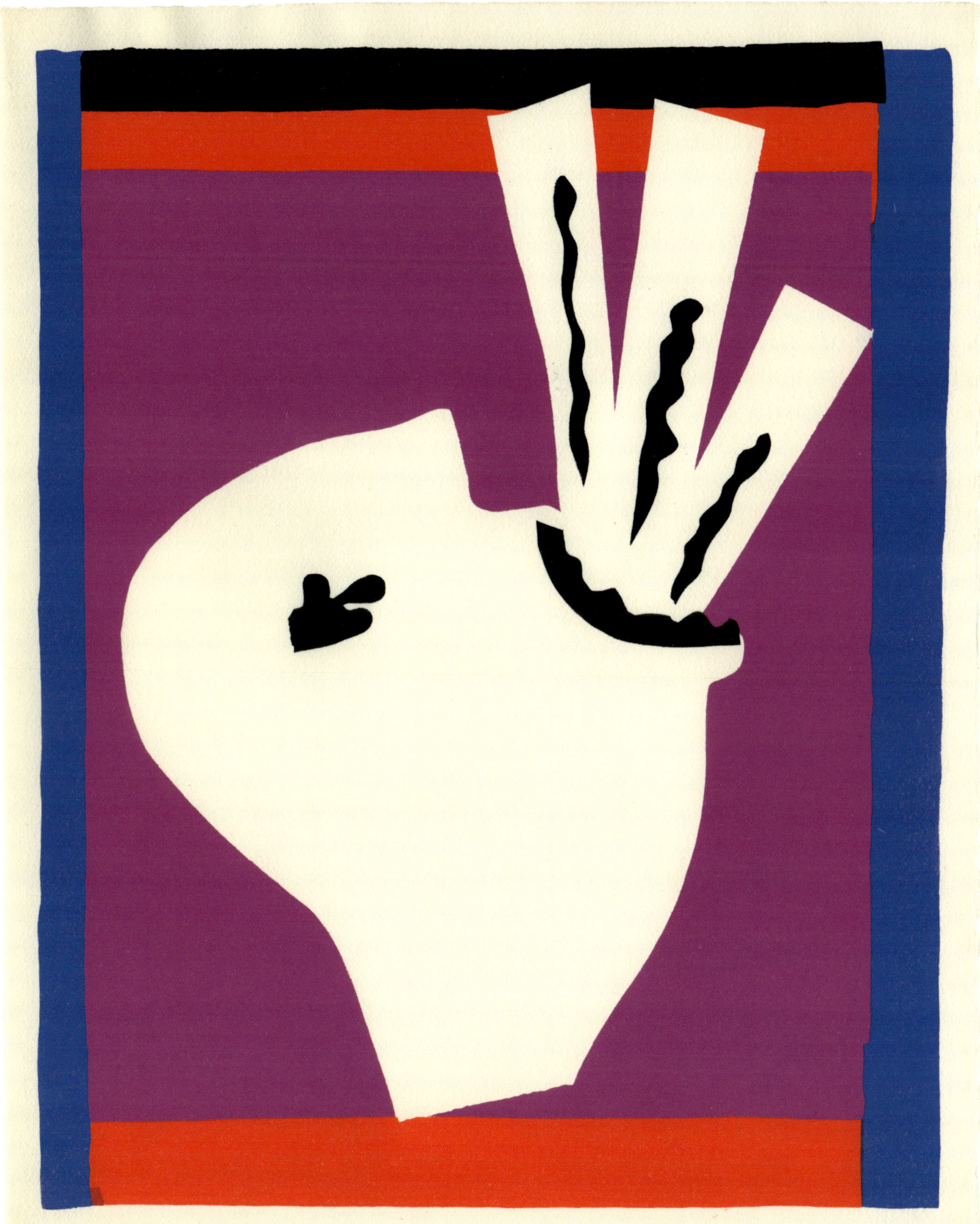

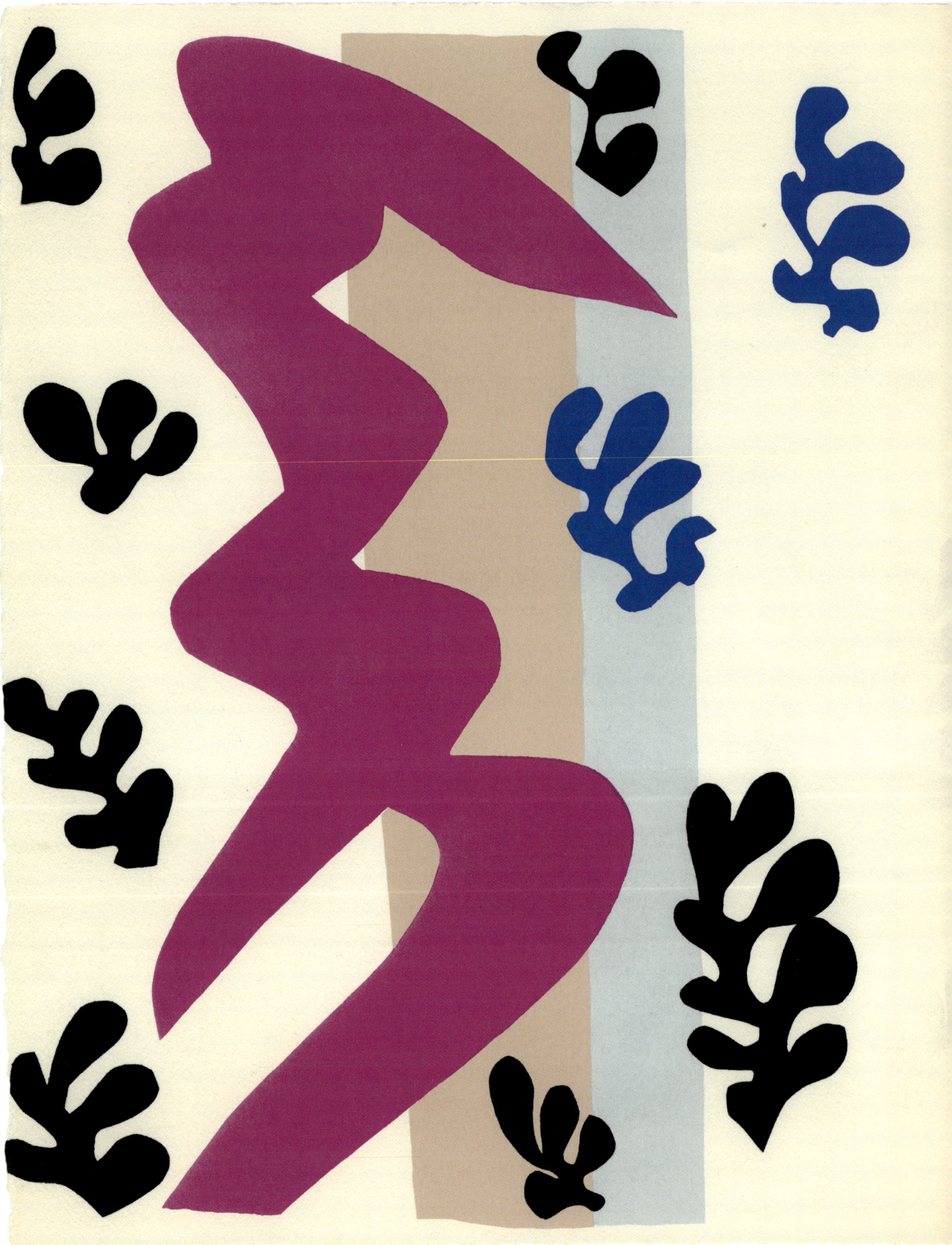

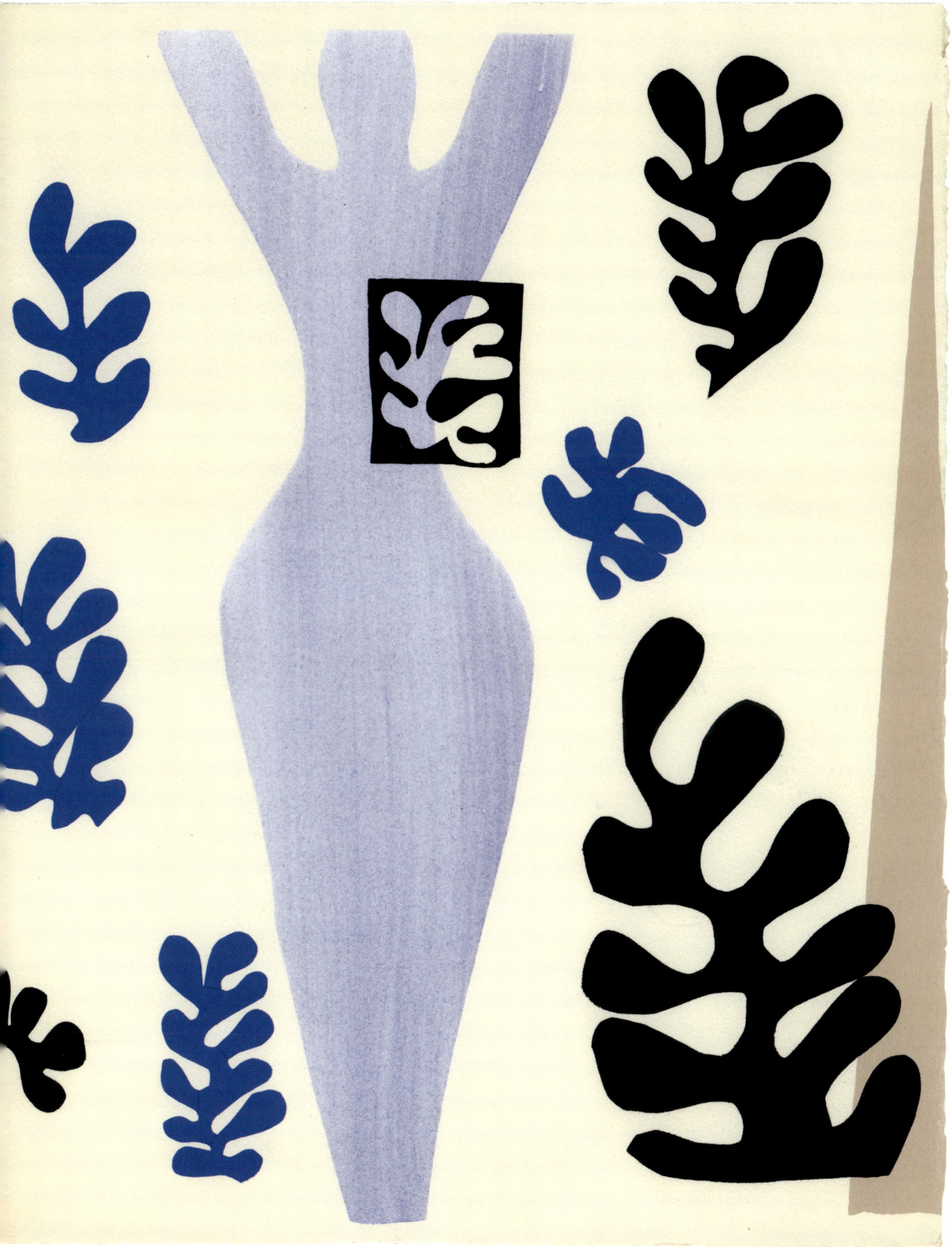

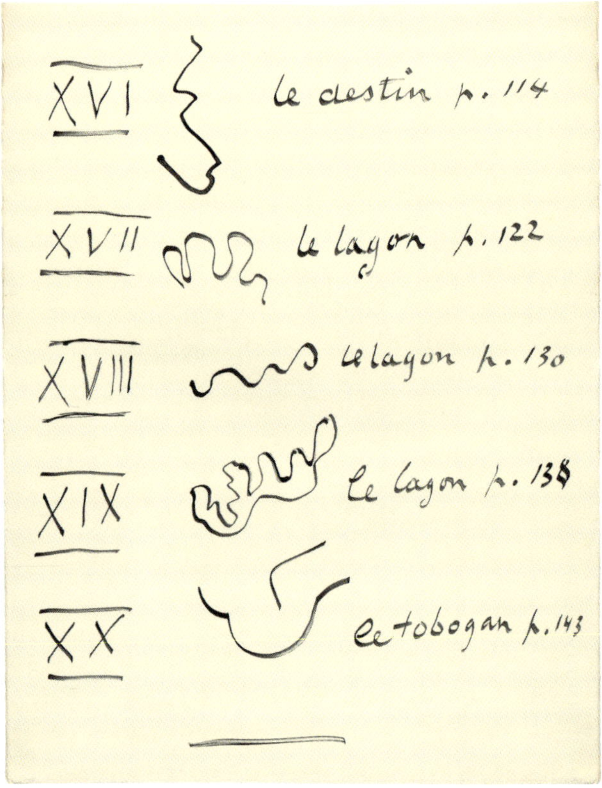

XVI le destin p. 114

XVII le lagon p. 122

XVIII le lagon p. 130

XIX le lagon p. 138

XX le tobogan p. 143

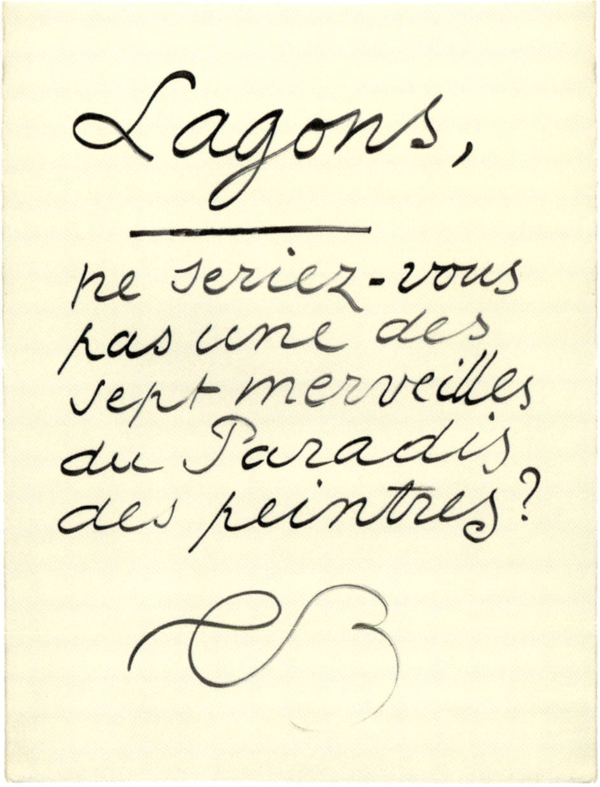

Lagons,

ne seriez-vous
pas une des
sept merveilles
du Paradis
des peintres?

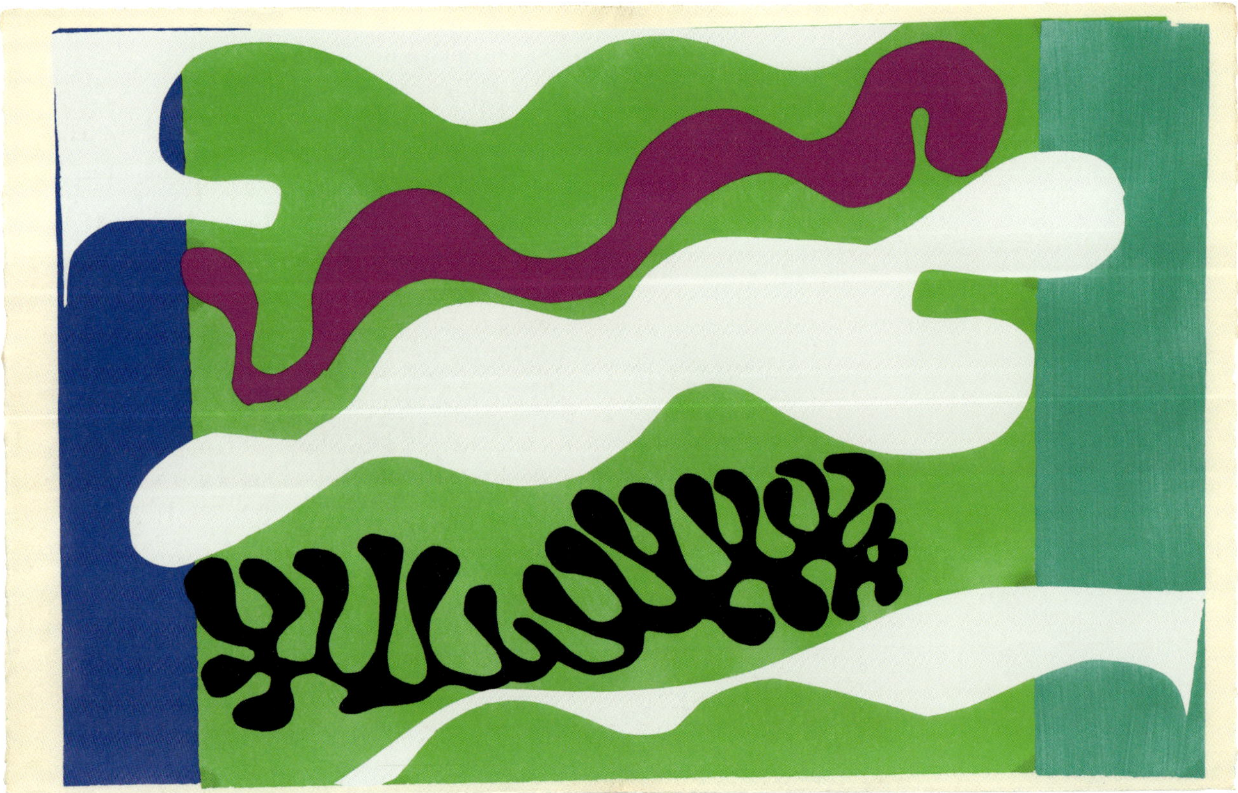

TOP
Page 4 of “Picture Index” and page 128 of *Jazz*

ABOVE AND PAGE 49
The Lagoon, *Jazz*, 1944, stencils

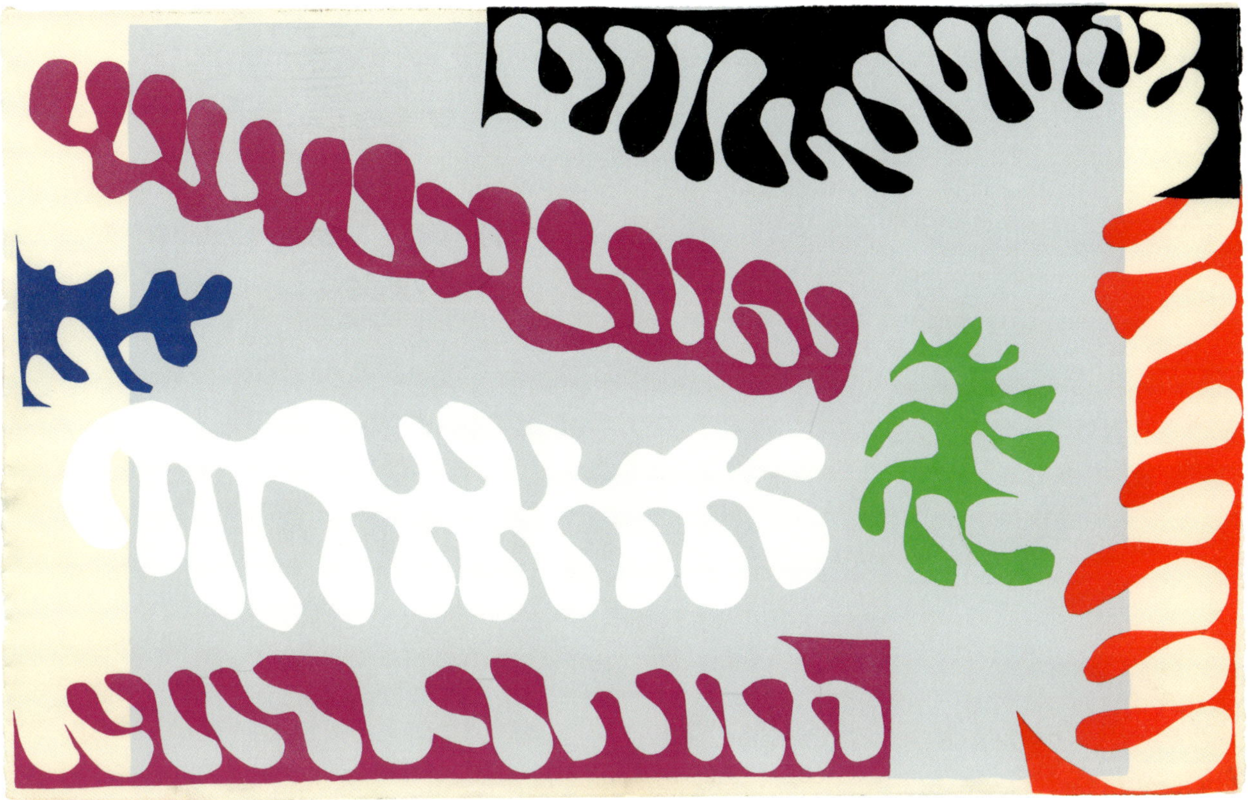

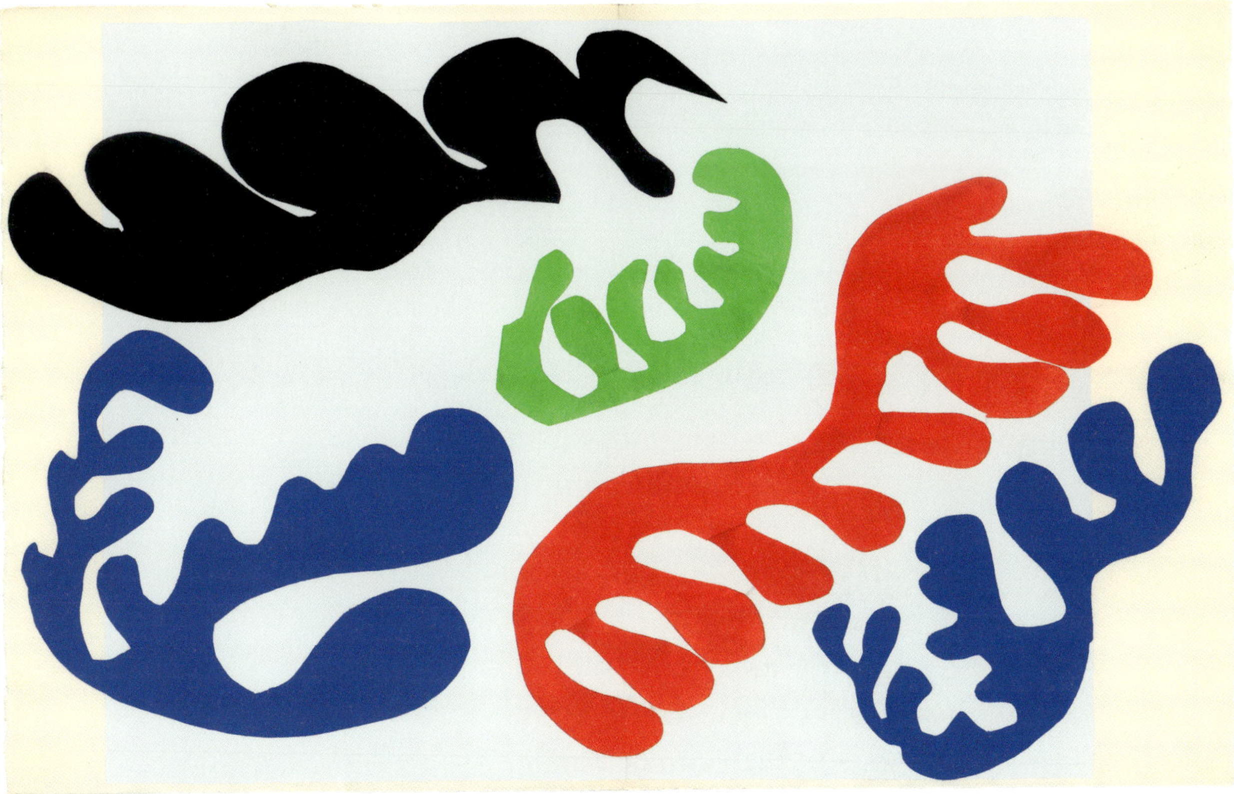

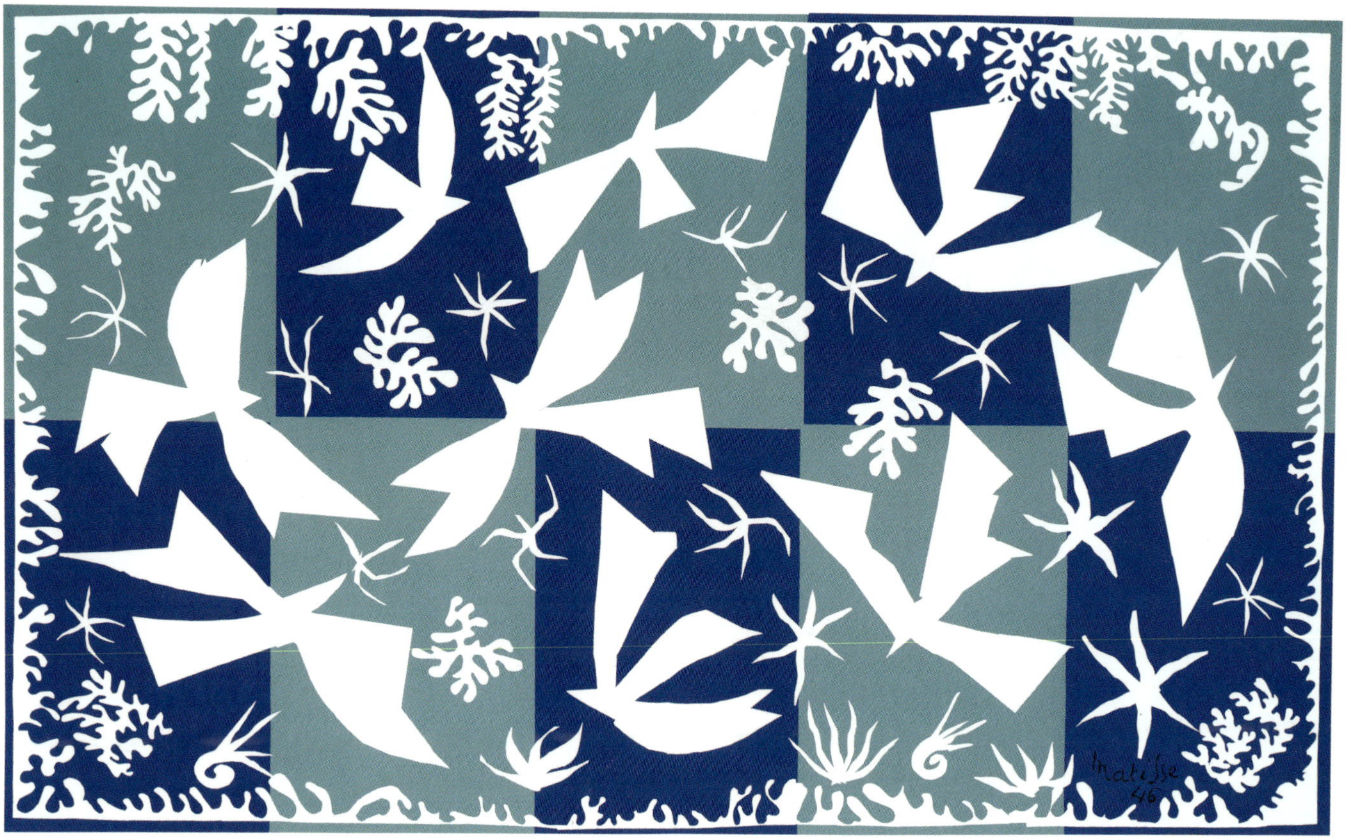

Polynesia, the Sky, 1946
Maquette for a woollen tapestry
Gouache on paper, cut and pasted
on canvas, 200 x 314 cm (78¾ x 123½ in.)
Paris, Musée national d'art moderne,
Centre Pompidou

Like a Flight of Doves …

After *Jazz* came a proliferation of gouache cut-outs of increasing size, which became first tapestries, then stained-glass windows or swimming-pool mosaics. One such is *Polynesia*, which is almost 4 metres (13 feet) in length and resulted from a commission by A. Ascher of London for a wall-hanging. "These successive flights of doves, their orbs and their curves glide within me, as if in a vast inner space," Matisse confided to André Verdet. "… The sensation of flight released in me helps to guide my hand when it directs the trajectory of my scissors. It is difficult to explain. I would say that it is a sort of linear, graphic equivalent to the sensation of flight. There is also the question of vibrant space."

Christmas Eve, 1952
Maquette for a stained-glass window
Gouache on paper, cut and pasted, mounted
on Homasote panel
322.6 x 135.9 cm (127 x 53½ in.)
New York, The Museum of Modern Art,
Gift of Time Inc.

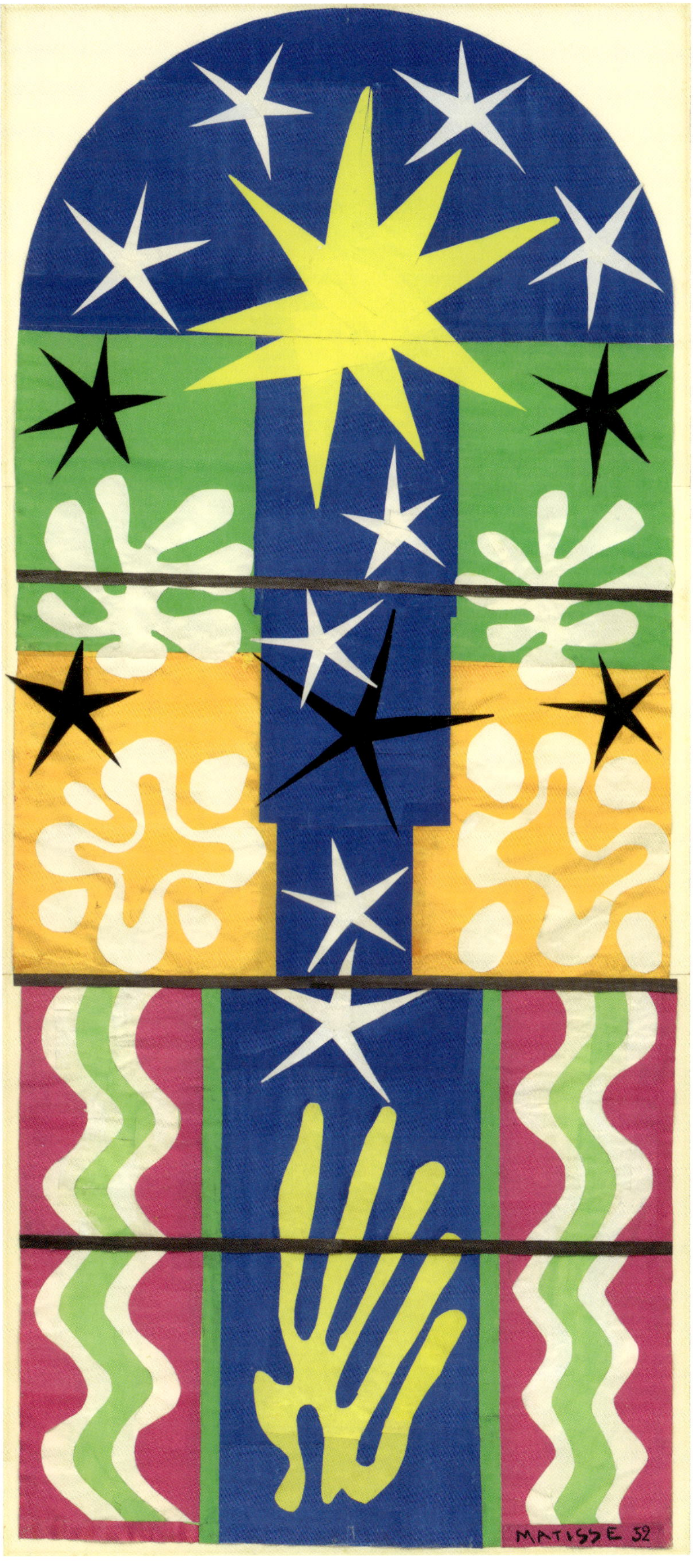
MATISSE 52

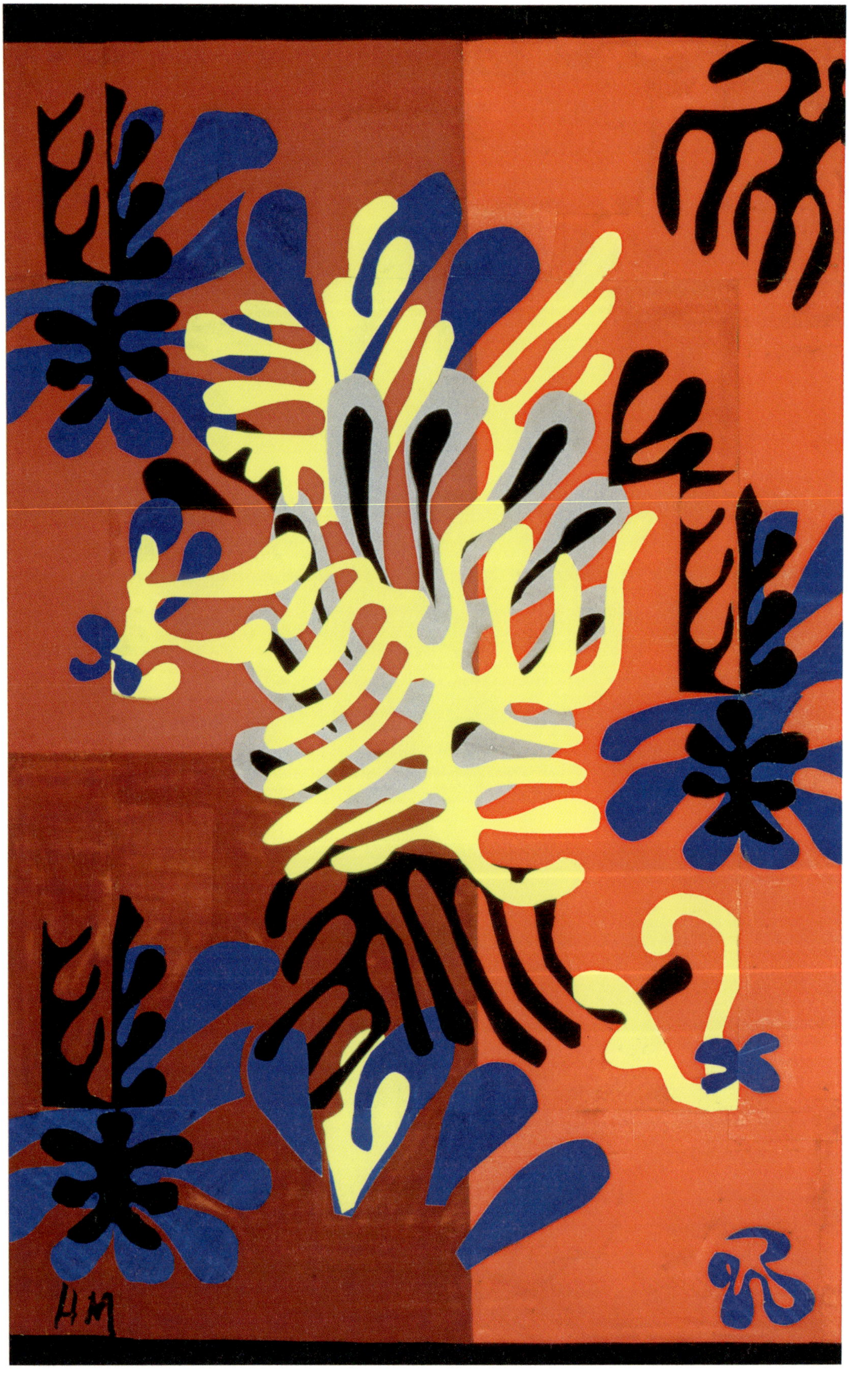

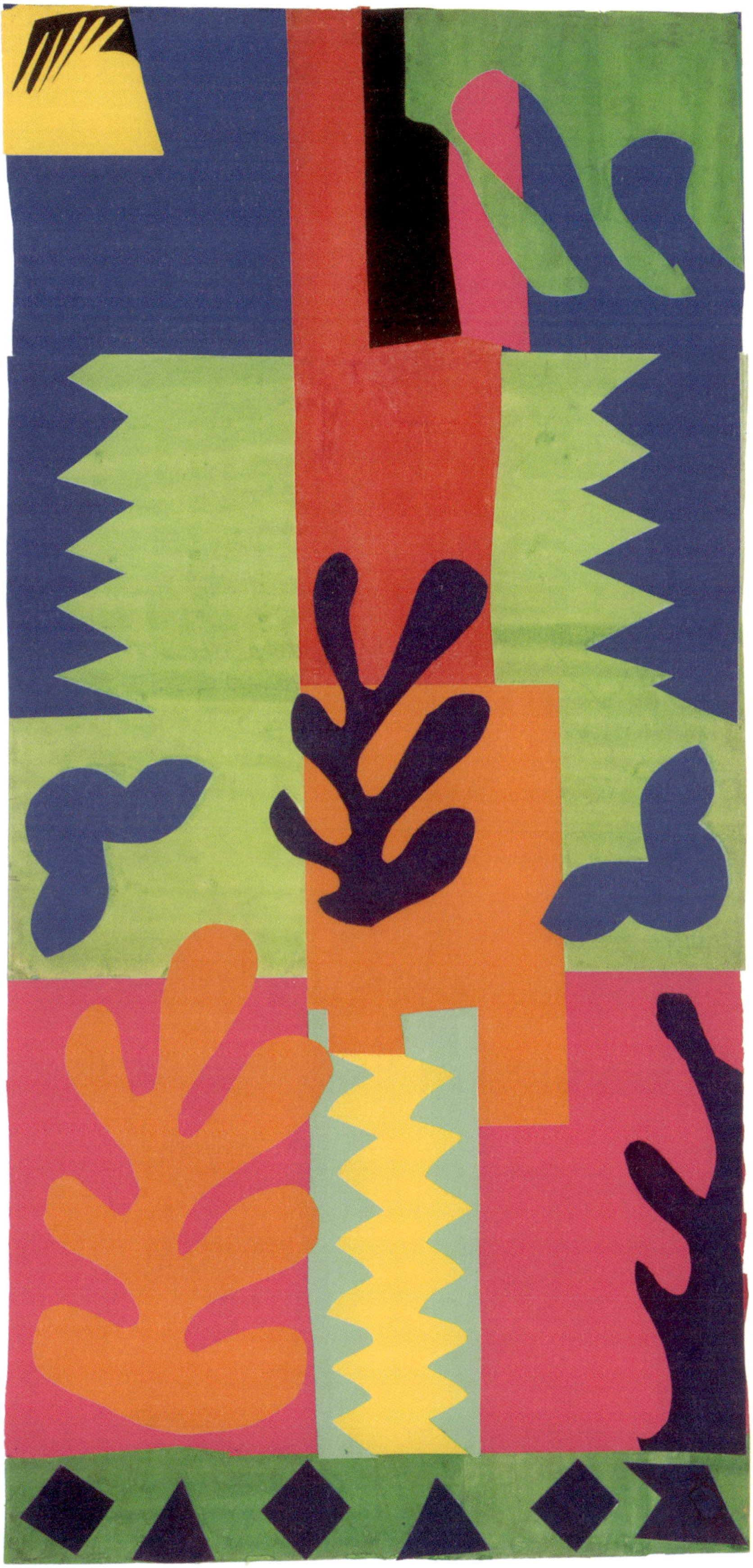

Mimosa, 1949–51
Maquette for a rug
Gouache on paper, cut and pasted on paper, on canvas, 148 x 96.5 cm (58¼ x 38 in.)
Itō City, Ikeda Museum of 20th Century Art

The Wine Press, *c.* 1951
Gouache on paper, cut and pasted on paper
175 x 82 cm (69 x 32¼ in.)
Private collection
Lithographic reproduction
of the original paper cut-out

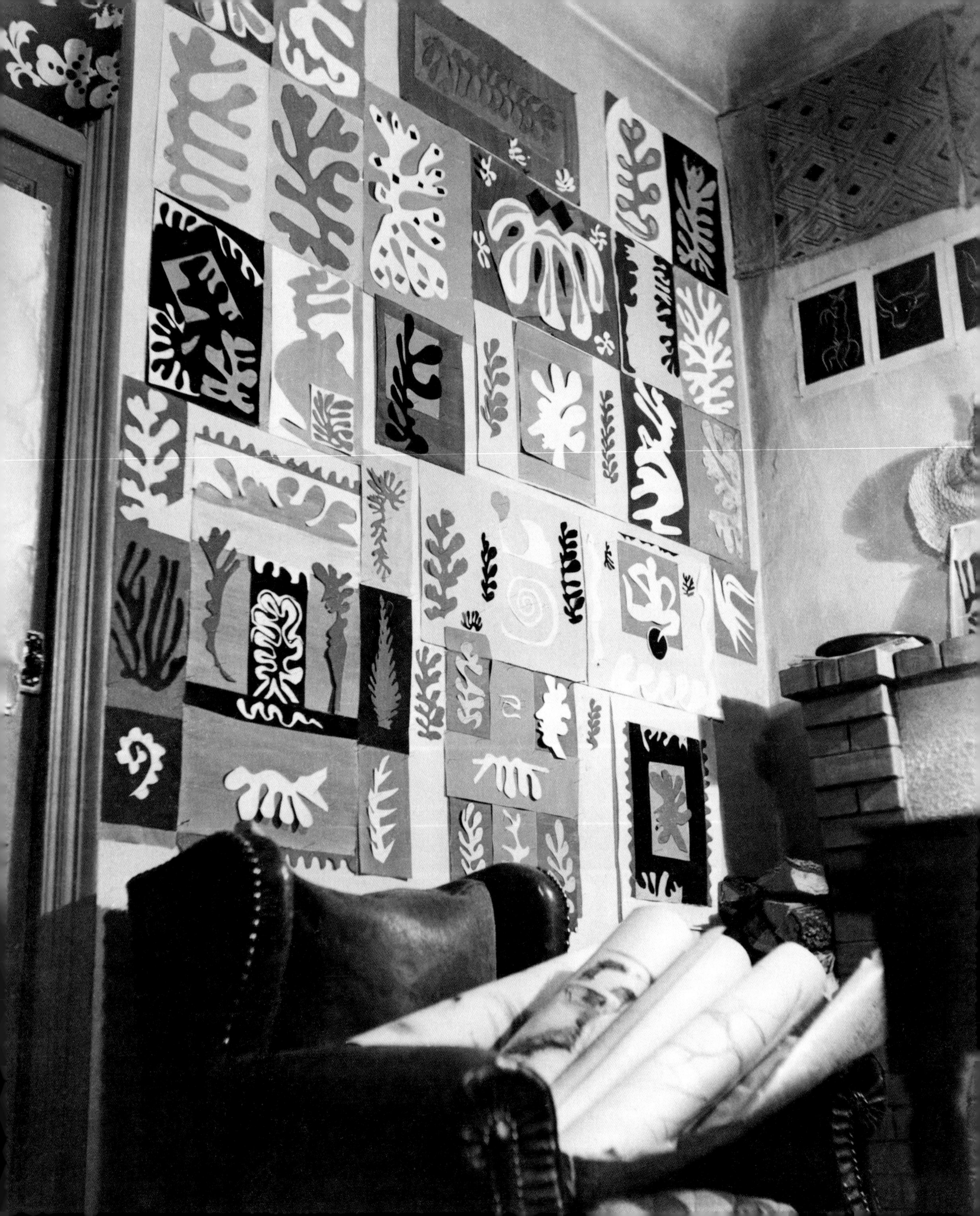

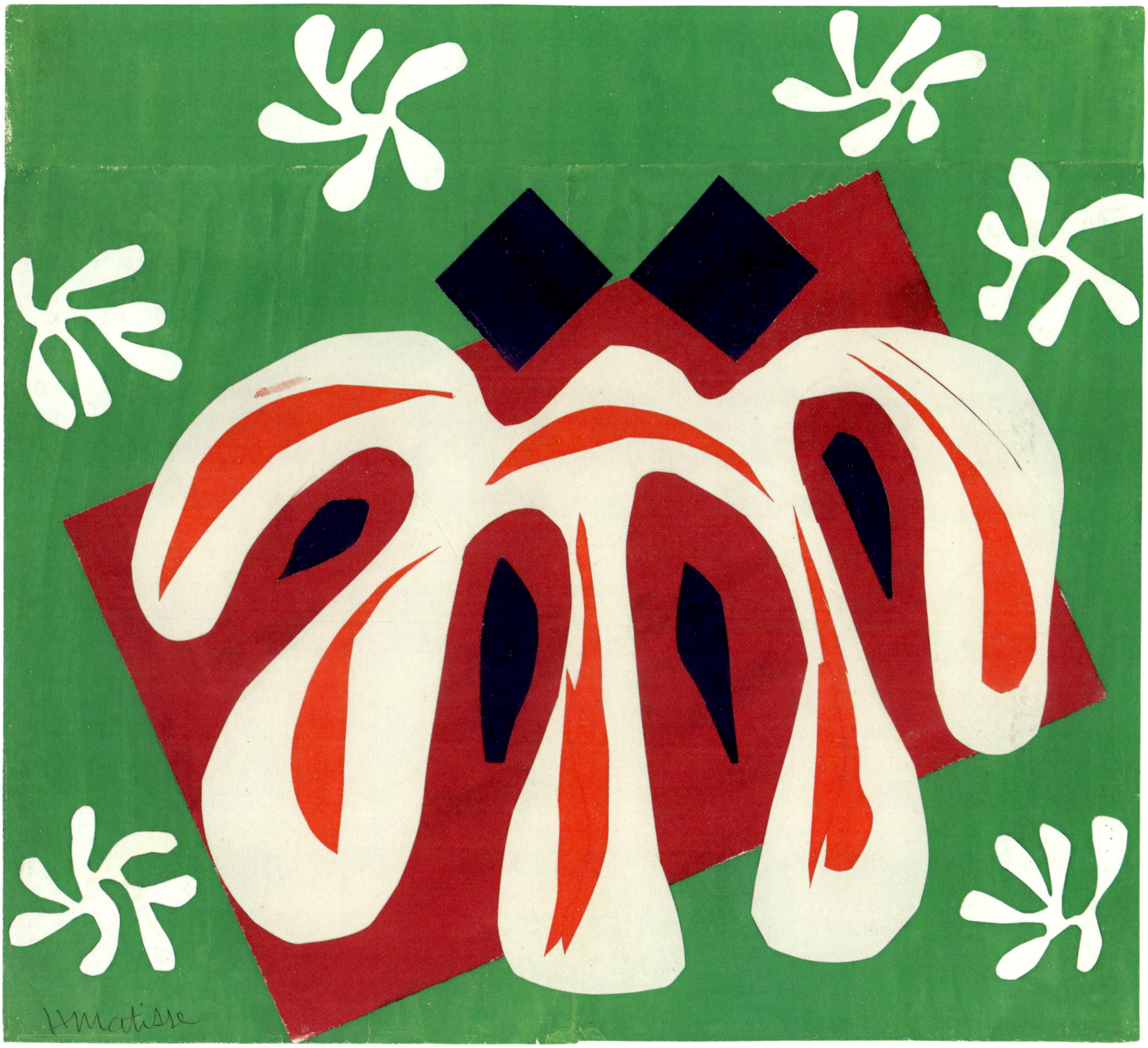

Villa "Le Rêve" with walls decorated
with gouache cut-outs
Vence, 1948

Two Masks (The Tomato), 1947
Gouache on paper, cut and pasted
on paper, 47.7 x 52 cm (18¾ x 20½ in.)
Private collection

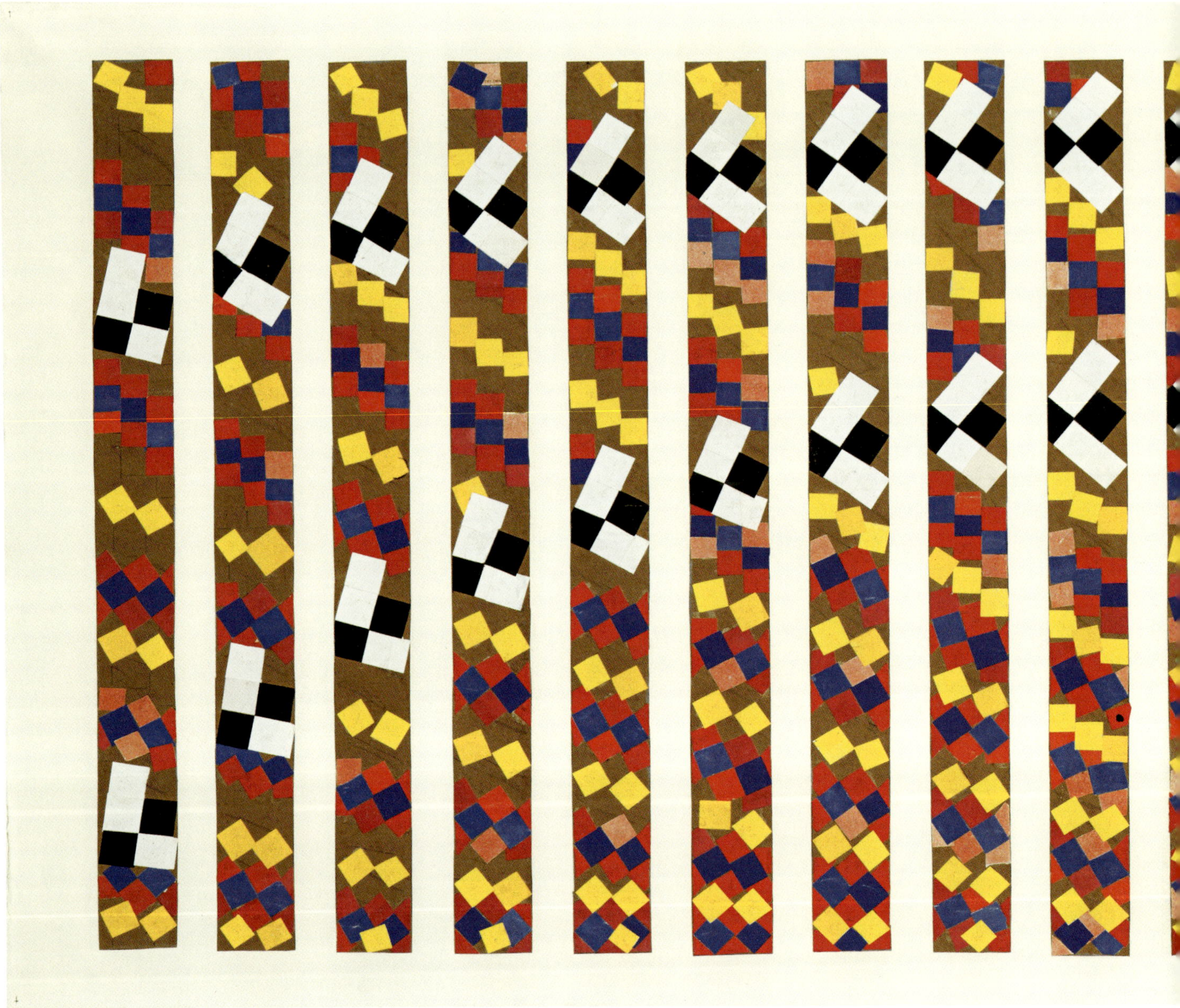

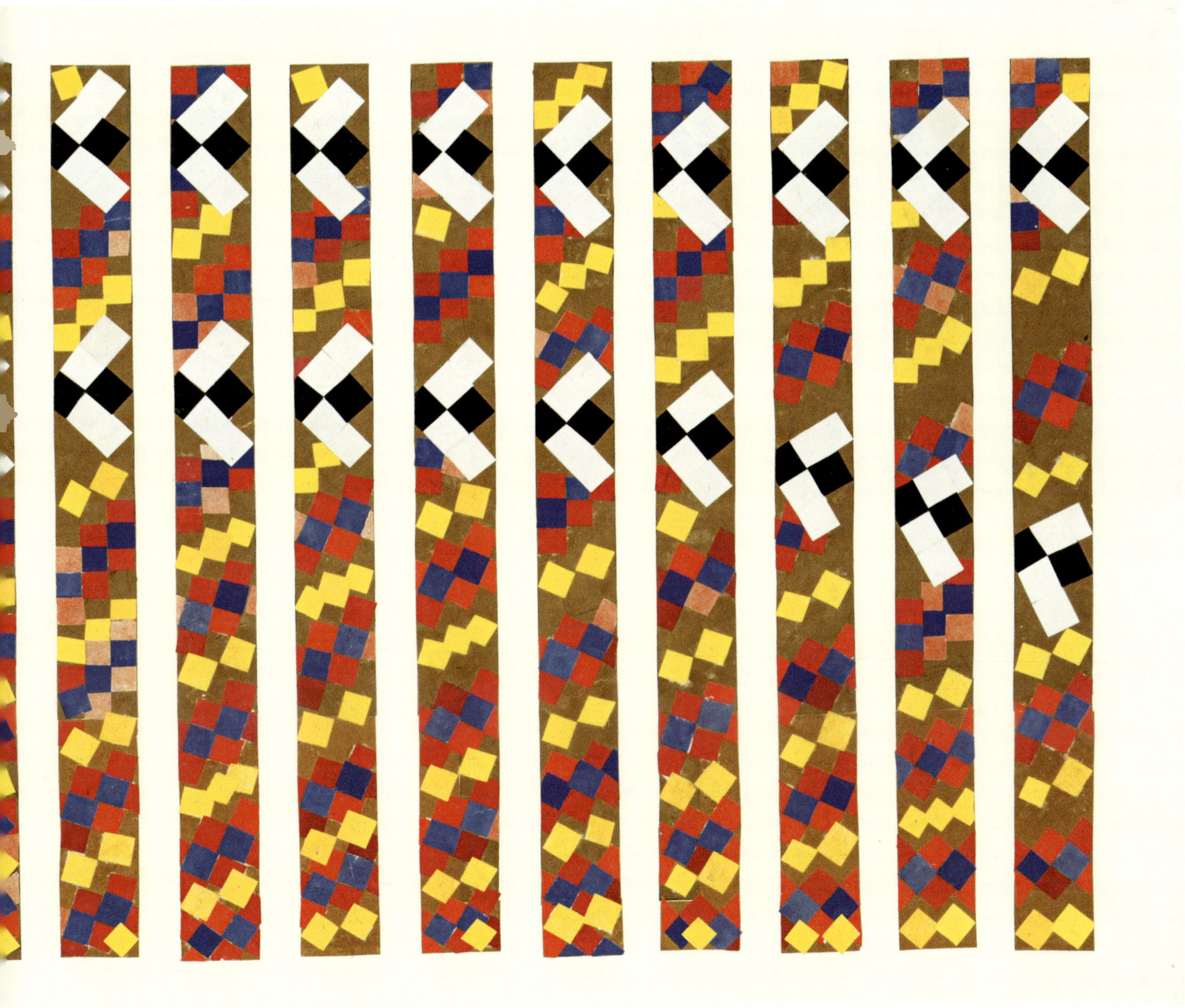

The Bees, Summer 1948
First maquette for the stained-glass windows of the Chapelle du Rosaire
Gouache on paper, cut and pasted on paper
101 x 241 cm (39¾ x 95 in.)
Nice, Musée Matisse

Like Cutting Glass …

Speaking of the stained-glass windows of his chapel, Matisse again referred to *Jazz*: "Those are stained-glass colours. I cut the gouached paper as one cuts glass; it is just that, there, the colours are arranged to reflect the light, whereas for the stained-glass they must be arranged so that the light comes through them."

The Tree of Life, 1949
Final maquette (3rd state) of the six windows of the nave
Gouache on paper, cut and pasted on paper
515 x 515 cm (202¾ x 202¾ in.)
Vatican City, Vatican Museums

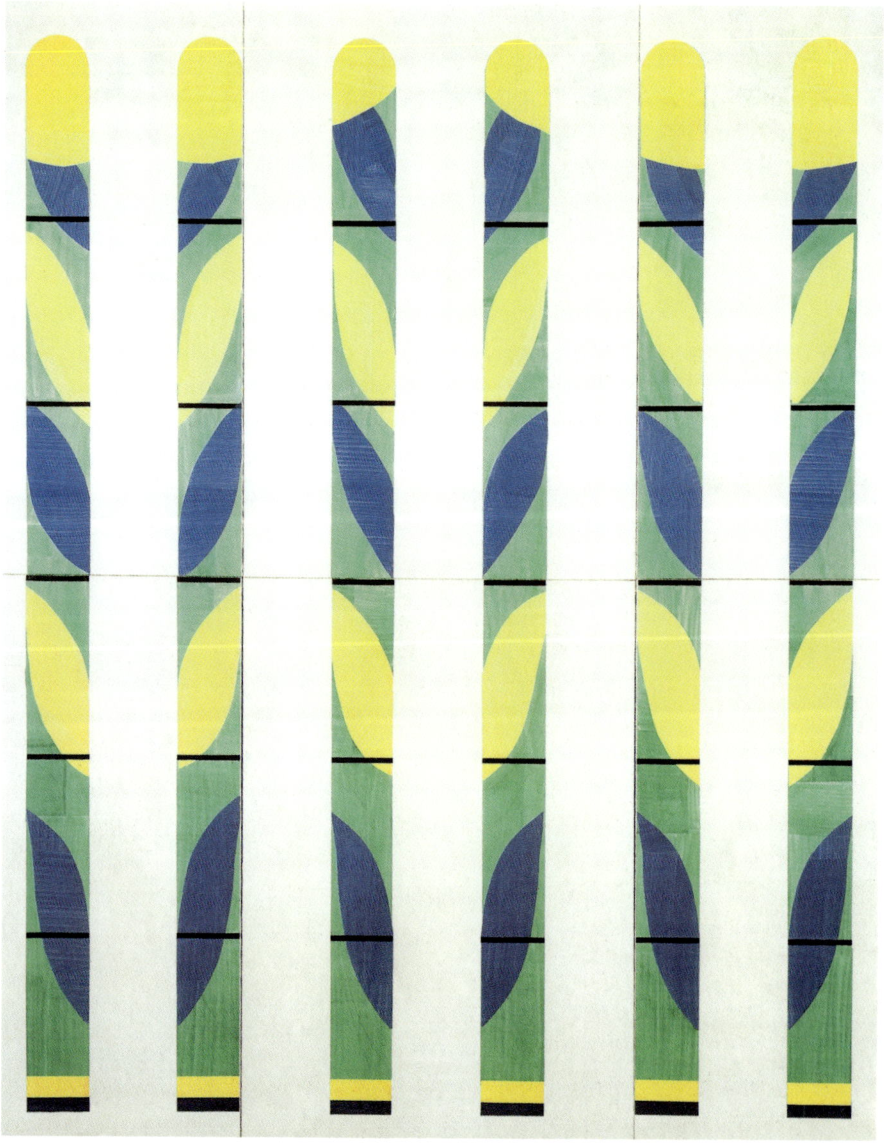

Matisse in front of ***The Tree of Life*** at the Chapelle du Rosaire, Vence, 1951
The tiles on the wall depict the "Stations of the Cross"
Photo: Dmitri Kessel

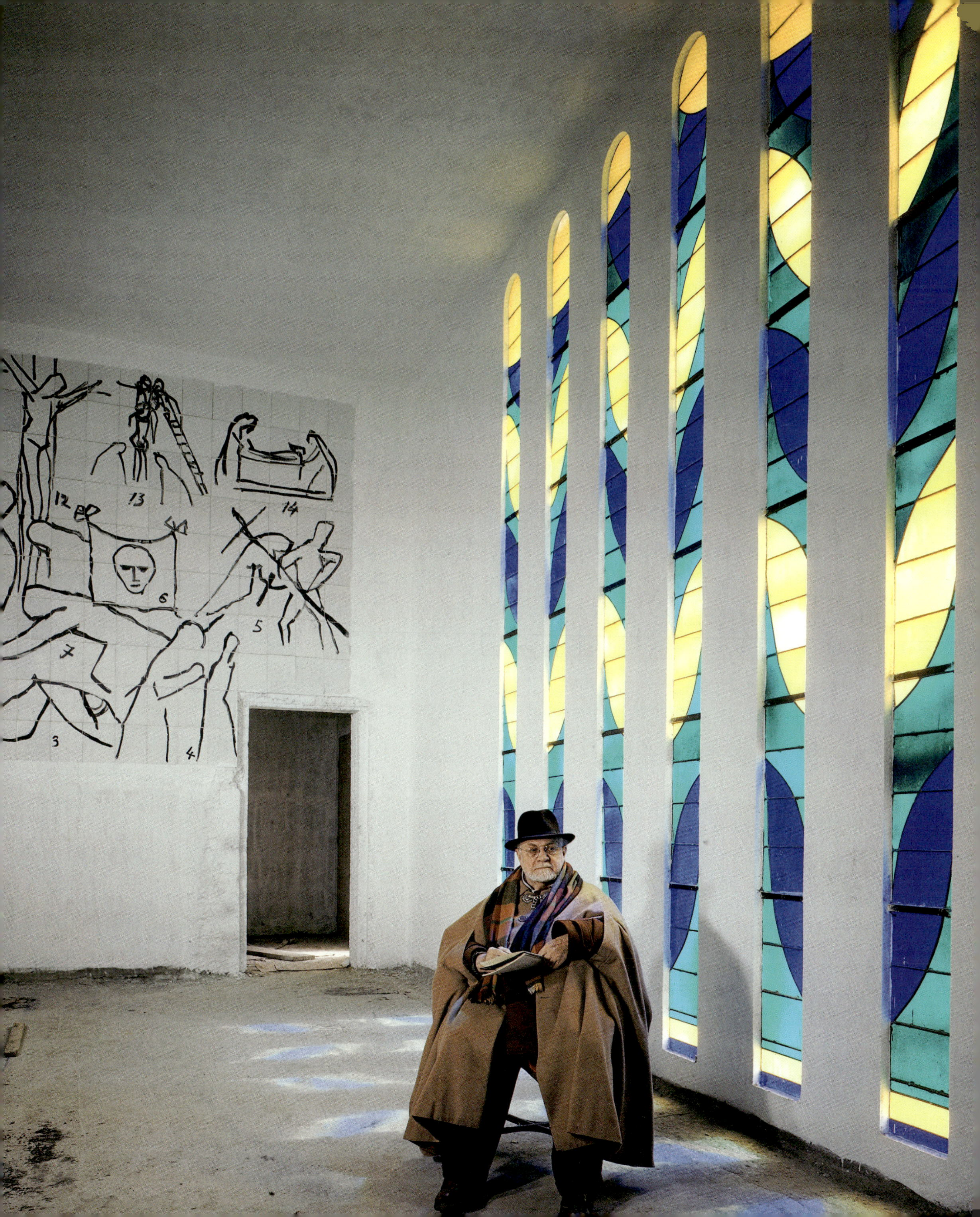
12
13
14
6
5
7
3
4

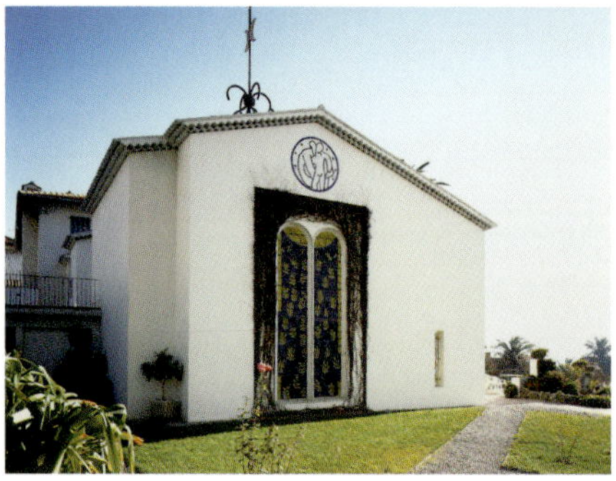

The entrance to the Chapelle du Rosaire, Vence, consecrated 25 June 1951 by the Bishop of Nice

The Tree of Life, Symbol of the Golden Age

The preparatory drawings for the stained-glass windows were thus created using gouache cut-outs. After long reflection, the theme was drawn from the Book of Revelation: "In the midst of the street of it, and on either side of the river, was there the tree of life, which … yielded her fruit every month: and the leaves of the tree were for the healing of the nations". The Tree of Life, symbol of the Golden Age! The tree, the flower! Is there any more beautiful leitmotif in the work of Matisse than this culmination of his habitual themes? Picasso was furious that Matisse was creating a church. "Why not do a market instead? You could paint the fruit and the vegetables!" Matisse confided to Father Couturier: "But I don't care: I have greens greener than pears and oranges more orange than pumpkins …"

The altar, with the stained-glass window of ***The Tree of Life*** to the left and St Dominick to the right.

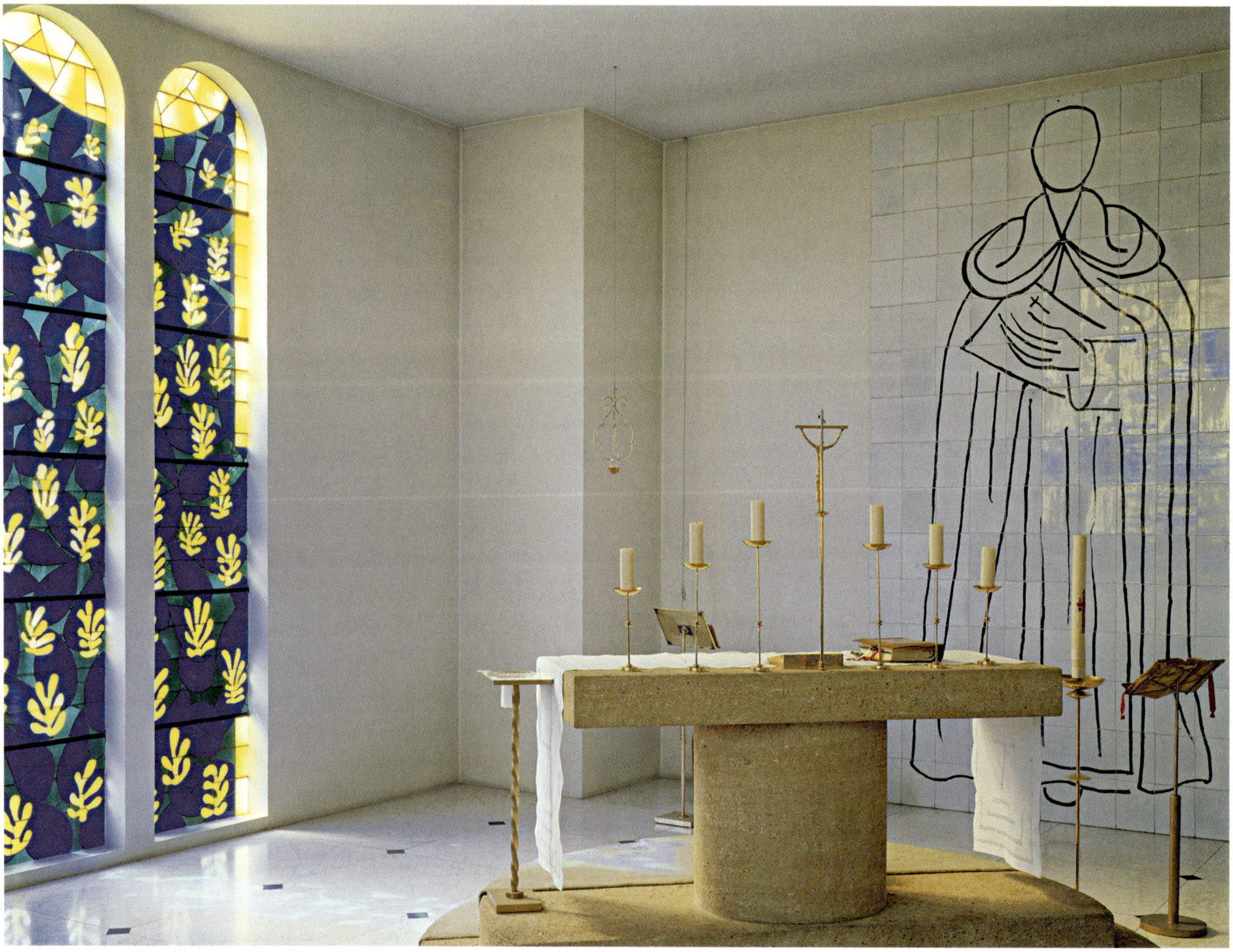

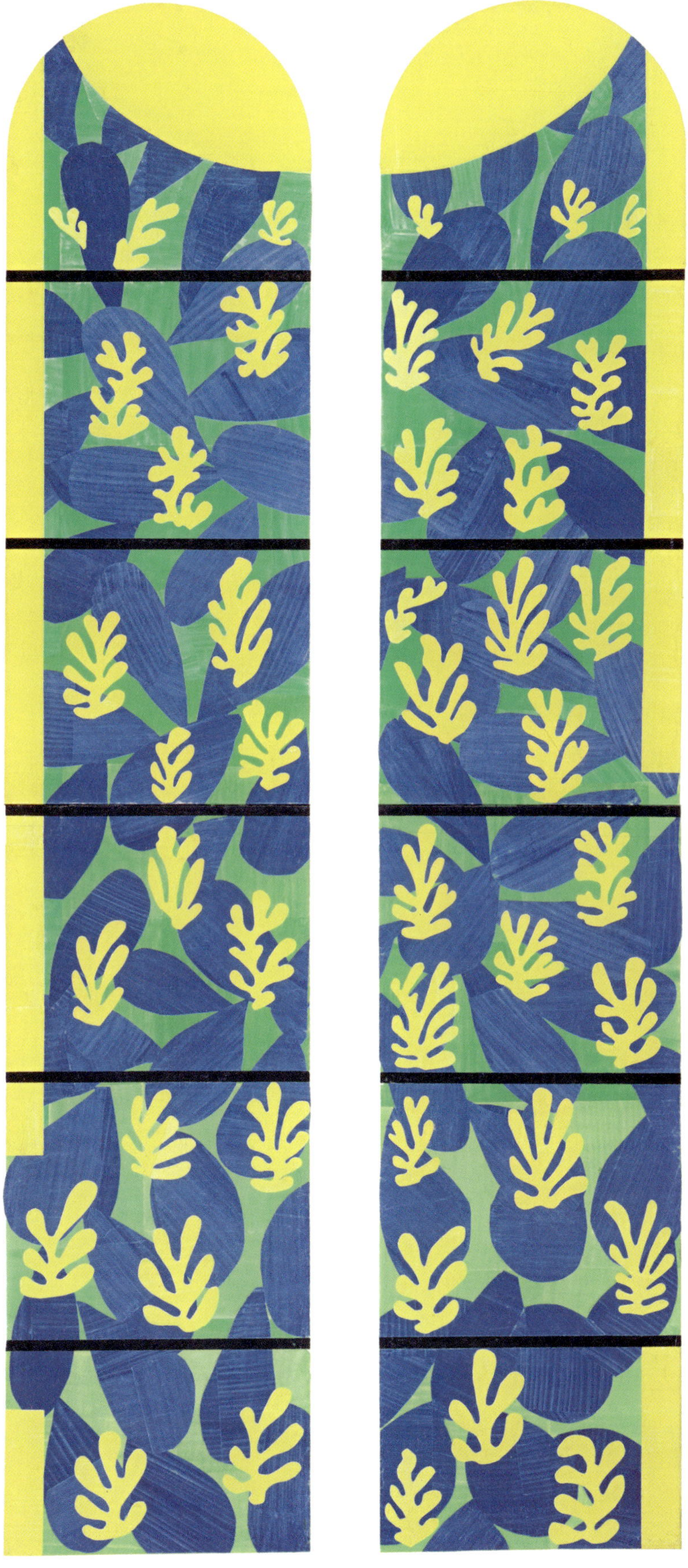

The Tree of Life, 1949
Third and final maquette for the stained-glass windows of the chapel
Gouache on paper, cut and pasted on canvas
515 x 252 cm (202¾ x 99¼ in.)
Vatican City, Vatican Museums

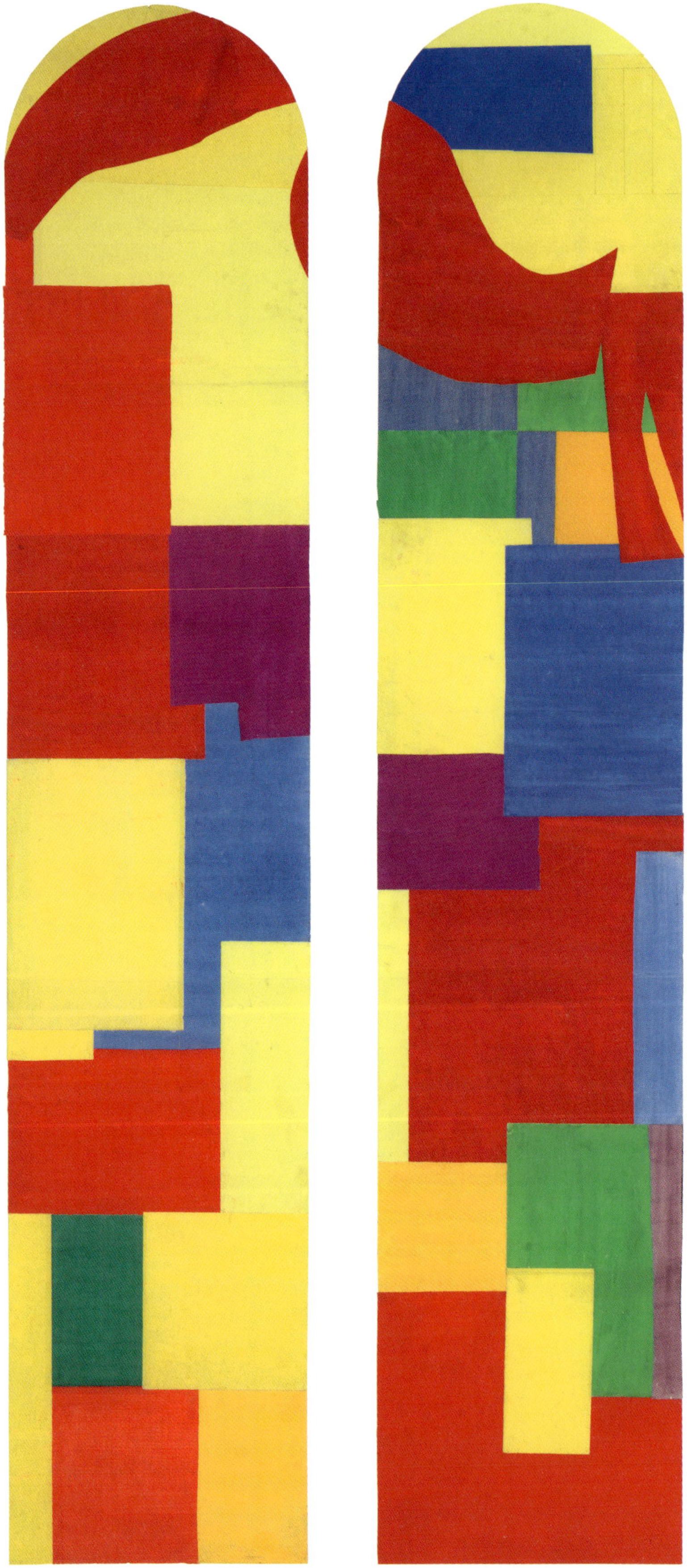

Celestial Jerusalem, 1948
First maquette, along with *The Bees*,
for the stained-glass windows of the chapel
Gouache on paper, cut and pasted on paper
270 x 130 cm (106¼ x 51¼ in.)
Paris, Musée national d'art moderne,
Centre Pompidou

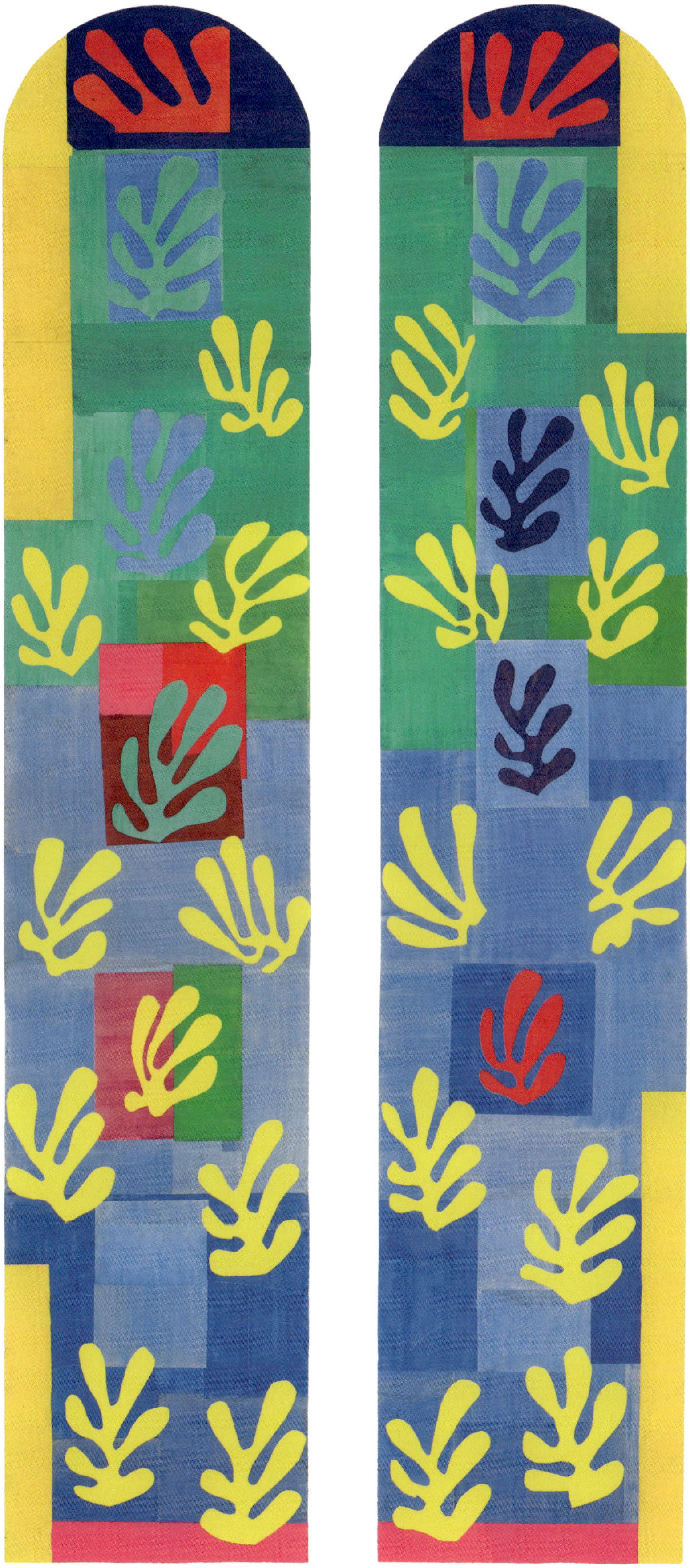

Light Blue Stained-Glass Window, 1949
Second maquette for the stained-glass windows of the chapel
Gouache on paper, cut and pasted on paper
509.8 x 252.3 cm (200¾ x 99¼ in.)
Paris, Musée national d'art moderne, Centre Pompidou

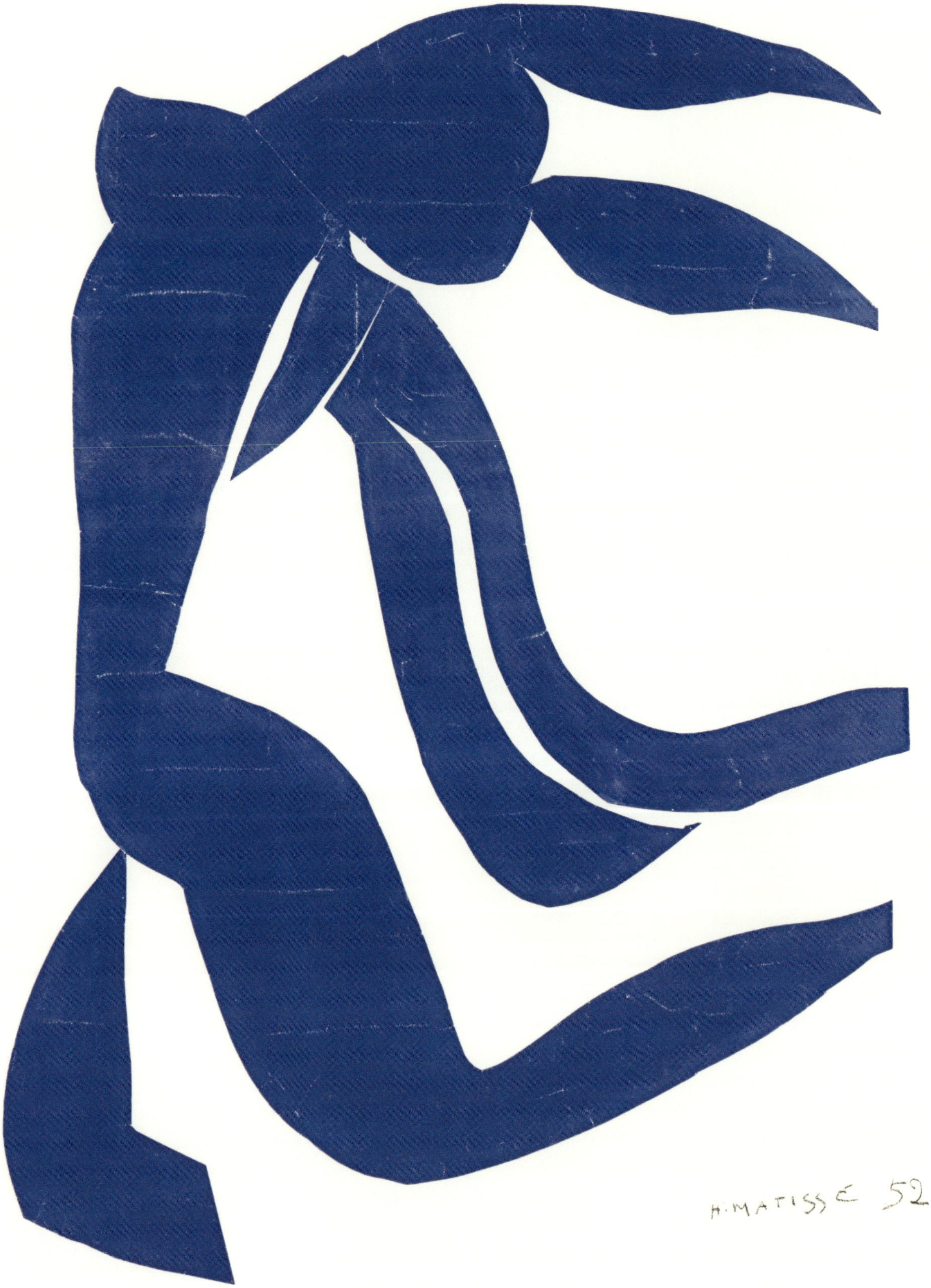
H. MATISSE 52

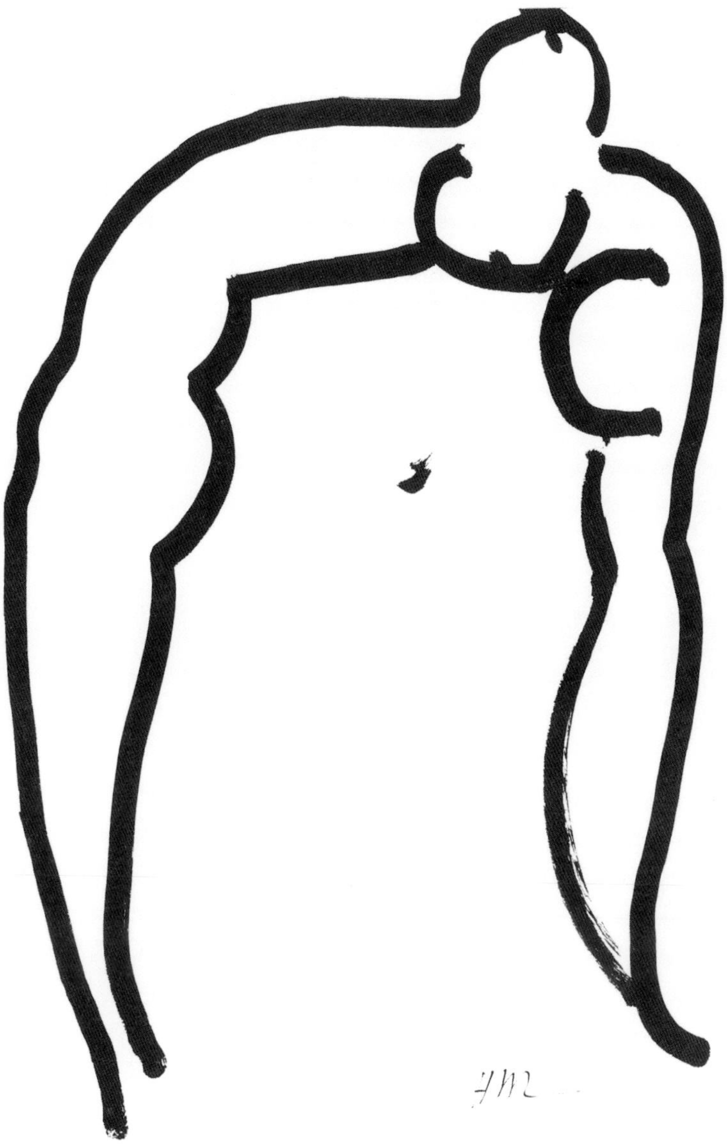

Acrobat, 1952
Brush and ink on paper
105 x 75 cm (41¼ x 29½ in.)
Illustration on p. 70, *Verve*, Nos. 35–36, 1958
Private collection

Dance and "Joie de vivre"
The pleasure that Matisse took in painting the joy of living made dance one of his major themes. "I had had this dance in me for a long time, and I had put it into *La joie de vivre,* then in the first big composition [for Shchukin] … It was like a rhythm within me that carried me along."

Flowing Hair, 1952
Gouache on paper, cut and pasted on paper
108 x 80 cm (42½ x 31½ in.)
Private collection

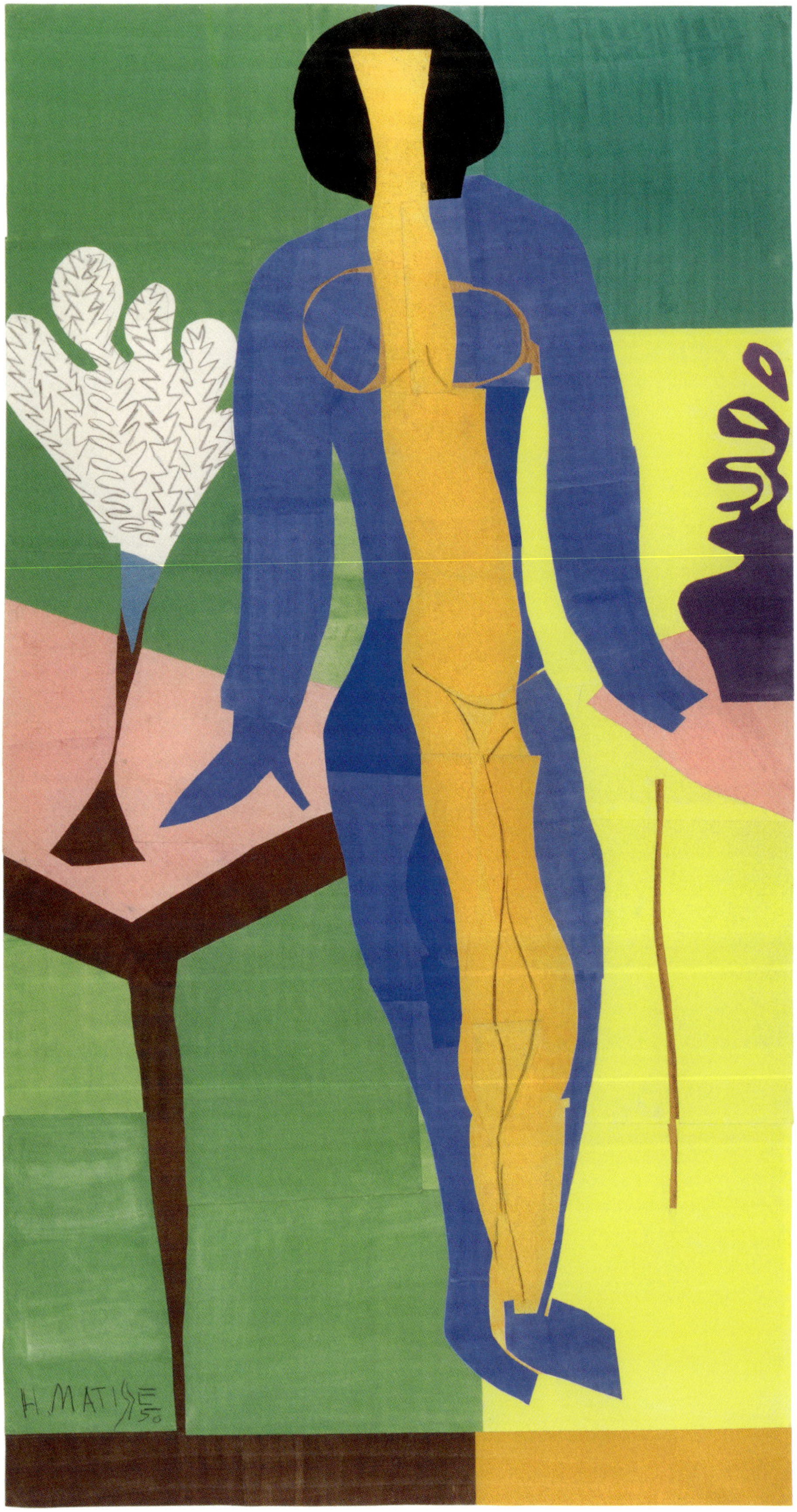
H. MATISSE 50

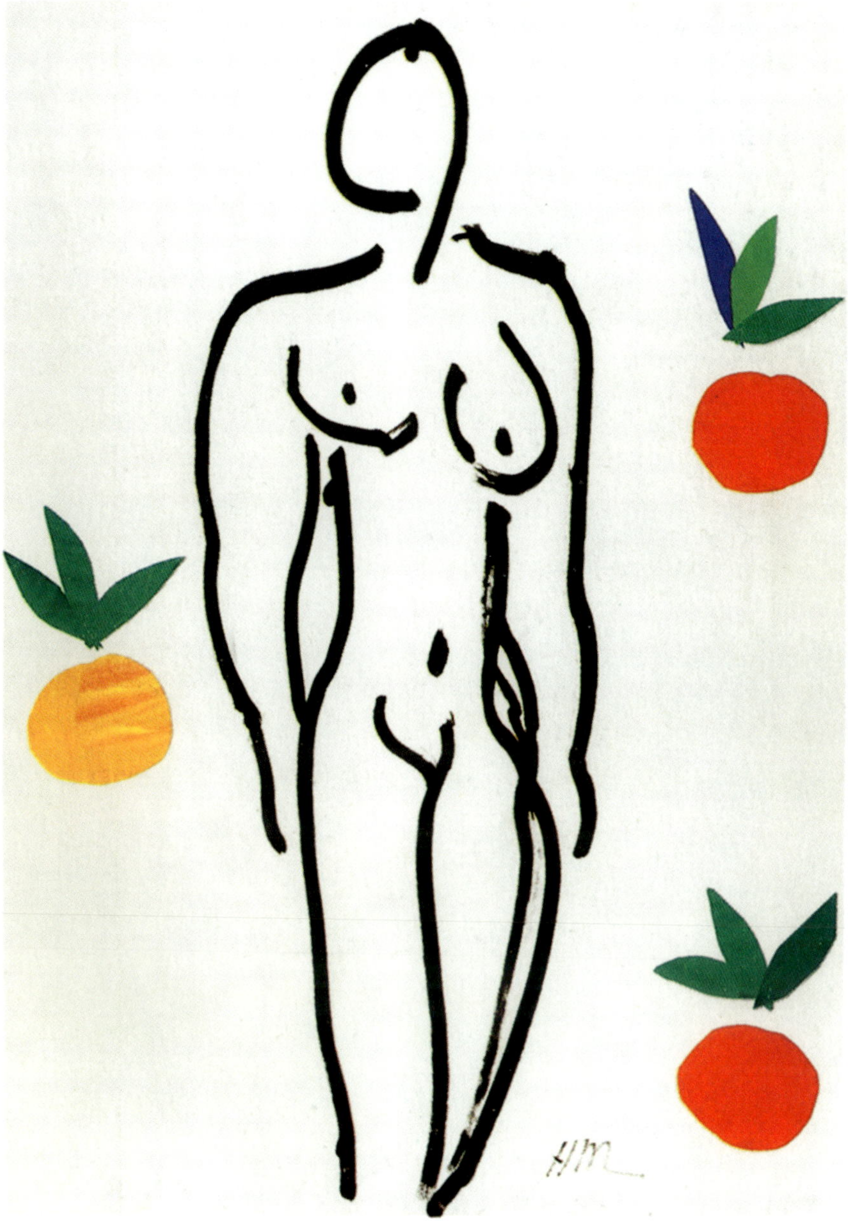

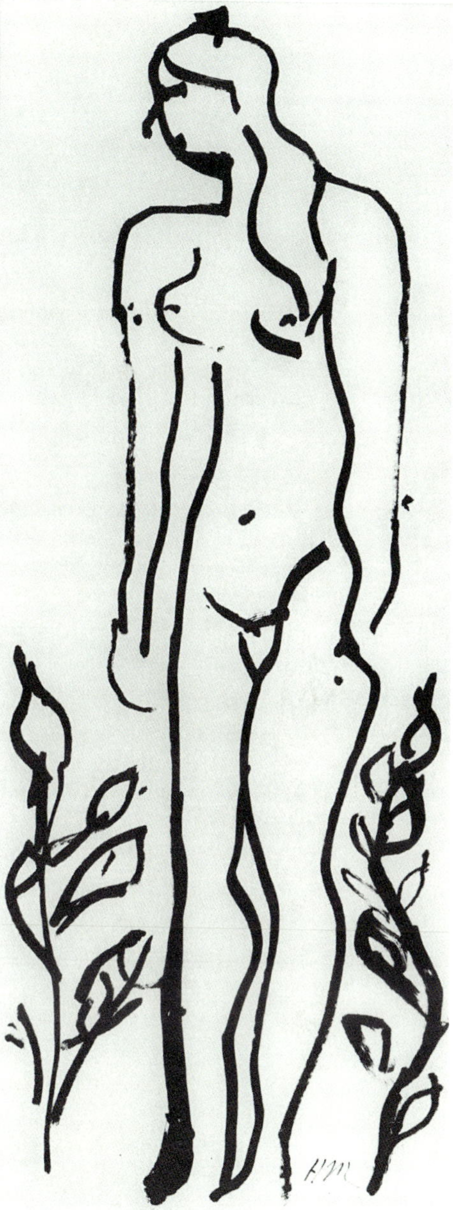

The Old Sage and the Young Giantesses

An old sage surrounded by young giantesses ("plane trees" in his description): Matisse endlessly modelled them, cut them out of vast sheets of coloured paper, or drew them in an earthly paradise reconstituted in the middle of the 20th century.

Nude with Oranges, 1953
Brush drawing and gouache on paper, cut and pasted on paper
155 x 108 cm (61 x 42½ in.)
Paris, Musée national d'art moderne, Centre Pompidou

Large Nude, 1952
Brush and Indian ink,
210 x 80 cm (82¾ x 31½ in.)
Illustration of front cover of *Verve,*
Nos. 35–36, 1958
Private collection

Zulma, 1950
Gouache on paper, cut and pasted, and pencil on paper, 238 x 133 cm (93¾ x 52¼ in.)
Copenhagen, Statens Museum for Kunst,
J. Rump Collection

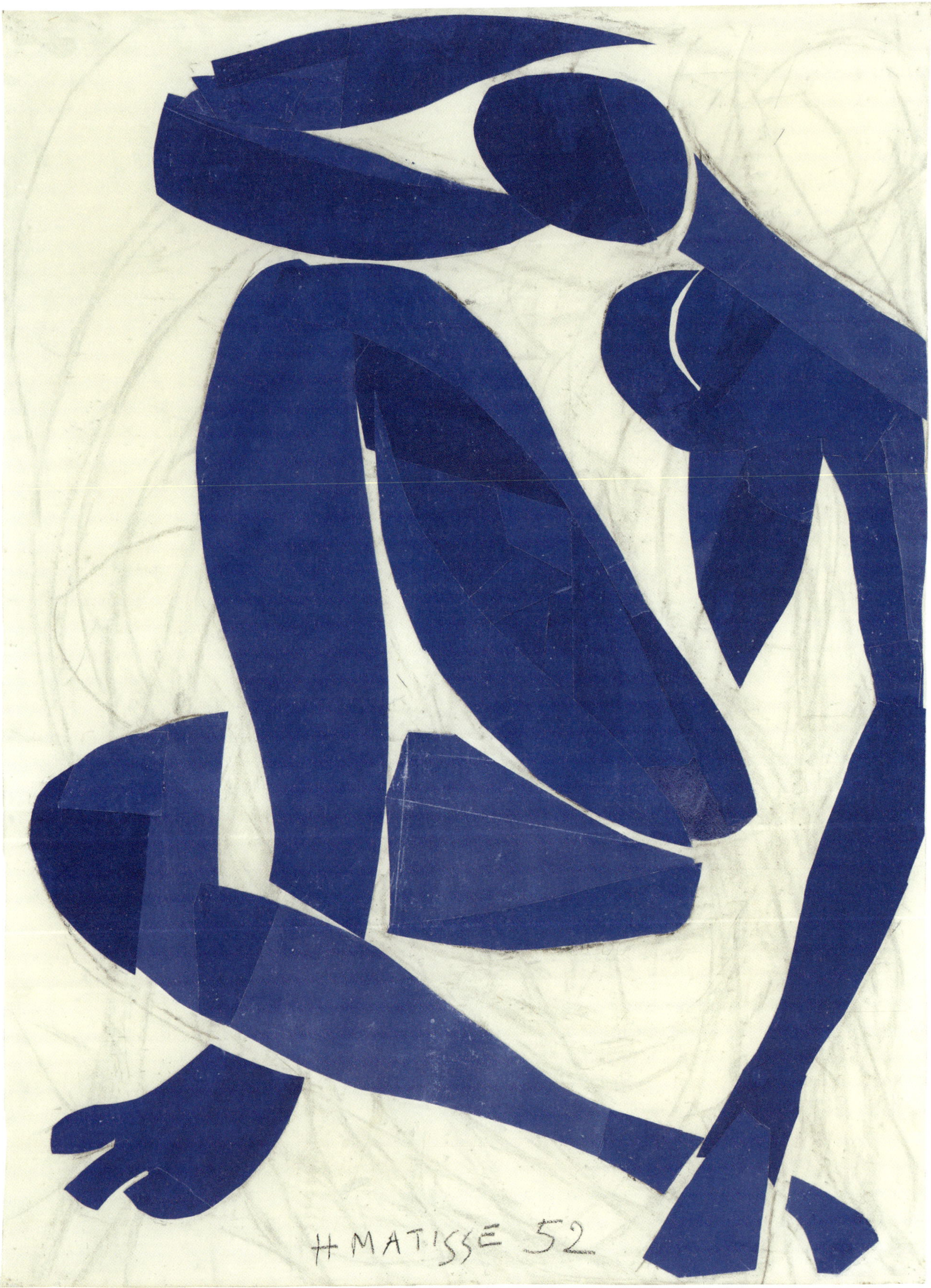
H MATISSE 52

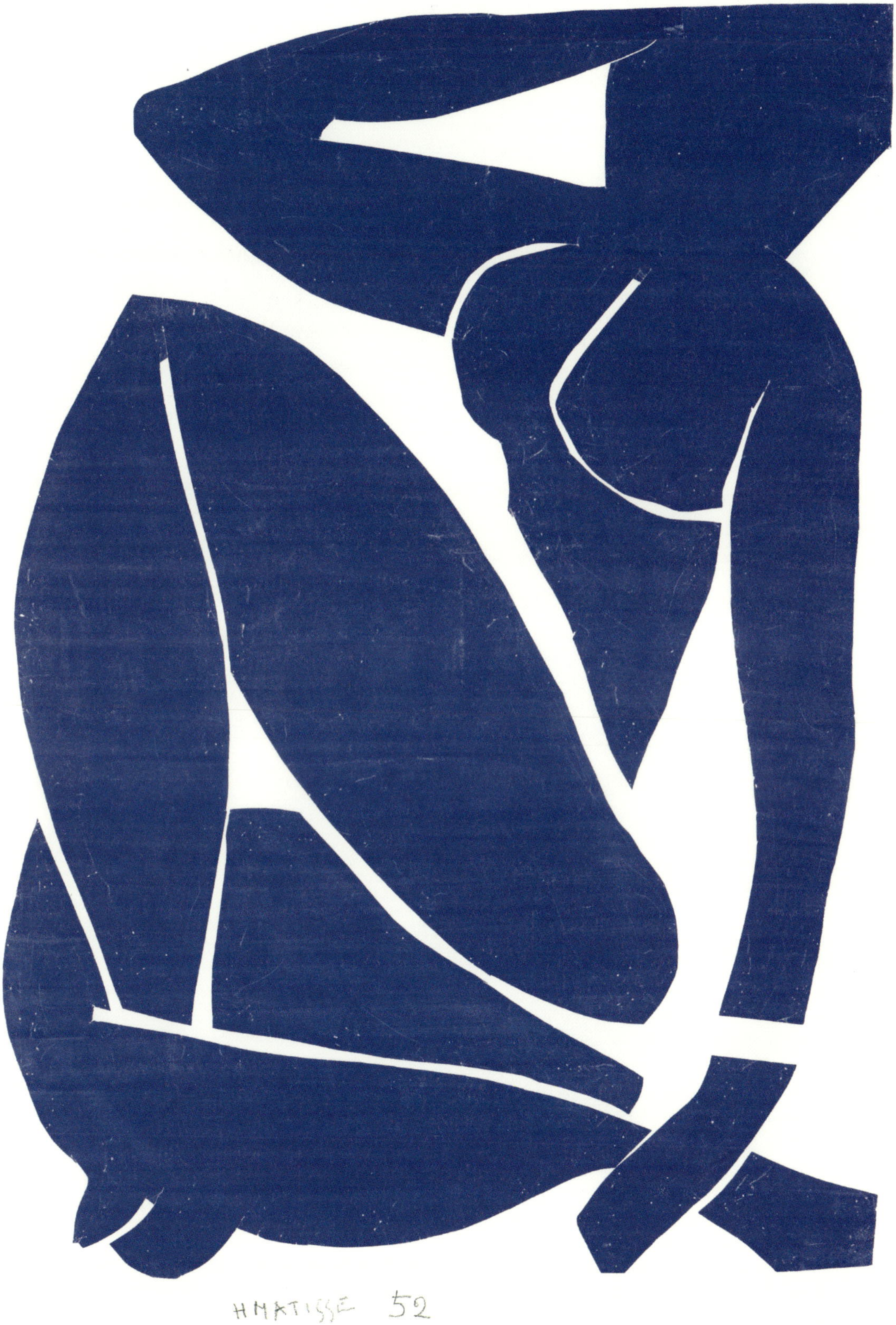
HMATISSE 52

PAGE 68
Blue Nude IV, 1952
Gouache on paper, cut and pasted on canvas
103 x 74 cm (40½ x 29¼ in.)
Nice, Musée Matisse

PAGE 69
Blue Nude III, 1952
Gouache on paper, cut and pasted on paper
112 x 73.5 cm (44 x 29 in.)
Paris, Musée national d'art moderne, Centre Pompidou

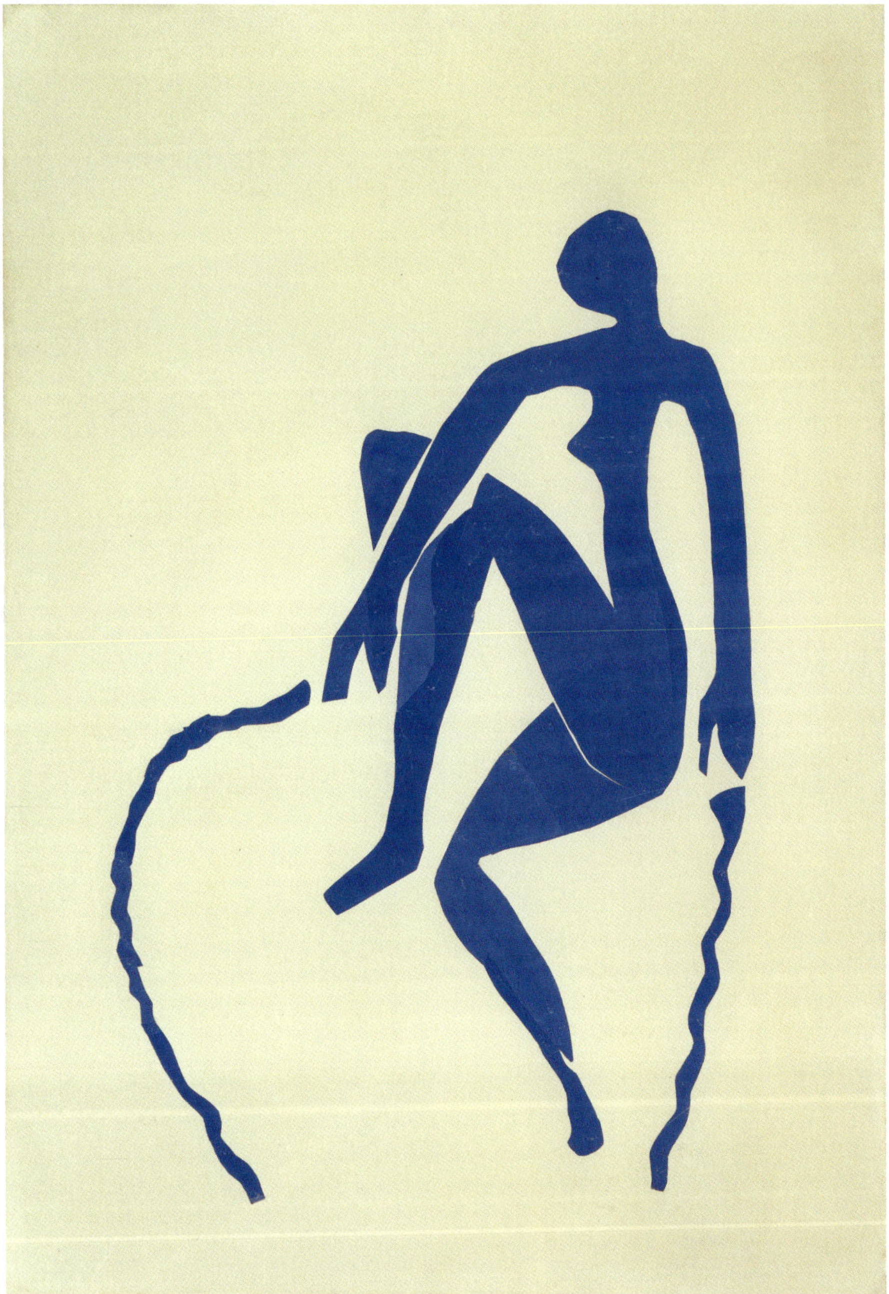

Blue Nude, Skipping, 1952
Gouache on paper, cut and pasted on paper
145 x 98 cm (57 x 38½ in.)
Nationalgalerie, Museum Berggruen, Staatliche Museen zu Berlin

Emblems of the Female Body

Dancer or acrobat, the figure of Woman finds its definitive sign in the œuvre of Matisse. The *Blue Nudes*, veritable emblems of the female body, act on our intimate feelings like the stroke of a gong, their power the greater for their simple inner form. The interstices of white suggest their kinship to sculpture. One thinks of Lao-Tzu's words in the Tao Te Ching: "Clay serves to make the vase. But only the space within allows its use."

Blue Nude with Green Stockings, 1952
Gouache on paper, cut and pasted on paper
260 x 168 cm (102¼ x 66¼ in.)
Paris, Fondation Louis Vuitton

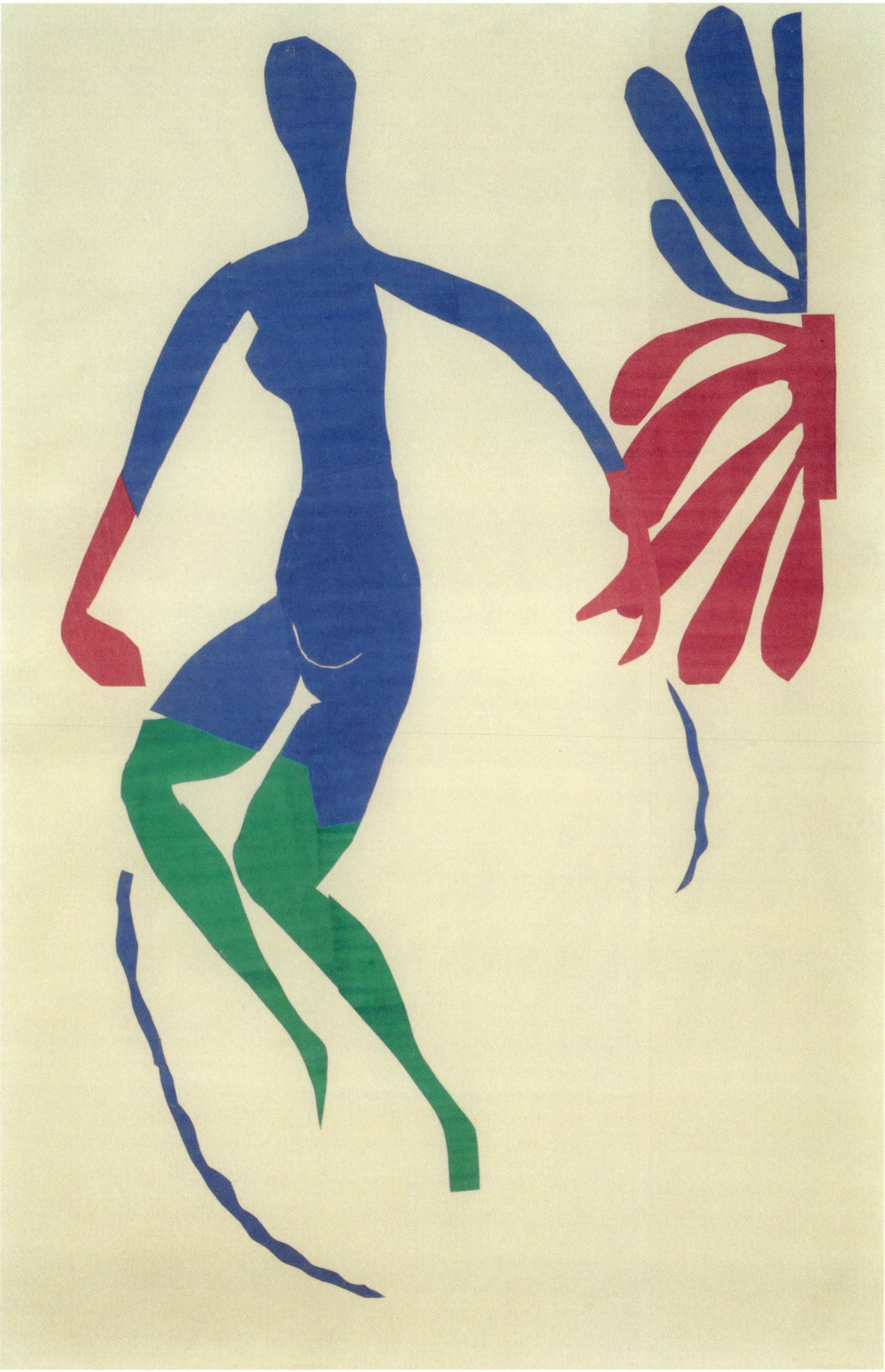

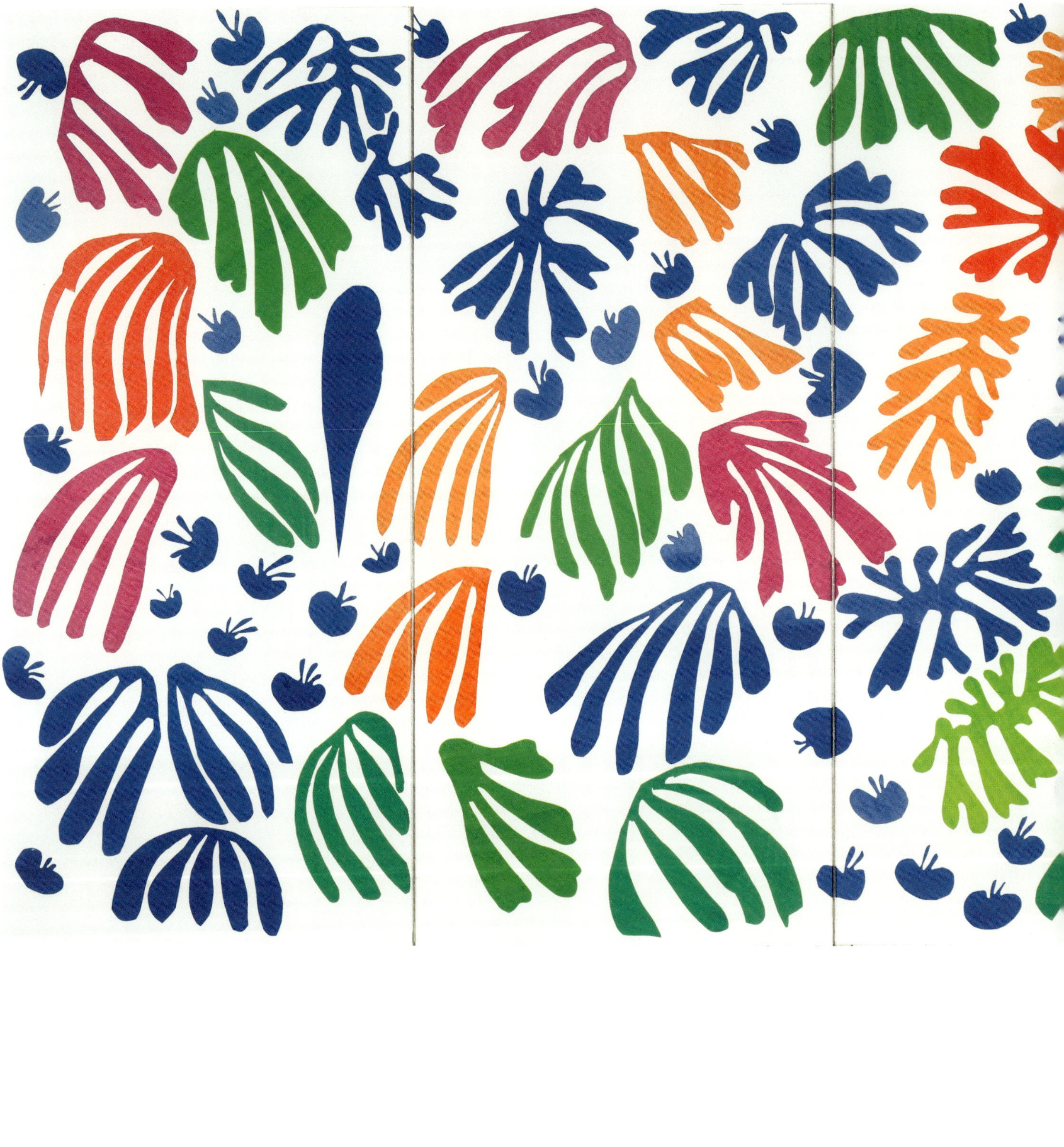

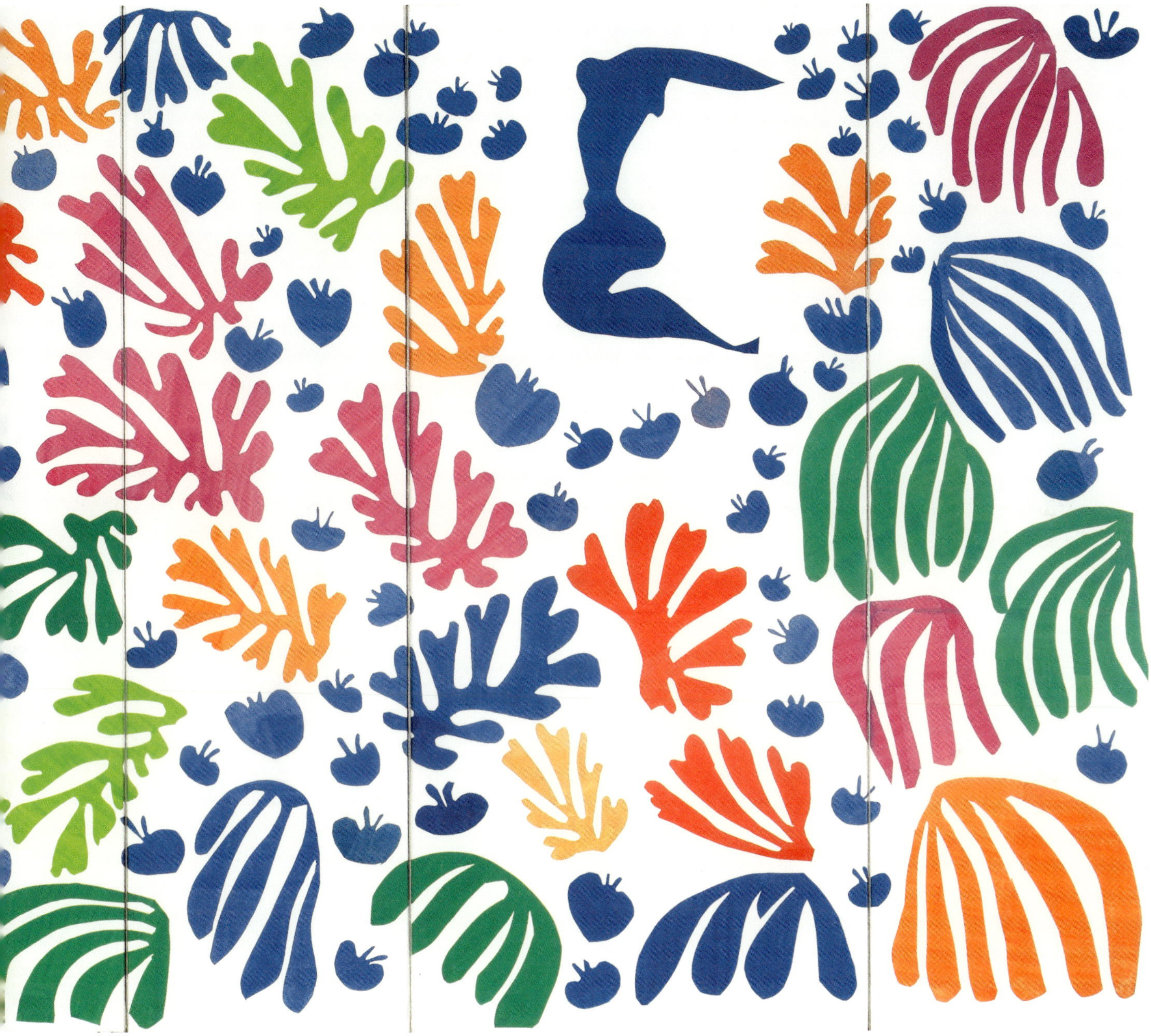

Vision of Earthly Paradise
Standing Blue Nude, Blue Nude, Skipping, Blue Nude with Green Stockings (it is said that supplies of blue gouached paper were lacking that day, so the legs were finished with green and the arms with red) are stepping-stones in the creation of large compositions. They recur in *The Swimming Pool* (pp. 84–85) and each in turn was tried as a counterpart to the budgerigar before the "siren" was chosen in their place.

The Budgerigar and the Siren, 1952
Gouache on paper, cut and pasted on paper, 337 x 768.5 cm (132¾ x 302½ in.)
Amsterdam, Stedelijk Museum

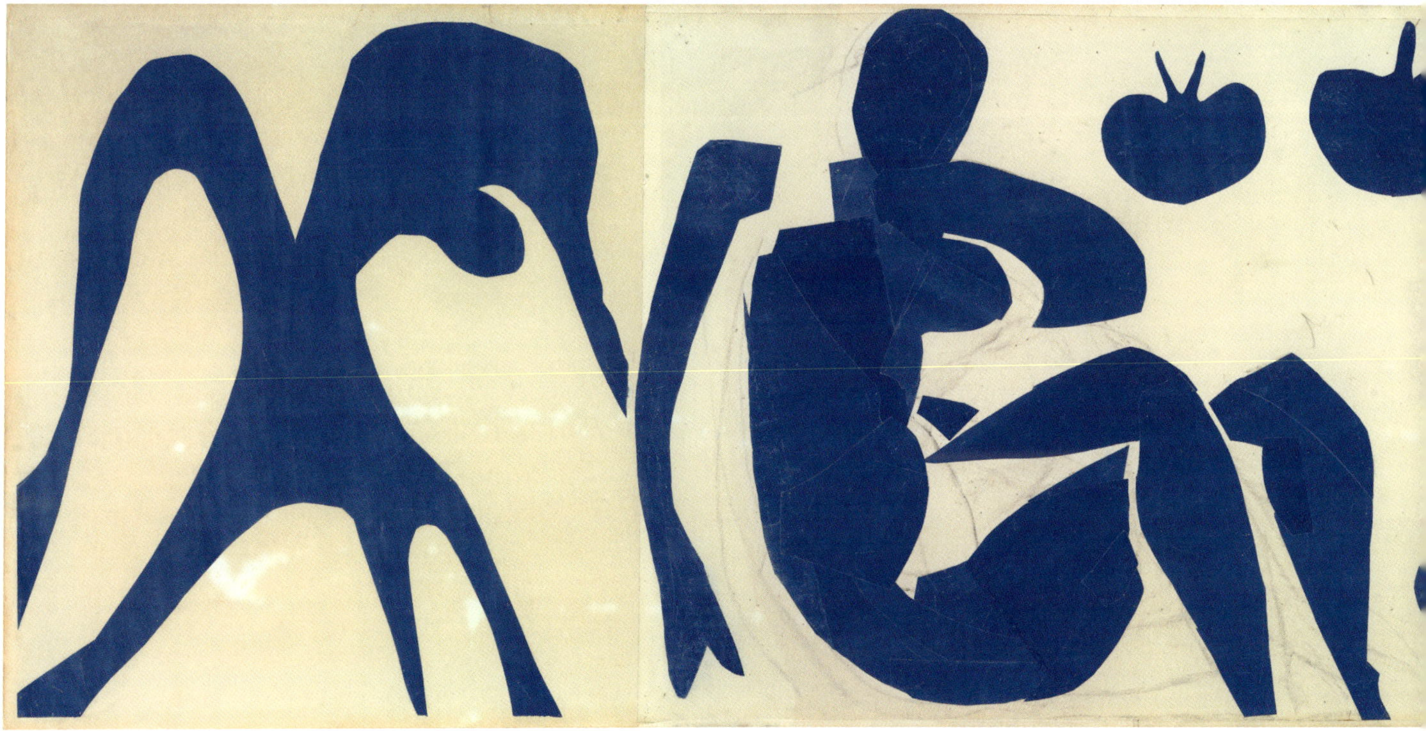

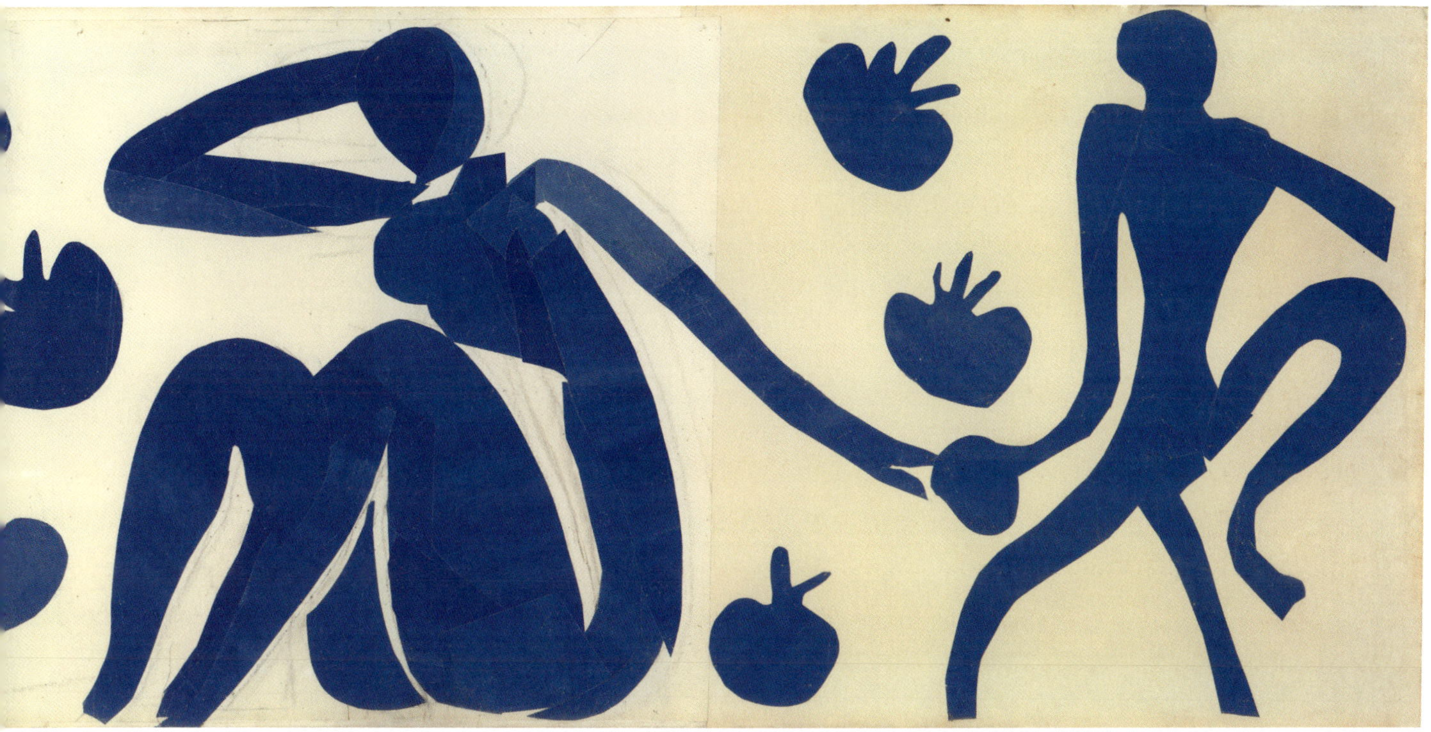

Eve's Costume is the Uniform of Love

Matisse avowed that the woman of *Women and Apes* was a link between the plant on the left and the hominoid on the right. More than ever, Matisse's works of 1952–53 suggest the Golden Age, the extraordinary garden of Earthly Paradise brimming with flowers and fruits among which, as myth prescribes, naked creatures wander. Is not Eve's costume the uniform of love?

Woman and Apes, 1952
Gouache on paper, cut and pasted, and charcoal on paper, 71.7 x 286.2 cm (28¼ x 112¾ in.)
Cologne, Museum Ludwig

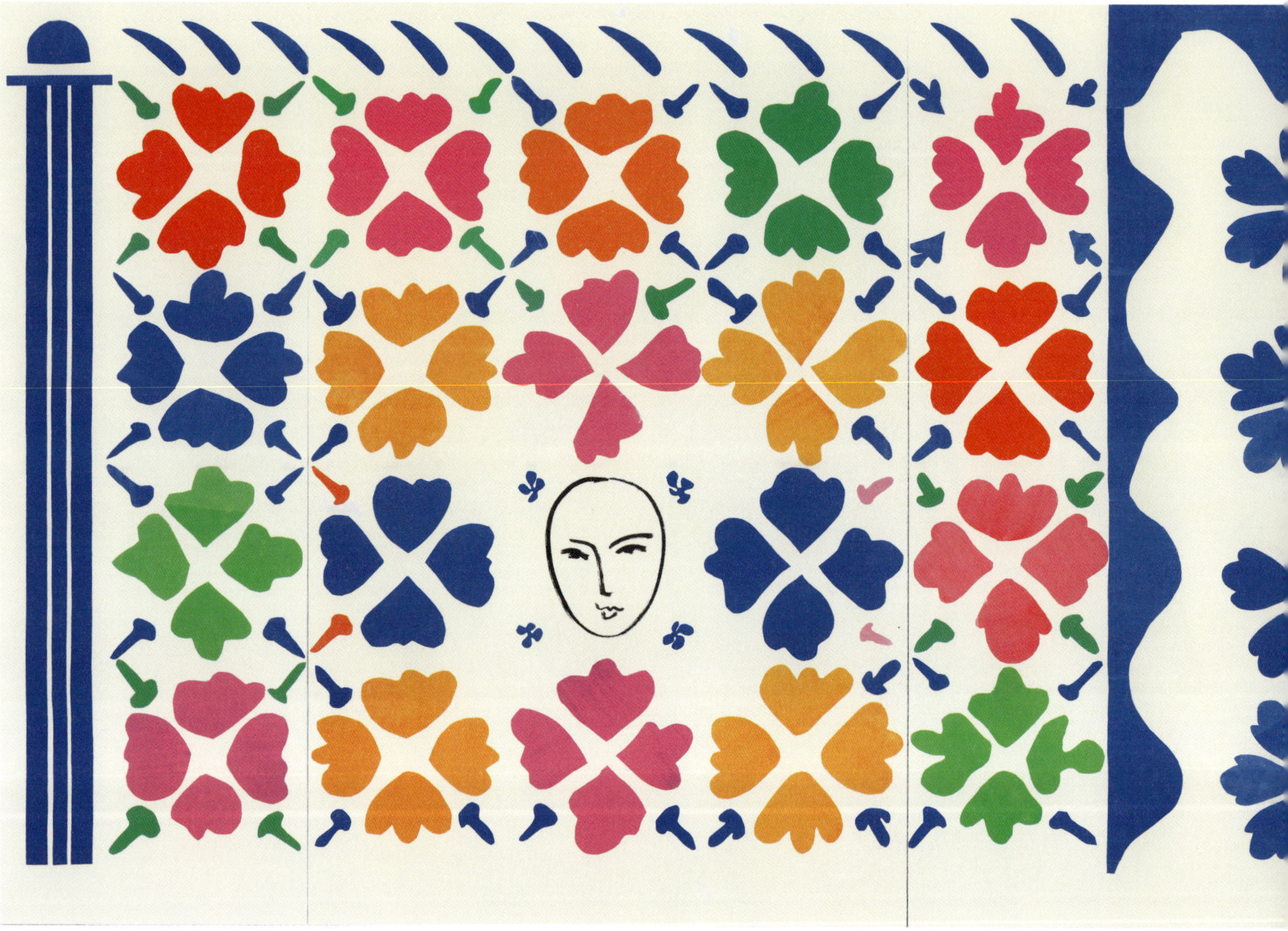

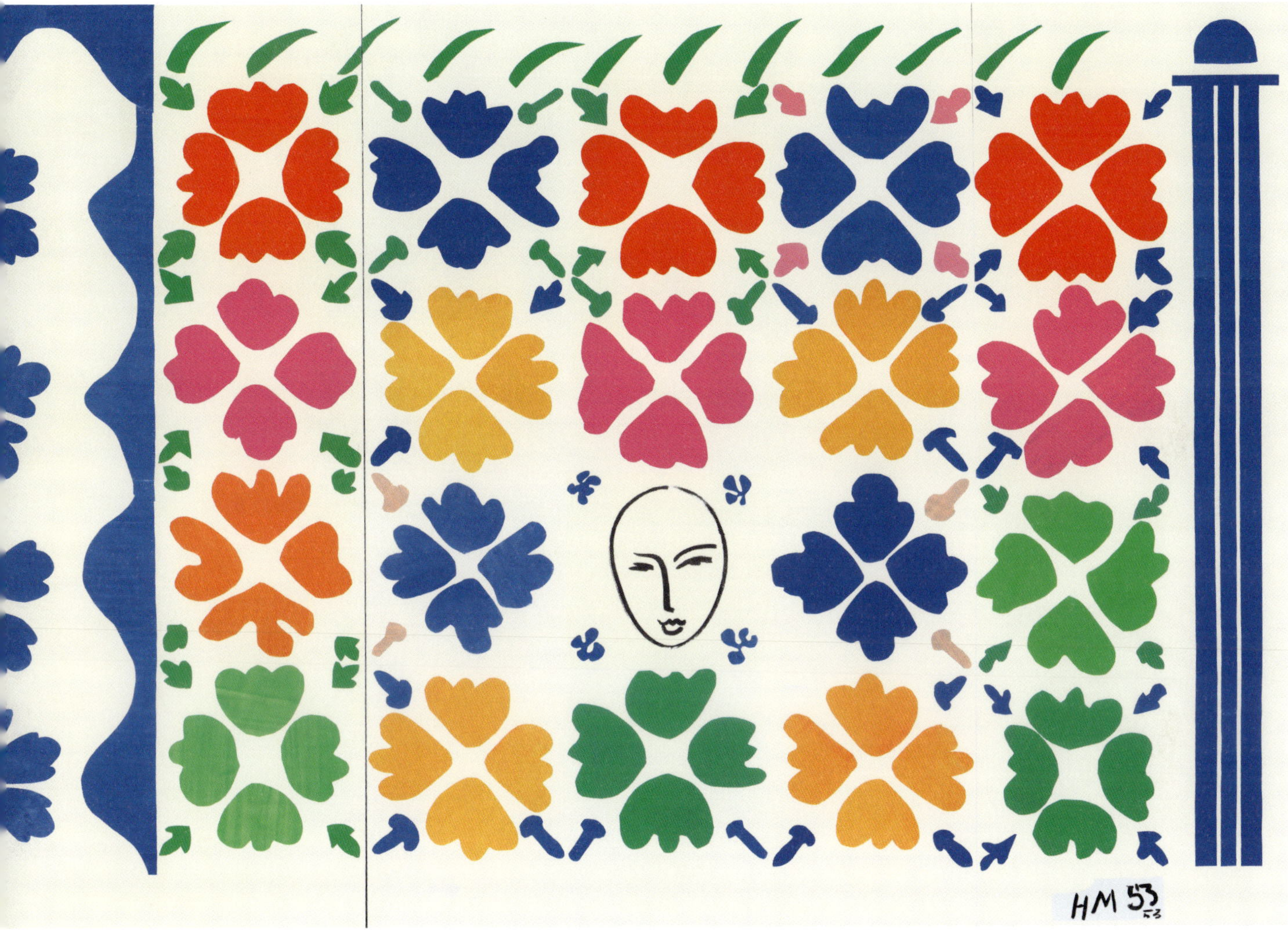

Large Composition with Masks, 1953
Gouache on paper, cut and pasted
on canvas, 353.6 x 996.4 cm (139¼ x 392¼ in.)
Lithographic reproduction of the
original paper cut-out
Washington, D.C., National Gallery of Art,
Ailsa Mellon Bruce Fund

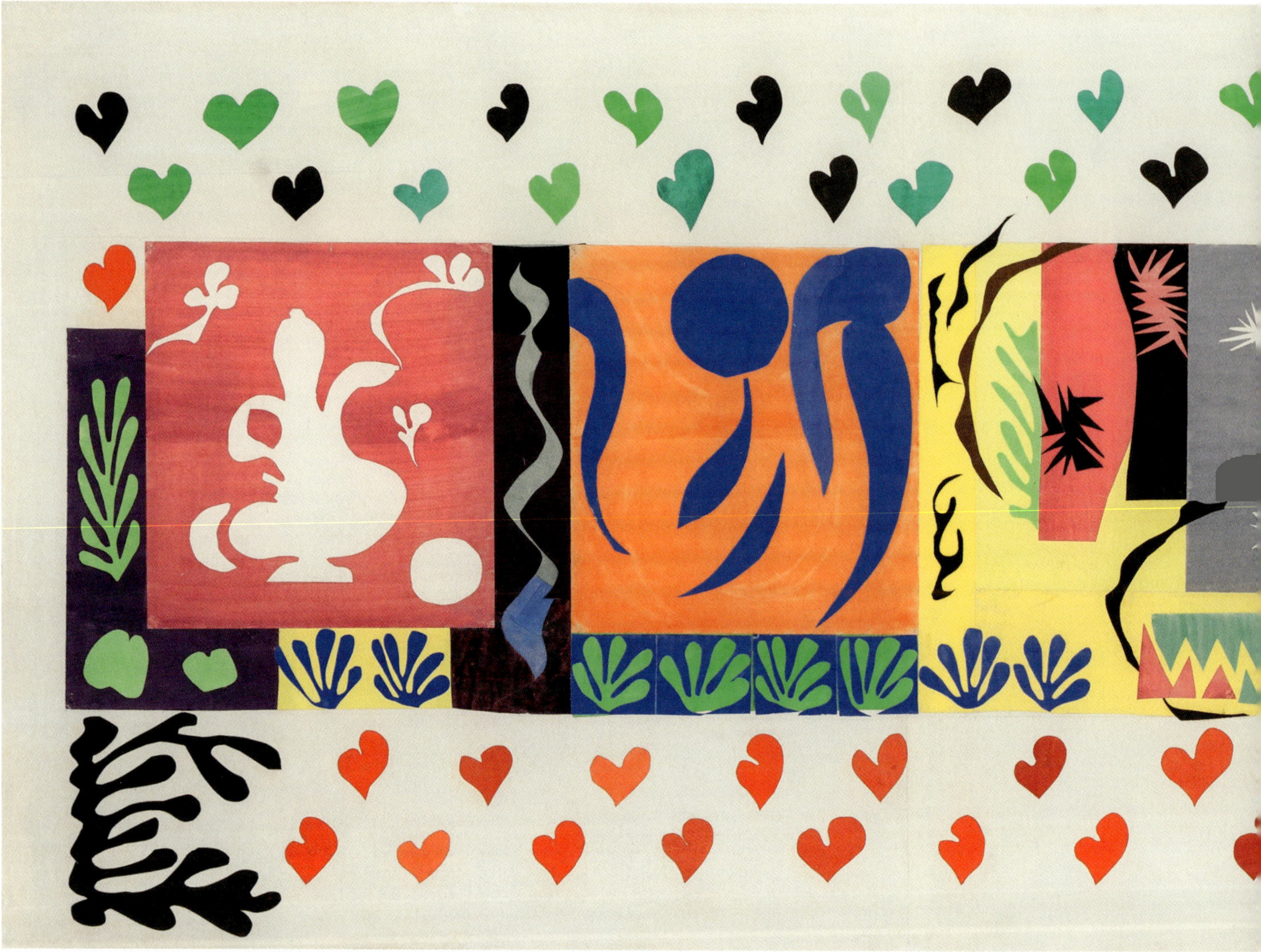

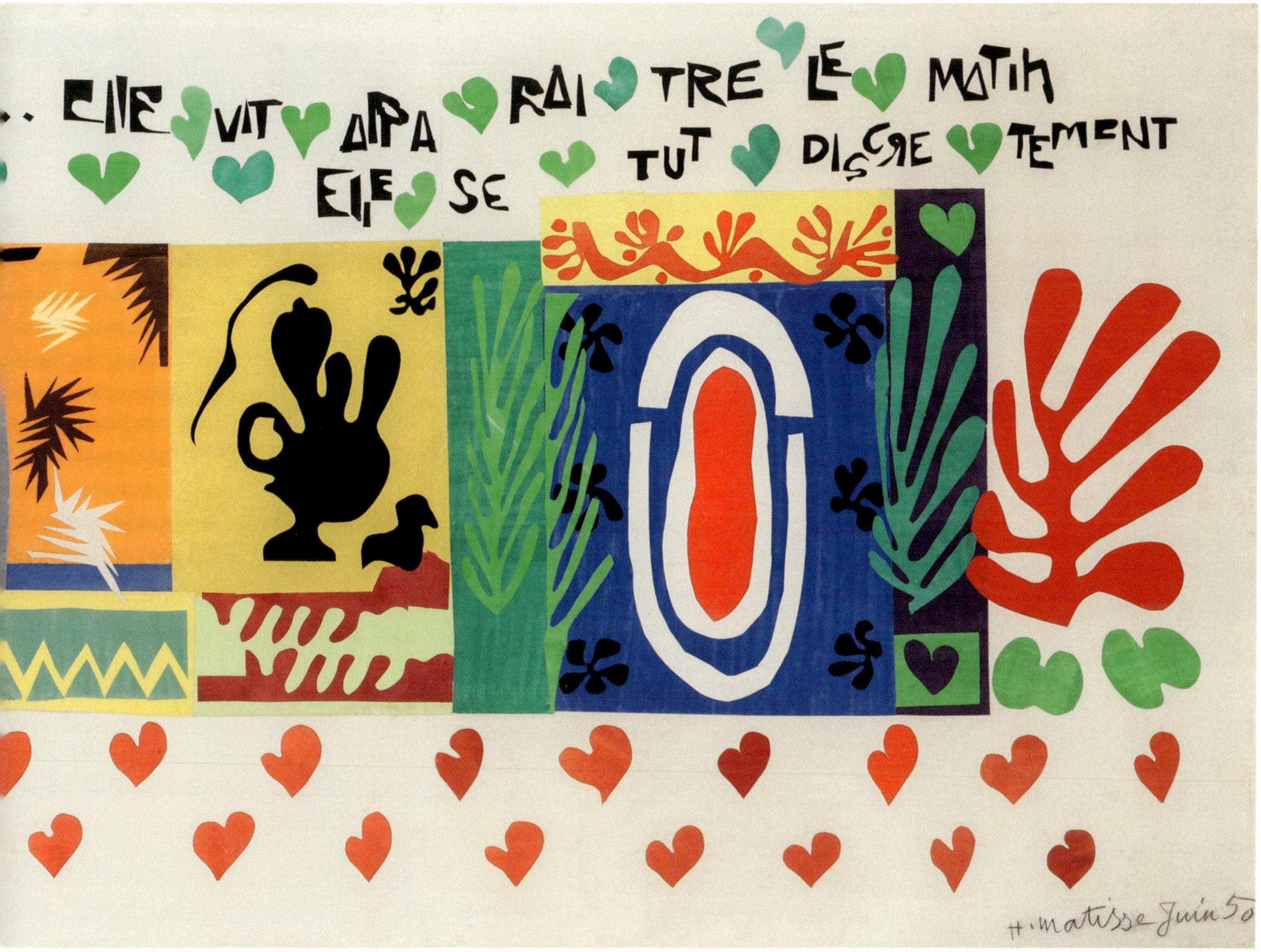

The Magical Creatures of Night

The Thousand and One Nights, like *The Beasts of the Sea* (p. 81), belongs to the group of works conceived as series of panels. There are links between them: Matisse would pin up their component pieces side by side on the wall of his studio in the Hôtel Régina. Like a cartoon strip of the tale improvised by Scheherazade, the successive images follow the narrative order through a night punctuated by the Persian lantern first alight (white on red), then extinguished (black on lemon). The broad ornamental border of hearts tells us clearly that this is a story of love. Deft as he was at using black to create light, Matisse recounts the magical creatures of night in the most dazzling colours.

The Thousand and One Nights, June 1950
Gouache on paper, cut and pasted, and pencil on paper, 139 x 374 cm (54¾ x 147¼ in.)
Pittsburgh, Carnegie Museum of Art,
Acquired through the generosity of the Sarah Mellon Scaife Family

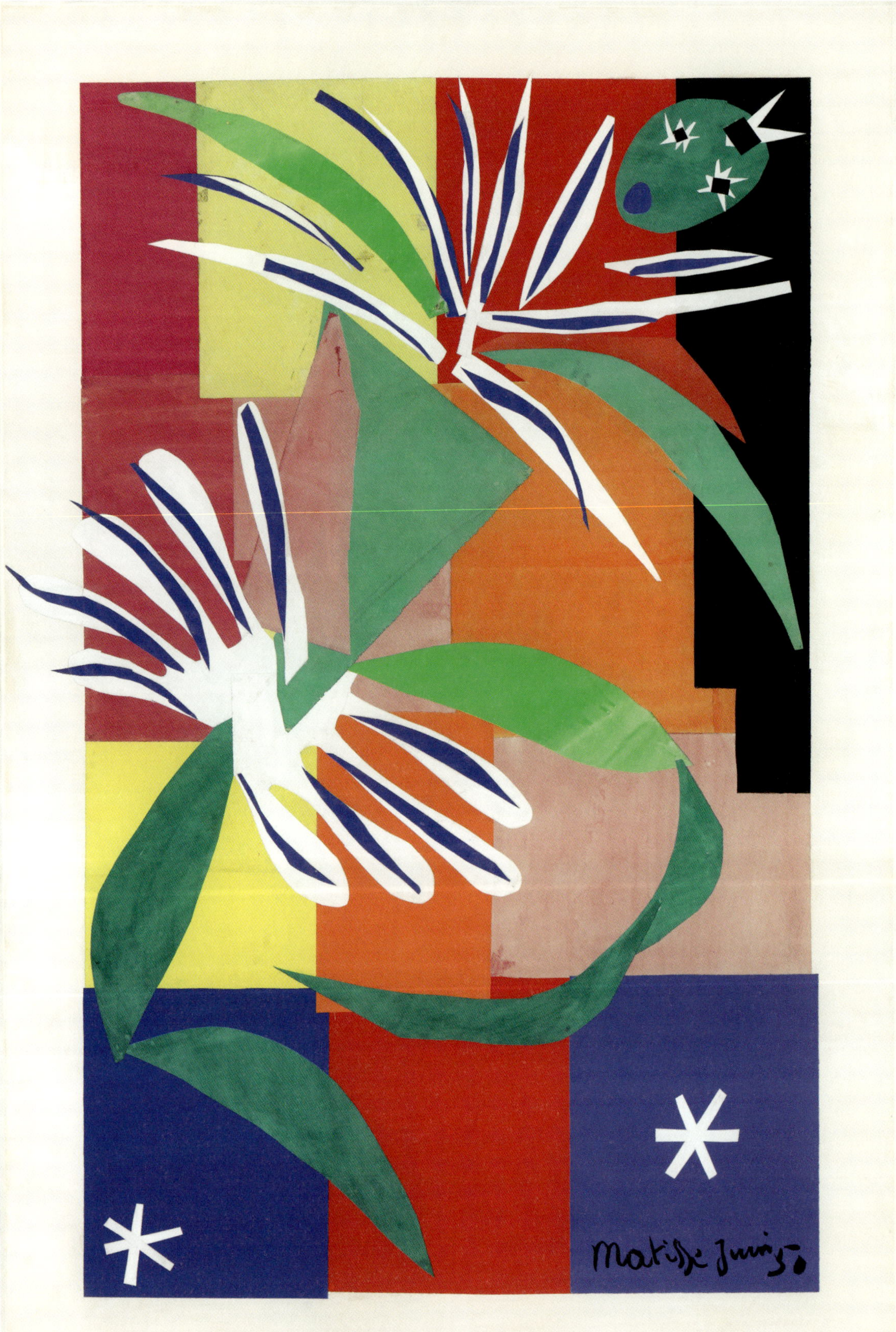
Matisse Juin 50

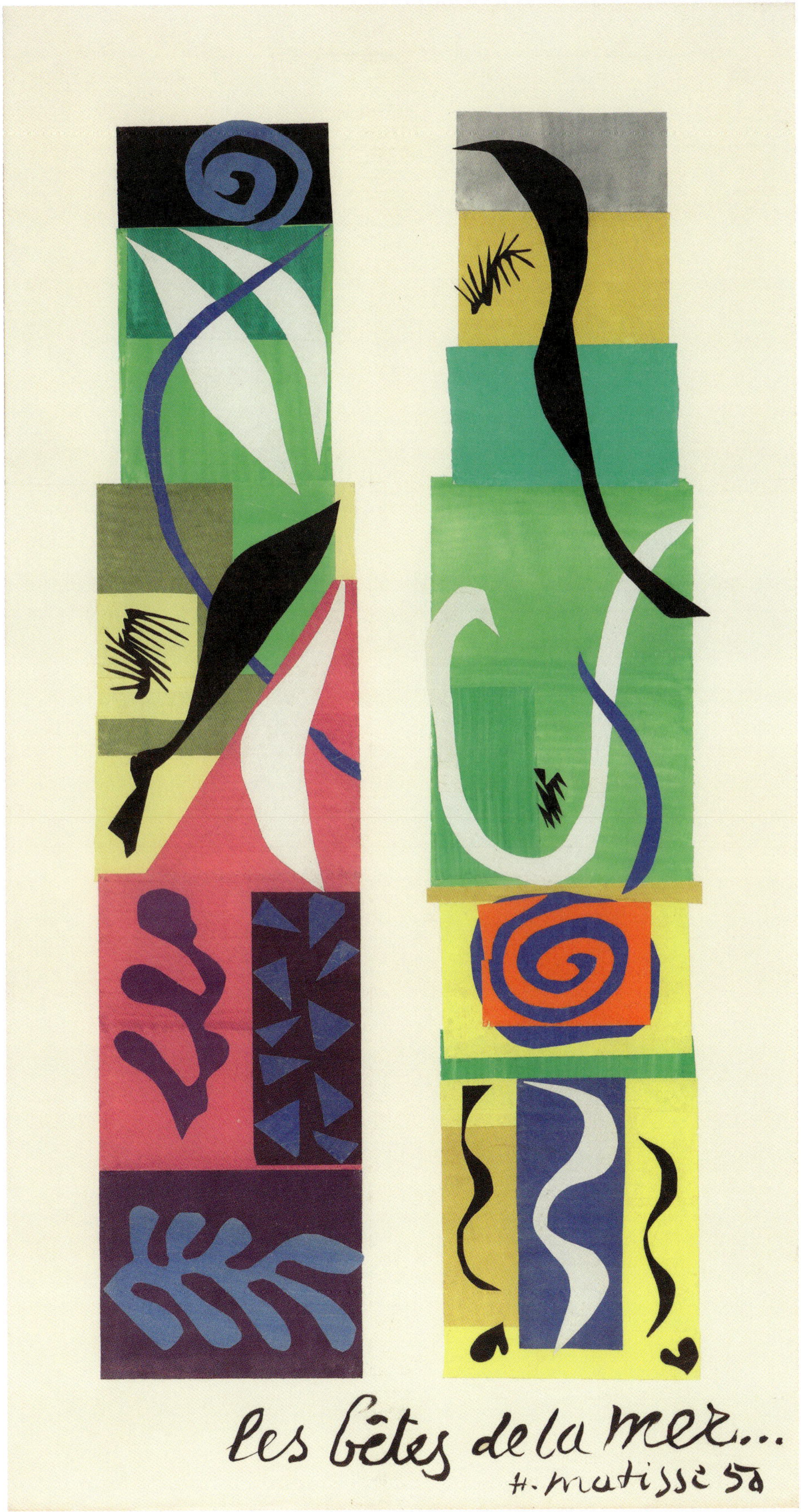

Creole Dancer, 1950
Gouache on paper, cut and pasted
on paper, 205 x 120 cm (80¾ x 47¼ in.)
Nice, Musée Matisse

The Beasts of the Sea, 1950
Gouache on paper, cut and pasted
on paper, 295.5 x 154 cm (116¼ x 60¾ in.)
Lithographic reproduction of the original
paper cut-out
Washington, D.C., National Gallery of Art,
Ailsa Mellon Bruce Fund

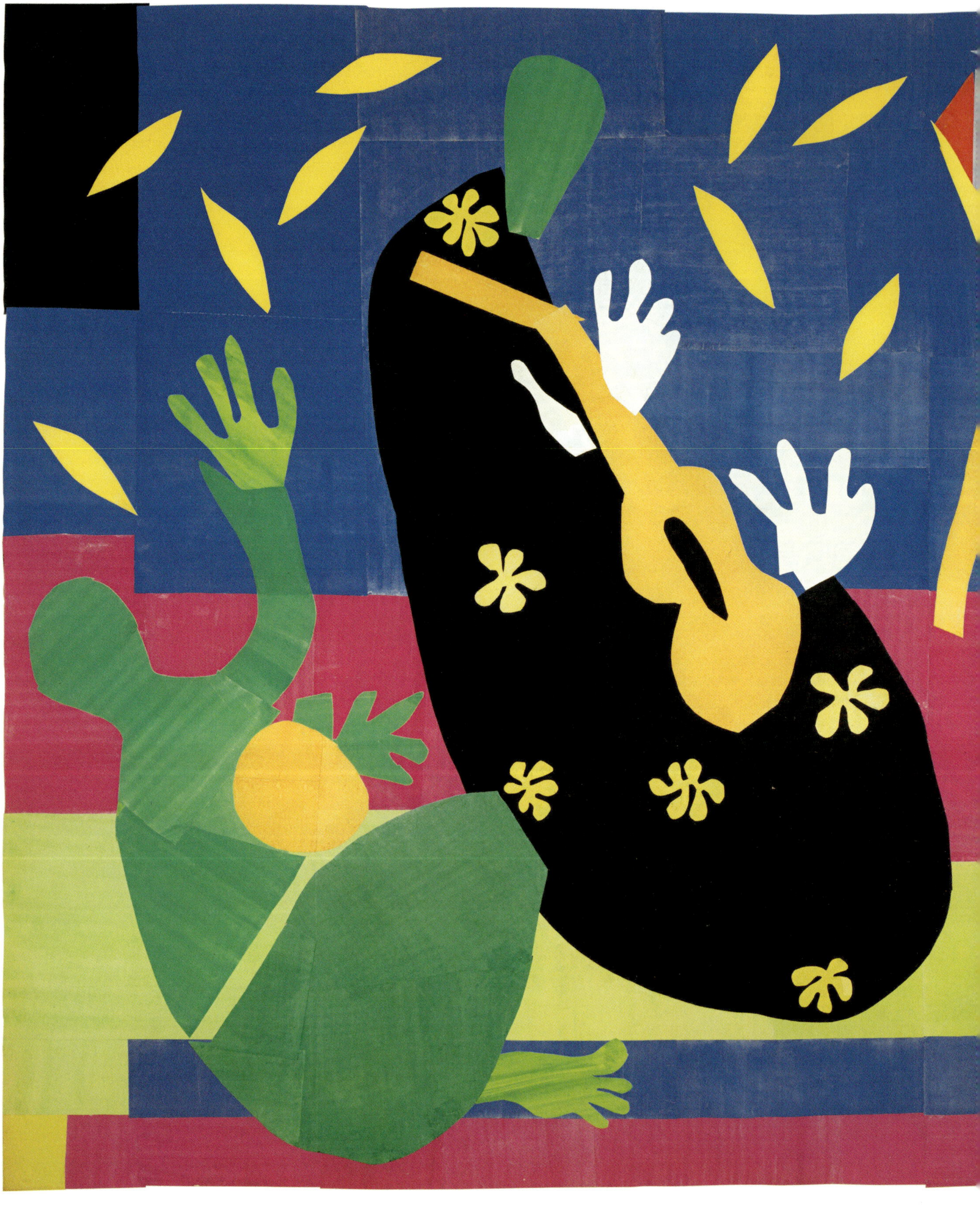

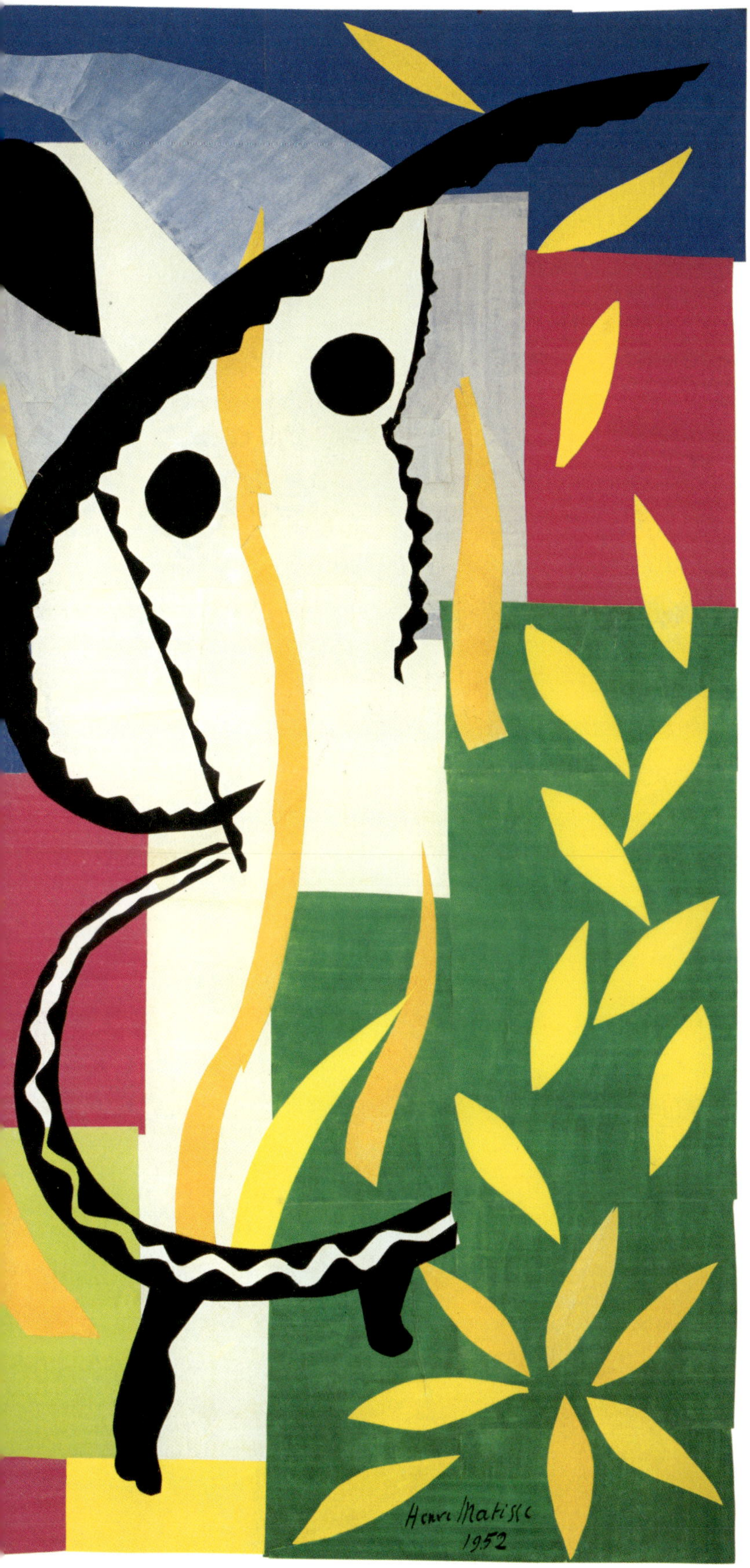

The Sorrows of the King, 1952
Gouache on paper, cut and pasted
on canvas, 292 x 386 cm (115 x 152 in.)
Paris, Musée national d'art moderne,
Centre Pompidou

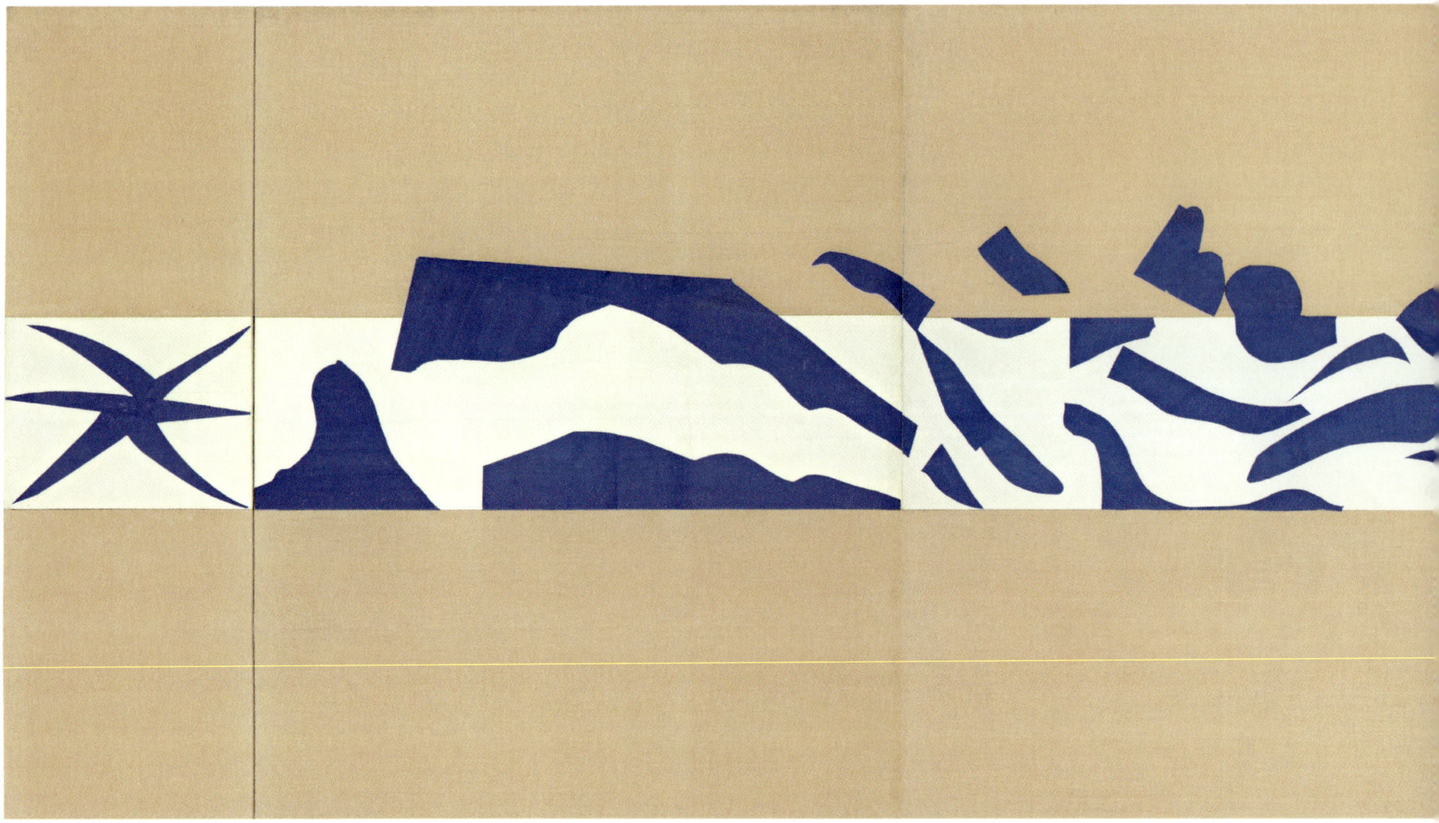

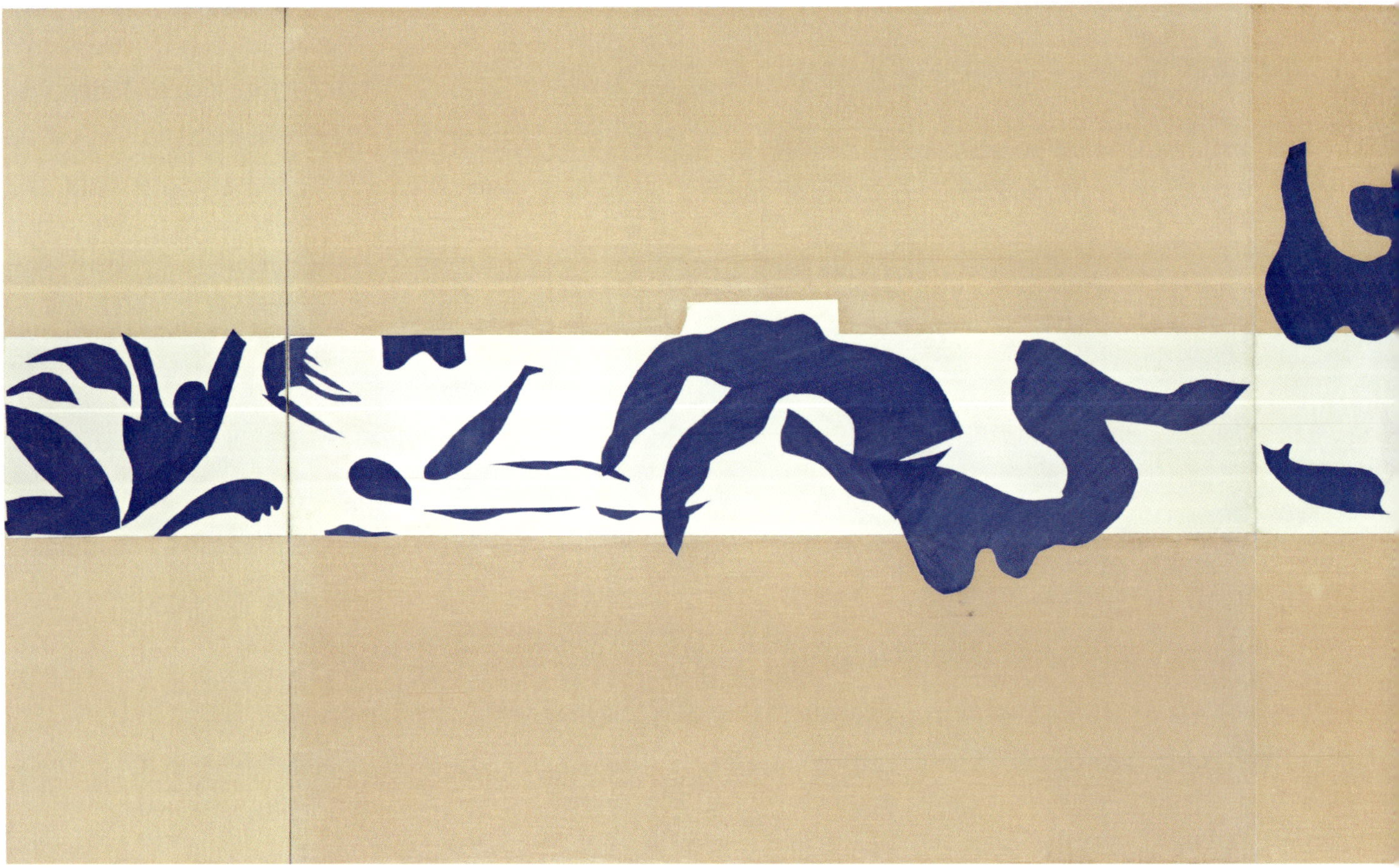

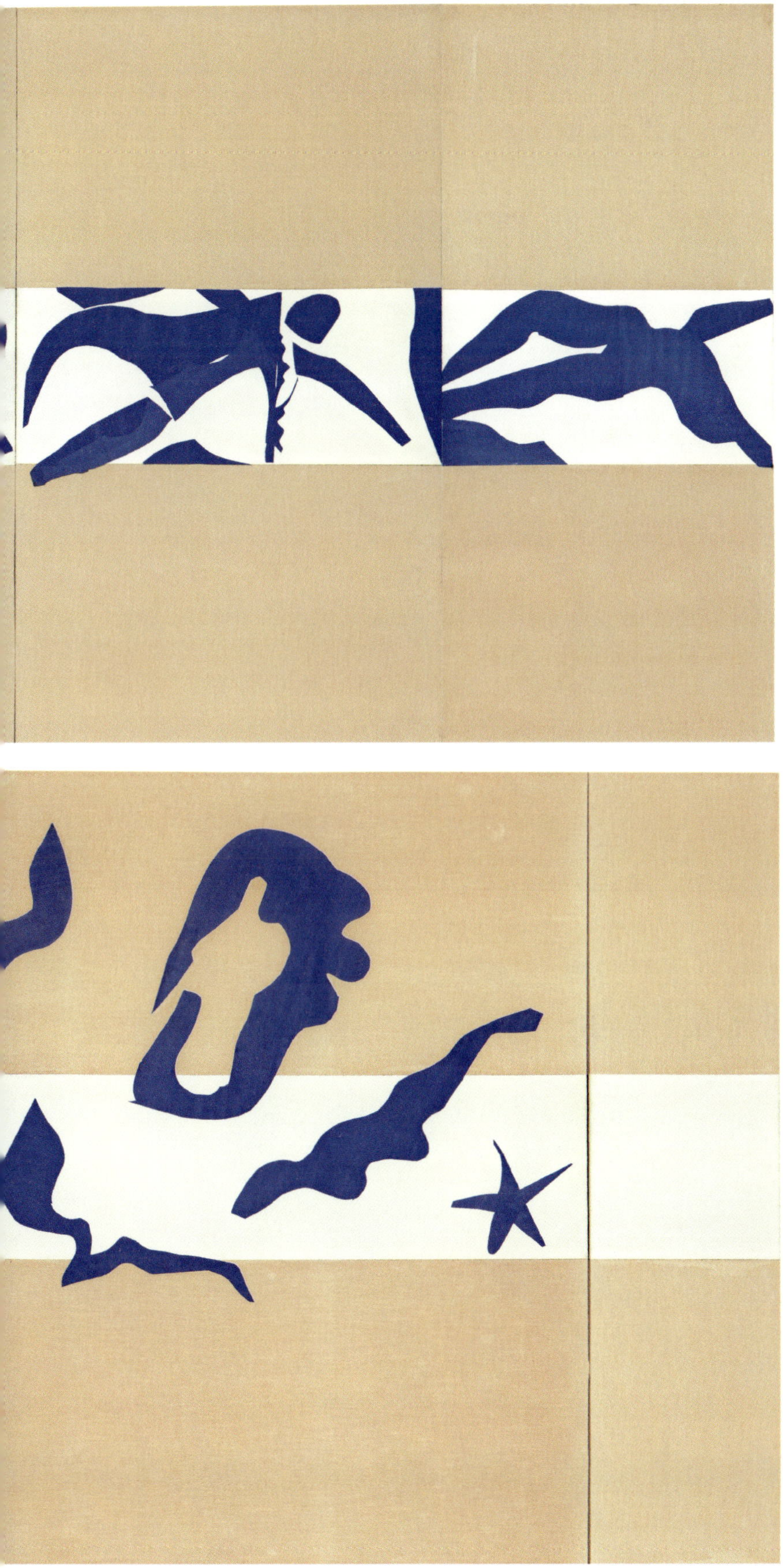

The Swimming Pool, 1952
Nine-panel mural in two parts: gouache on paper, cut and pasted on white painted paper, mounted on burlap
230.1 x 1645 cm (90½ x 647¾ in.)
New York, The Museum of Modern Art, Mrs Bernard F. Gimbel Fund

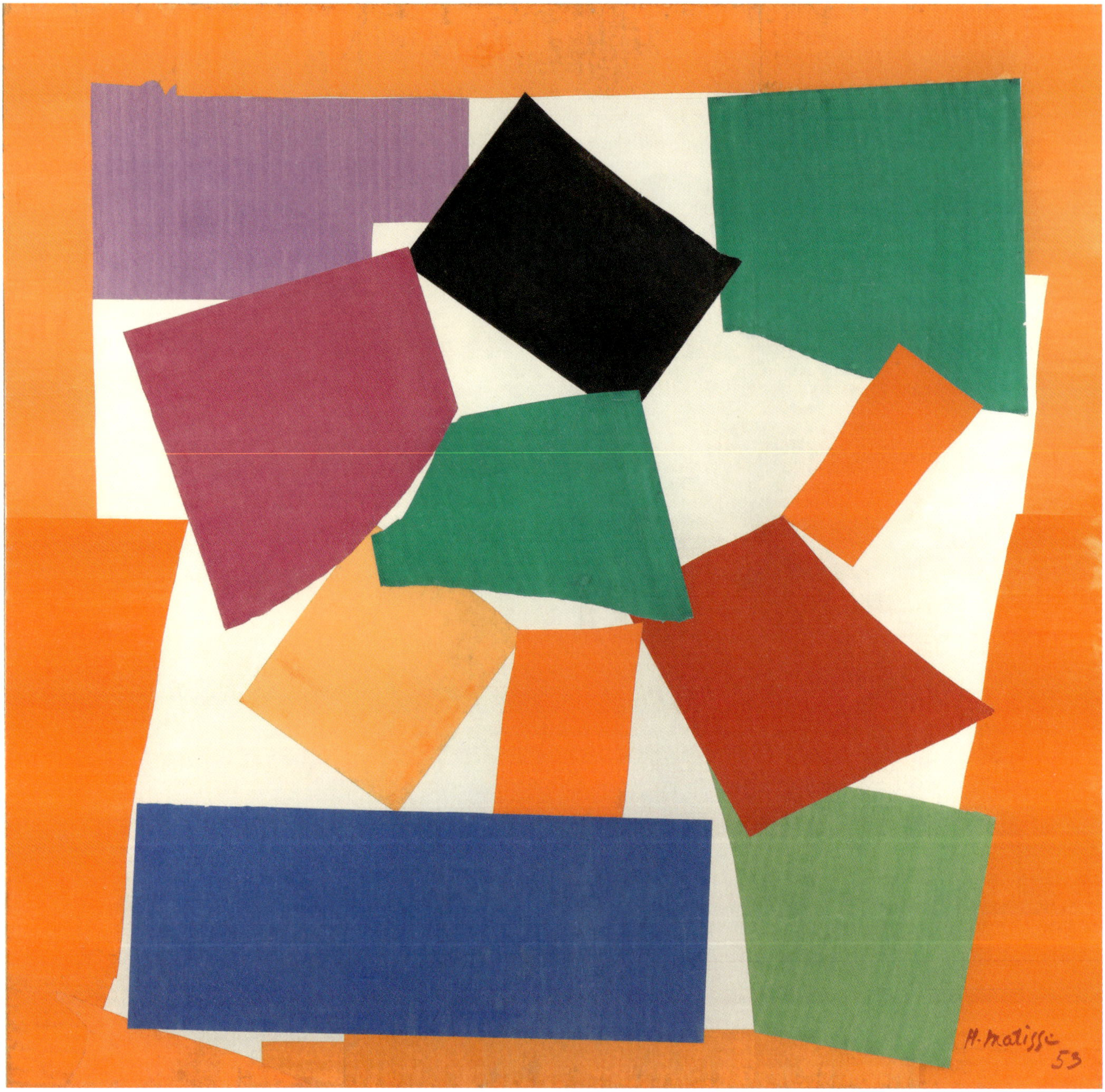

The Snail, 1953
Gouache on paper, cut and pasted
on paper, 286 x 287 cm (112½ x 113 in.)
London, Tate

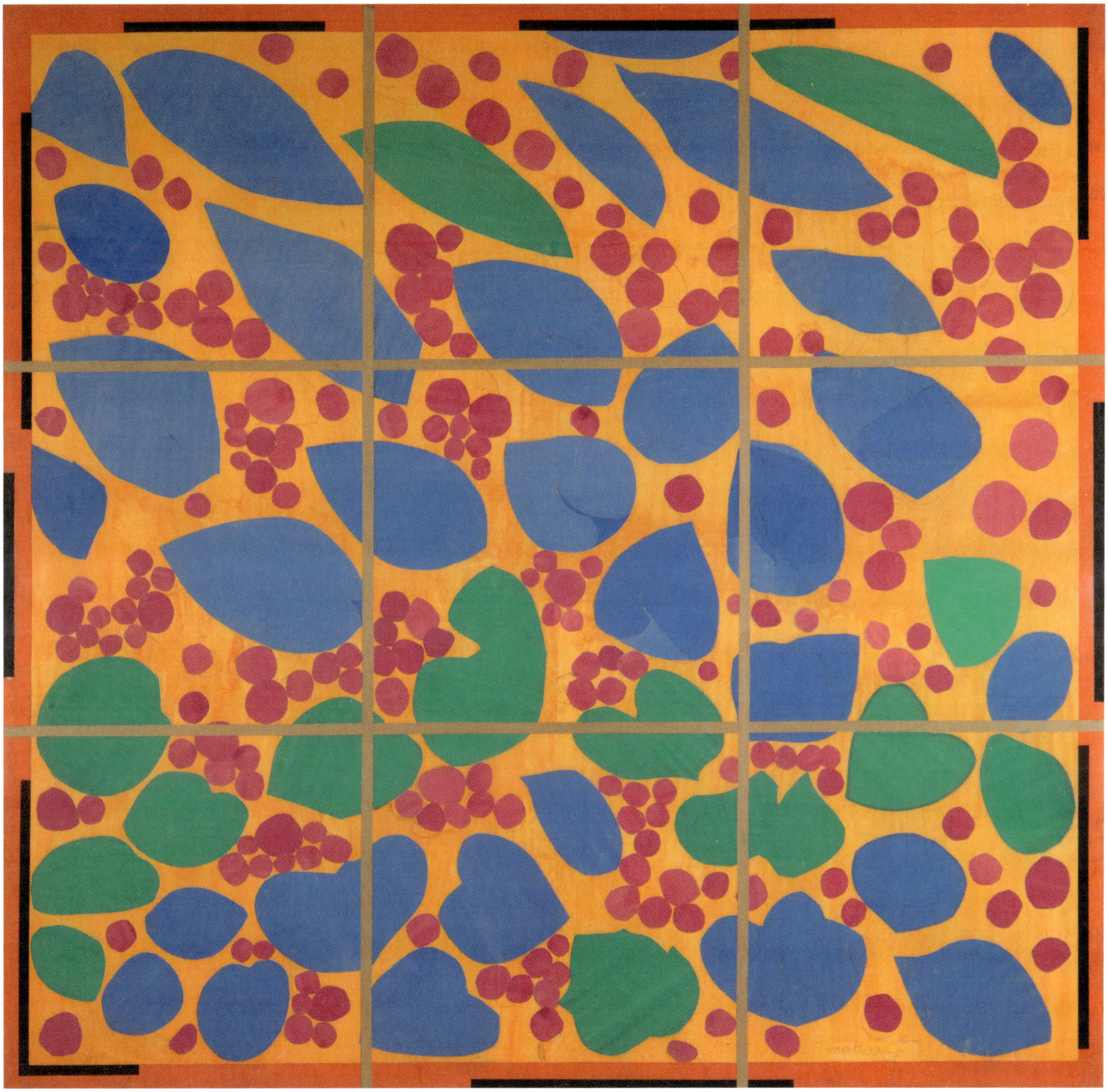

Ivy in Flower, 1953
Maquette for a stained-glass window envisaged for the mausoleum of Albert Lasker
Gouache on paper, cut and pasted, and pencil on paper, 284.5 x 284.5 cm (112 x 112 in.)
Dallas Museum of Art, Foundation for the Arts Collection, Gift of the Albert and Mary Lasker Foundation

"A pair of scissors is a … wonderful instrument … Working with scissors in this paper is an occupation I can lose myself in … My pleasure in cutting things out grows ever greater. Why didn't I think of it earlier? More and more, I feel that one can express with the simplest cut-out what one might want to express as a draughtsman or painter … By entering into the object one comes into one's own. I had to make this budgerigar with coloured paper. Well, I have become a budgie! And in the work, I found myself. The Chinese sage said that one must grow with the tree. I know nothing truer … But I know that only much later will people realize how much what I do today was in accord with the future."

HENRI MATISSE

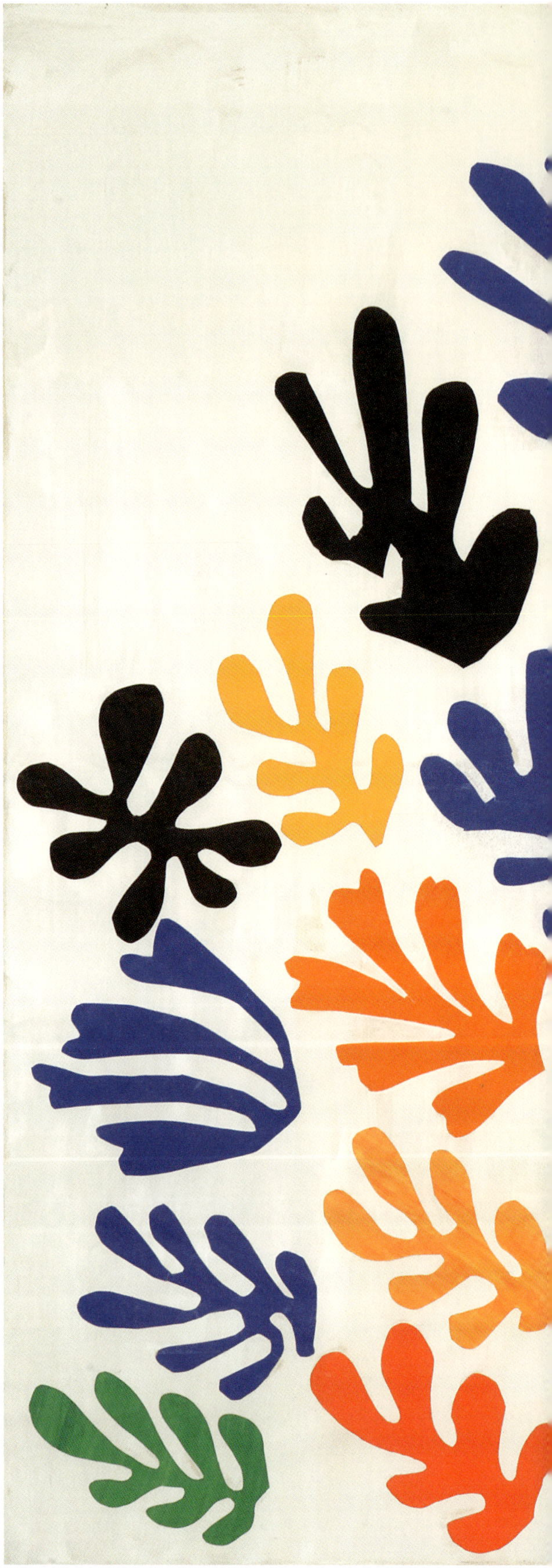

The Sheaf, 1953
Maquette for the ceramic of the same name
Gouache on paper, cut and pasted
on paper, 294 x 350 cm (115¾ x 137¾ in.)
Los Angeles, Hammer Museum, UCLA,
Gift of Mr and Mrs Sidney F. Brody

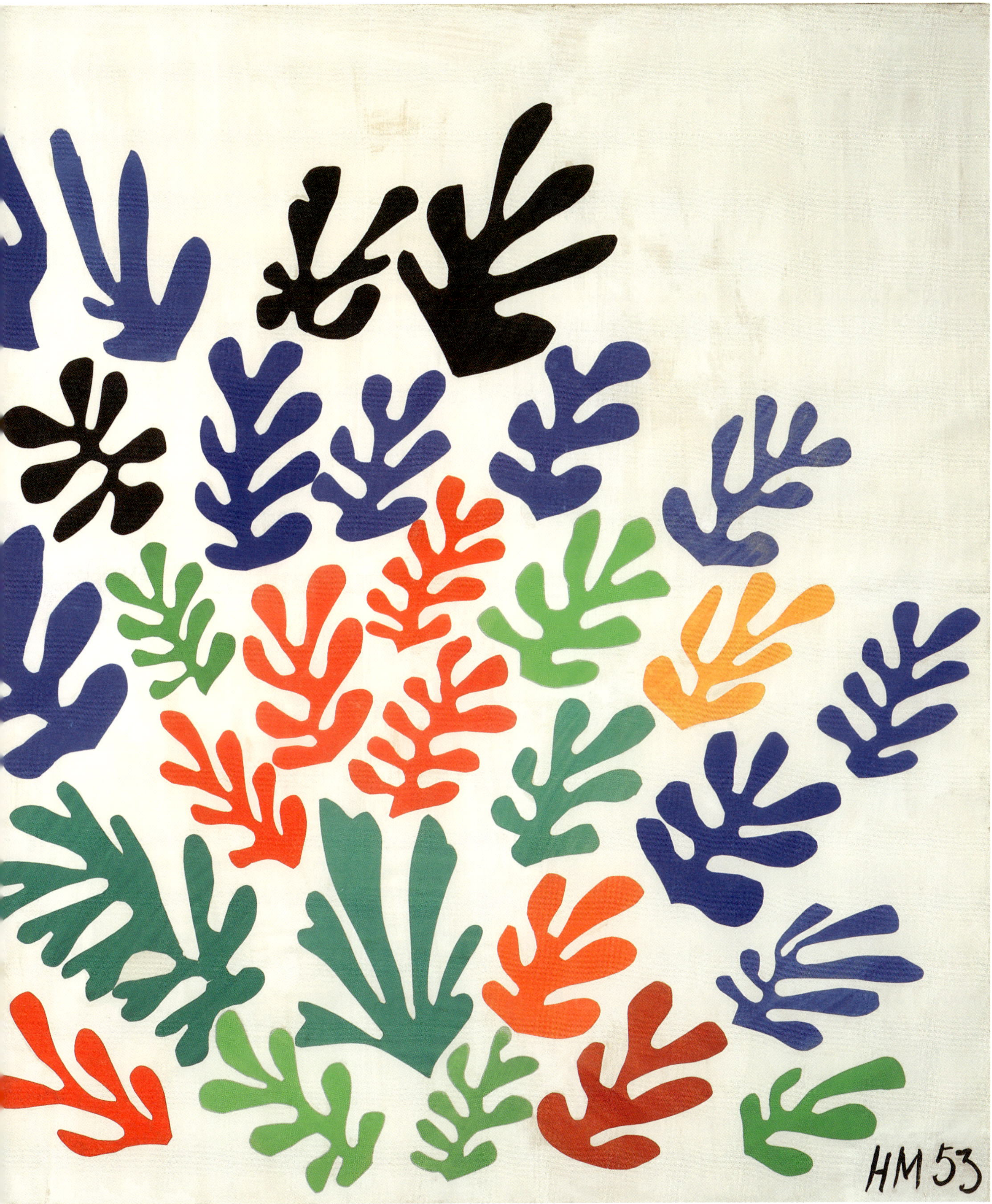
HM 53

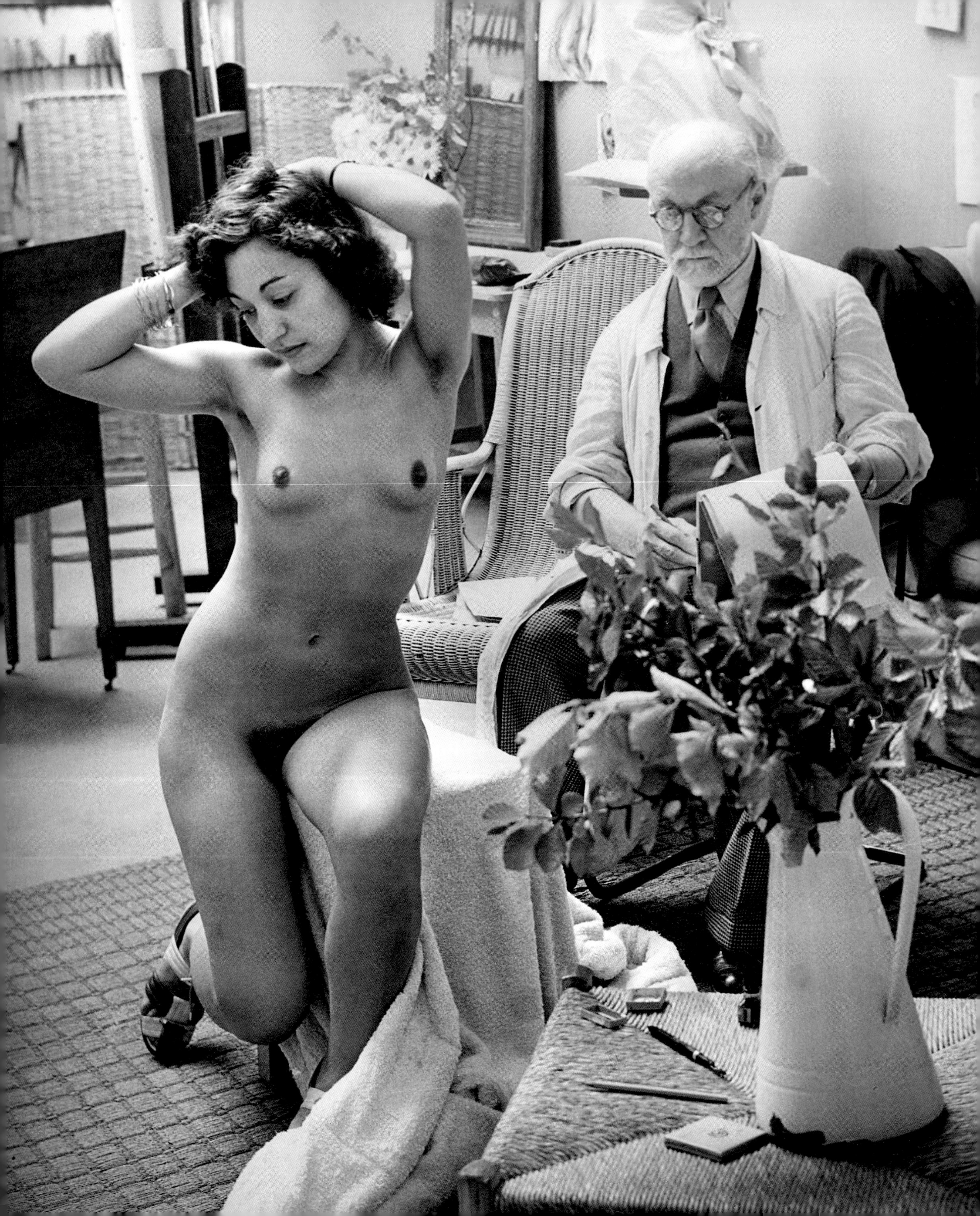

Henri Matisse
1869–1954
Life and Work

1869 Birth of Henri Emile Benoît Matisse at Cateau-Cambrésis on 31 December.

1887 Matisse arrives in Paris to study law.

1889 Takes a job as attorney's clerk in Saint-Quentin.

1890 After an appendectomy, he is confined to bed for months, and begins to draw to entertain himself. Immediately he has recovered, takes drawing lessons at the Maurice-Quentin Delatour School, while returning to Maître Duconseil's legal practice.

1891 Matisse gives up law to devote himself to his art. Moves to Paris and enrols at the Académie Julian where William Adolphe Bouguereau and Louis Ferrier teach.

1892 Leaves the Académie Julian for Gustave Moreau's studio at the École des Beaux-Arts. There meets Georges Rouault, then Charles Camoin and Henri Manguin. He enrols for the École des Arts Décoratifs.

1894 His mistress, Caroline Jobleau, gives birth to a daughter: Marguerite Emilienne.

1895 He is officially admitted to the École des Beaux-Arts and spends the summer at Belle-Île-en-Mer. Visits the Corot and Cézanne exhibitions at Paris.

1896 Exhibits for the first time at the Salon des Cent, organised by *La Plume*, and at the Salon de la Société Nationale des Beaux-Arts of which he is an associate member. The French state buys *Woman Reading* for the Château de Rambouillet. Again spends the summer at Belle-Île and meets the Australian John Russel who introduces him to Rodin and Pissarro. Takes an interest in Impressionist painting.

1897 End of his liaison with Caroline Jobleau. Meets Camille Pissarro; they become friends. *The Sideboard* is exhibited at the Salon de la Société Nationale and much criticised.

1898 He marries Amélie Pareyre and spends several months in London (where he discovers William Turner), in Toulouse, and in Corsica.

1899 After the death of Gustave Moreau, works for a while under the directon of Cormon, and creates his first sculptures. Buys Cézanne's *The Three Bathers*, Gauguin's *Head of a Boy* and a Rodin cast from Ambroise Vollard. Birth of his son Jean.

1900 Major financial problems. Another child is born: Pierre. Matisse works at the Académie de la Grande Chaumière, under the direction of Antoine Bourdelle; also attends the workshop of Eugène Carrière, where he meets André Derain and Jean Puy. His wife opens a fashion boutique.

1901 Exhibits at the Salon des Indépendants. Derain introduces him to Maurice de Vlaminck.

1902 One-man exhibition at Berthe Weill's. Toulouse-Lautrec retrospective at the Salon des Indépendants.

1903 Matisse takes part in the first Salon d'Automne and makes his first etchings. A Gauguin retrospective follows Gauguin's death.

1904 First exhibition at Ambroise Vollard. Spends part of the summer in Saint-Tropez, with Paul Signac and Henri Edmond Cross; paints *Luxe, calme et volupté* (Musée d'Orsay), experimenting with neo-Impressionist technique.

1905 Spends the summer at Collioure with Derain. Exhibiting at the Salon d'Automne, where he, Albert Marquet, de Vlaminck, Derain, Kees van Dongen and others cause uproar with their juxtaposed planes of pure violent colours. The critic Louis Vauxcelles having dubbed them "fauves" ("wild beasts"), the group immediately

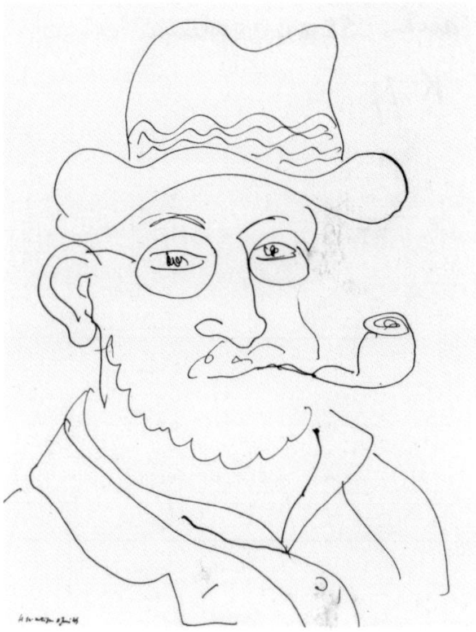

Self-portrait, 1945
Pen and Indian ink, 51.5 x 40.5 cm (20¼ x 16 in.)
Private collection

Brassaï
Matisse and his model at the Villa d'Alésia, Paris, 1939

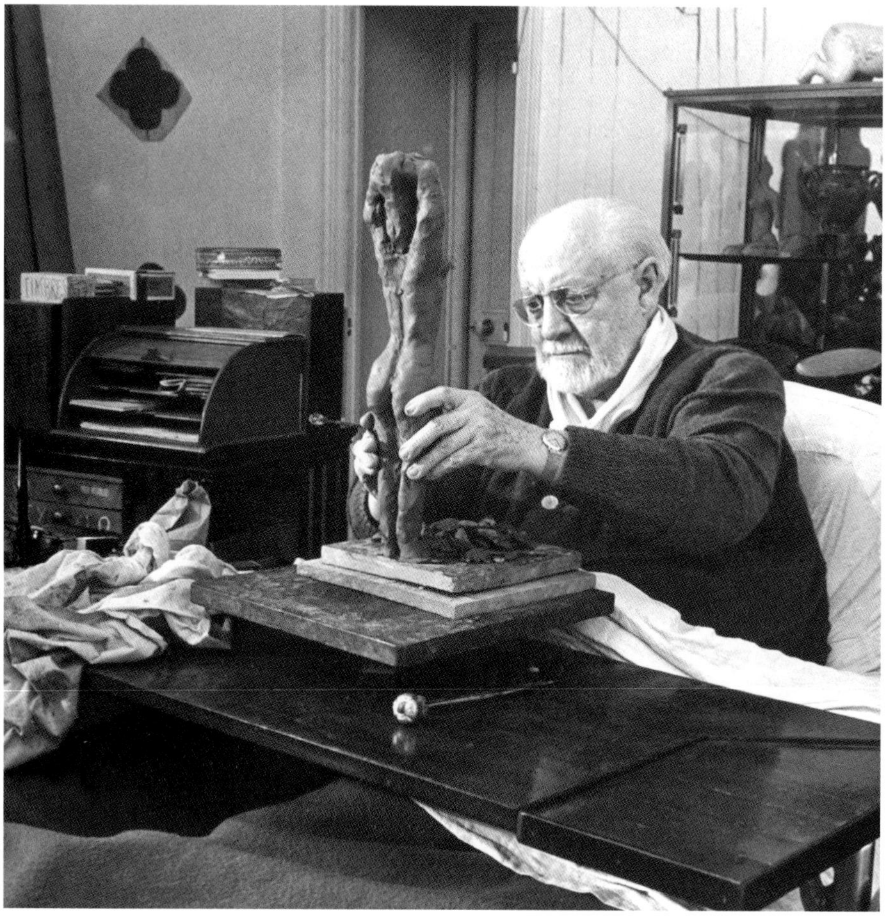

Henri Matisse sculpting a nude female figure, November 1951
Photo: Dmitri Kessel

PAGE 93
Self-portrait, 1934/35
Brush and Indian ink,
24.2 x 20.3 cm (9½ x 8 in.)
Private collection

adopts the term in defiance. Matisse meets the Stein family, who buy *Woman with Hat*, the painting that triggered the scandal. Signac buys *Luxe, calme et volupté*.

1906 Takes part in the Salon de la Libre Esthétique in Brussels and a further Fauve exhibition at the Salon d'Automne. Matisse meets Pablo Picasso at Gertrude Stein's; Picasso shows him an African sculpture which was to influence *Les Demoiselles d'Avignon*.

1907 Travels in Italy with Leo and Gertrude Stein. Exchanges pictures with Picasso, who is working on *Les Demoiselles d'Avignon*.

1908 Starts an open drawing course at the Convent des Oiseaux, then at the Hôtel de Biron, to which foreign students come in droves. The class closes in 1911. Exhibits at the first Golden Fleece Salon in Moscow. Publishes "Notes of a Painter" in *La Grande Revue*.

1909 Exhibition of his works in Berlin, in the gallery of Paul Cassirer. The Russian collector Sergei Shchukin commissions two large decorative panels: *The Dance* and *The Music*.

1910 First major exhibition, at the Bernheim-Jeune gallery in Paris. Visits Munich with Marquet for the Islamic art exhibition, then travels in Spain. First exhibitions in London and New York.

1911 On Shchukin's invitation, goes to New York to be present at the installation of *The Dance* and *The Music*; discovers Russian icons, which become a great source of inspiration.

1912 Twice travels in Morocco with Marquet and Camoin.

1913 Some works by Matisse are exhibited at the Armory Show in New York and at the Berlin Sezession.

1914 Moves to Collioure with his family. Marquet joins them; they meet Juan Gris, to whom Matisse is of financial assistance. Matisse takes violin lessons. Paints *Notre-Dame* and *French Windows at Collioure*.

1916 Spends part of the winter at Nice. In Paris, takes part in a banquet given in honour of the "assassinated" poet Guillaume Apollinaire. Exhibition in London.

1918 Matisse decides to remain on the Côte d'Azur, which he considers a "paradise". Meets Renoir at Cagnes. Exhibits with Picasso at the Galérie Paul Guillaume.

1919 Igor Stravinsky and Sergei Diaghilev request costumes and décor for *The Song of the Nightingale,* choreographed by Léonide Massine for the Ballets Russes, and performed in London. *The Black Table* with Antoinette for model.

1920 Marcel Sembat publishes the first monograph on Matisse. Décor and costumes for *Song of the Nightingale* performed by Diaghilev's Ballets Russes. Summer in London, then in Etretat.

1922 Series of *Odalisques*.

1923 Exhibition at the Galérie Paul Guillaume.

1924 Exhibition in New York, retrospective in Copenhagen.

1925 Exhibits several works at the Exposition internationale des Arts décoratifs et industriels modernes. Made Chevalier de la Légion d'honneur. *Decorative Figure on Ornamental Background*.

1927 In New York, Matisse retrospective (1890–1926) organized by his son Pierre at the Valentine Gallery. Receives the Carnegie Prize at Pittsburgh.

1930 In the USA, Matisse meets Dr Albert Coombs Barnes, who commissions a large decorative mural for his museum. Ends his trip with a stay in Tahiti.

1931 Retrospective at the Museum of Modern Art, New York. Albert Skira asks him to illustrate works by Stéphane Mallarmé.

1933 Returns to the USA for the installation of *The Dance* at Merion. Meets Fernand Léger.

1934 He works on illustrations to James Joyce's *Ulysses*.

1935 Matisse's assistant Lydia Delectorskaya becomes his model, in particular for *The Dream* and *Pink Nude*. Visits Pierre Bonnard at Cannel.

1936 The Paris municipality buys the first version of *The Dance*, through the good offices of Raymond Escholier, Director of the Petit Palais.

1937 He starts work on the costumes and décor of *L'Étrange Farandole* (or *Red and Black)* for the Ballets Russes of Monte Carlo. For the first time, he uses the technique of cutting out gouached paper for certain of the maquettes.

1939 Lavishes praise on Jean Renoir for his film *La Règle du jeu.*

1940 Decides to remain in France. Separates from Amélie. Paints *The Romanian Shirt* and *The Dream.*

1941 Ill with cancer, he enters the Clinic du Parc in Lyon. Suggests illustrating the *Amours* of Pierre de Ronsard to Skira. Meets Aragon and Elsa Triolet.

1942 His nurse, Monique Bourgeois – later Sister Jacques-Marie – becomes his model. He uses the technique of cut-outs and starts the *Jazz* series, published in 1947. On the evacuation of Nice, goes to Vence.

1943 Moves permanently to Vence, to the Villa "Le Rêve", where he lives till 1948.

1944 Madame Matisse is imprisoned and his daughter deported for acts of resistance.

1945 Major retrospective at the Salon d'Automne. The French state buys six paintings for the new Musée d'Art Moderne. Exhibits with Picasso at the Victoria and Albert Museum, London. Exhibits recent pictures, with photographs of their successive stages, at the Maeght Gallery.

1946 Maquettes for the tapestries *Polynesia, the Sky* and *Polynesia, the Sea.*

1947 Made Commandeur de la Légion d'honneur. First meeting with the Dominican friar Rayssiguier concerning the decoration of the Chapelle du Rosaire at Vence. Deaths of Bonnard and Marquet.

1948 Devotes himself to the decoration of the Chapelle du Rosaire.

1950 Matisse receives First Prize at the XXVth Venice Biennale where he is the French representative.

1951 The Chapelle du Rosaire at Vence is consecrated. Léger designs the stained-glass windows of the church of Andincourt. Exhibitions at the Museum of Modern Art, New York, at Cleveland, Chicago, San Francisco and Tokyo.

1952 Inauguration of the Musée Matisse at Cateau-Cambrésis, the town of his birth. Creates *The Sorrows of the King* and the series of *Blue Nudes.*

1954 Alberto Giacometti draws a dozen portraits of Matisse for the Monnaie de Paris. Matisse dies 3 November at Nice and is buried in the Cimiez cemetery in a plot donated by the town.

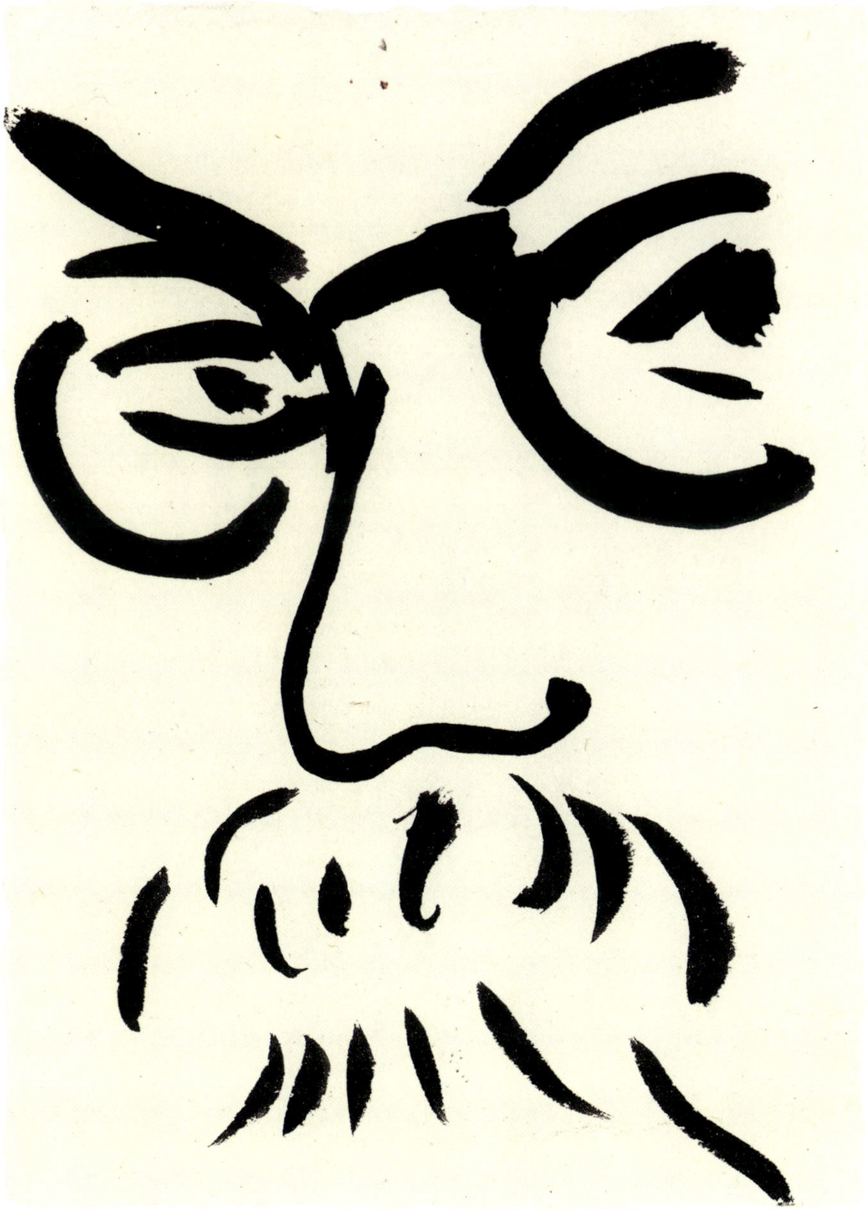

PAGE 94
The Sculpture of Henri Matisse, 1952
Poster for the exhibition at the Tate, London
82 x 57.5 cm (32¼ x 22¾ in.)

PAGE 95
Madame de Pompadour, 1951
Poster for the ball of the École des Arts Décoratifs at Paris
Gouache on paper, cut and pasted, and Indian ink on paper,
88.9 x 73.7 cm (35 x 29 in.)
Los Angeles County Museum of Art, Gift of Mrs Sidney F. Brody

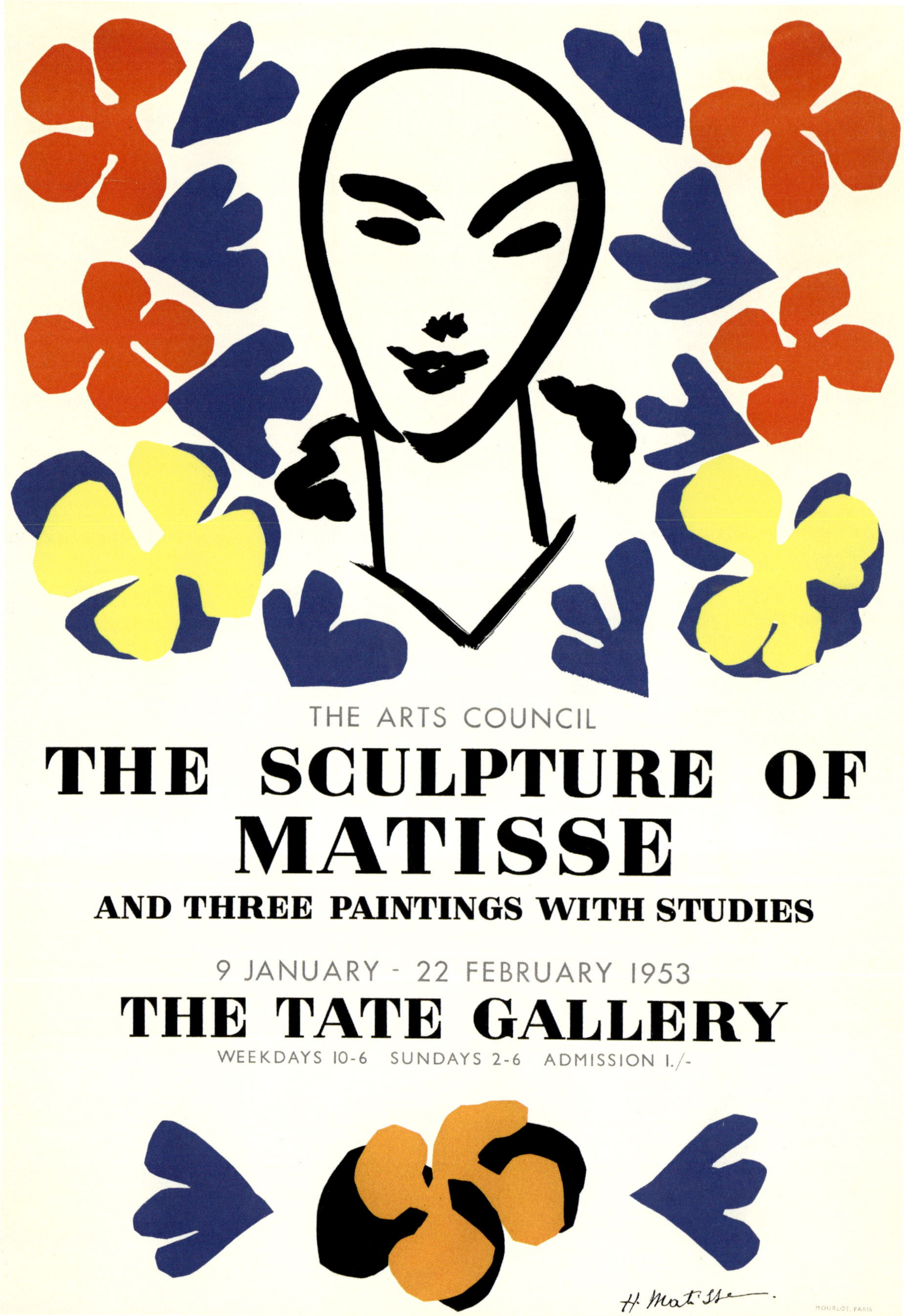
THE ARTS COUNCIL
THE SCULPTURE OF
MATISSE
AND THREE PAINTINGS WITH STUDIES
9 JANUARY - 22 FEBRUARY 1953
THE TATE GALLERY
WEEKDAYS 10-6 SUNDAYS 2-6 ADMISSION 1./-
H. Matisse

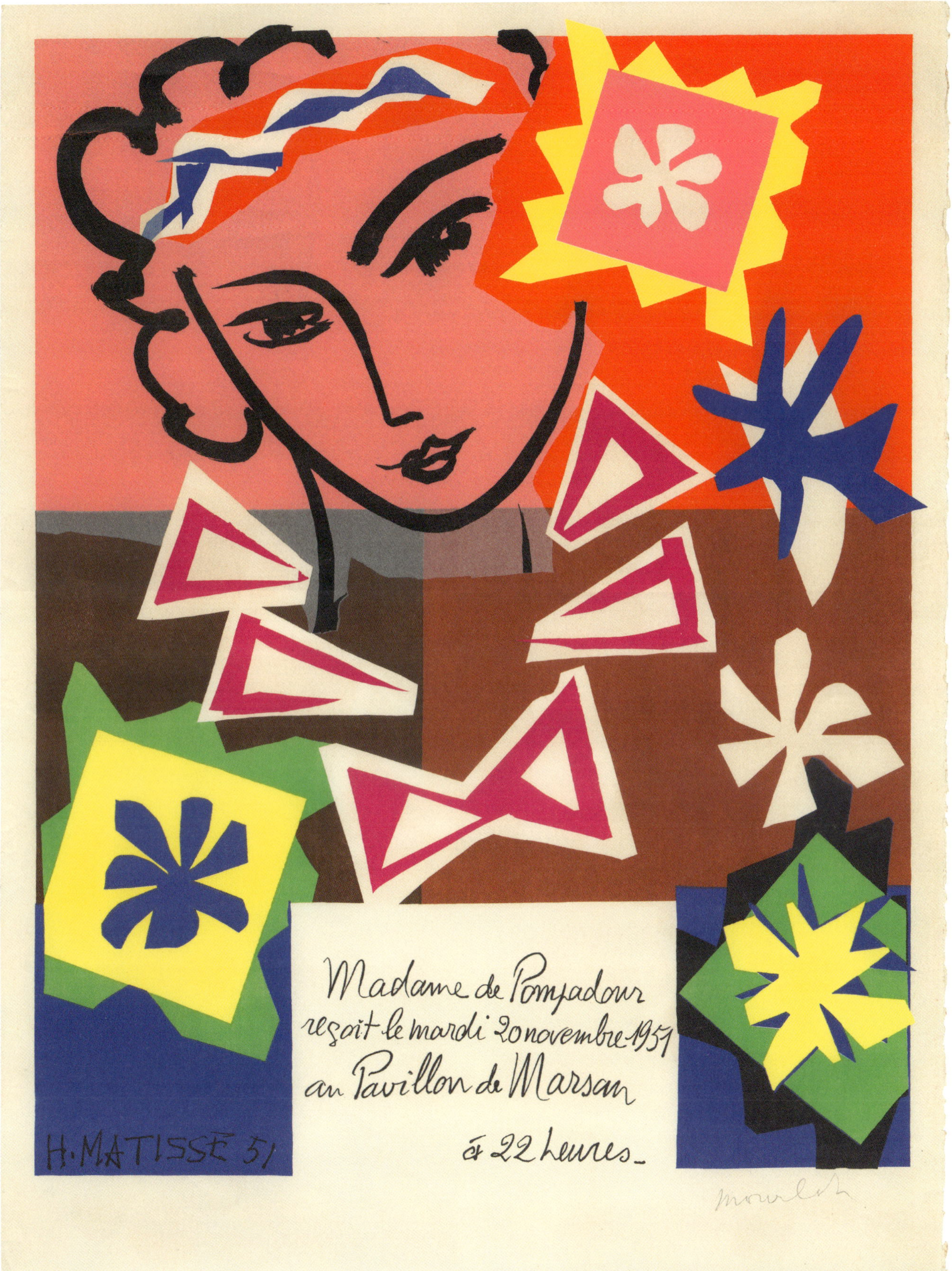
Madame de Pompadour
reçoit le mardi 20 novembre 1951
au Pavillon de Marsan
à 22 heures
H. MATISSE 51

Copyright

Photo credits

The publisher would like to thank the Succession H. Matisse for its invaluable help. All reproductions come from the Archives Matisse, with the exception of:

© akg-images/Bianconero: 7, 54
© bpk | Nationalgalerie, SMB, Museum Berggruen | Jens Ziehe: 94
© Cliché Documentation générale du Centre Pompidou, MNAM © Fonds Hélène Adant, Bibliothèque Kandinsky, centre de recherche et de documentation, MNAM / CCI, Centre G. Pompidou, Paris: 17, 94
© Getty Images / Time Life Pictures, Photo © Dmitri Kessel: 59, 92
© Musée National d'Art Moderne, Centre Pompidou, Paris: 67 left
© National Gallery of Art Washington, Image © Bord of Trustees: 14/15
© CNAC / MNAM Dist. RMN: 28, 33, 39, 69, 82/83
© RMN, Paris – Gérard Blot: 50
Musei Vaticani, Rome: 58
© Photo: Lydia Delectorskaya: 2, back cover
© RMN – Henri del Olmo: 60
© Rheinisches Bildarchiv, Cologne: 64, 74/75
© Roger-Viollet, Paris: 8/9 top
The Phillips Collection, Washington: 12 top
© Stedelijk Museum, Amsterdam: 72/73
© The Museum of Modern Art, New York/ Scala, Florence. Digital Image: 12, 51, 84/85
Archives of the author: 12 bottom, 13 right, 38, 90

The author

Gilles Néret (1933–2005) was an art historian, journalist, writer and museum correspondent. He organised several art retrospectives in Japan and founded the SEIBU Museum and the Wildenstein Gallery in Tokyo. He directed art reviews such as *L'Œil* and *Connaissance des Arts* and received the Élie Faure Prize in 1981 for his publications. His TASCHEN titles include *Salvador Dalí: The Paintings*, *Matisse*, and *Erotica Universalis.*

FRONT COVER
Dancer, 1937–38
Study for the curtain of the ballet *L'Étrange Farandole*
Gouache on paper, cut and pasted on paper, 61 x 61 cm (24 x 24 in.)
Private collection
Lithographic reproduction of the original paper cut-out

BACK COVER AND PAGE 2
Henri Matisse working on the monumental cut-outs, Cimiez-Nice 1952
Photo: Lydia Delectorskaya

PAGE 4
Verve, No. 23, 1949
Front cover: *Cœur d'amour épris*
Drawing and handwritten text by Matisse for *Jazz*

Imprint

EACH AND EVERY TASCHEN BOOK PLANTS A SEED!
Each year, we offset our annual carbon emissions with carbon credits at the Instituto Terra, a reforestation program in Minas Gerais, Brazil, founded by Lélia and Sebastião Salgado. To find out more about this ecological partnership, please check: www.taschen.com/institutoterra.
Inspiration: unlimited.
Carbon footprint: (almost) zero.

Want to see more? Visit *taschen.com* to view our current publications, browse our latest magazine, and subscribe to our newsletter.

Hohenzollernring 53, D–50672 Köln
www.taschen.com

Original edition:

English translation: Chris Miller, Oxford

Printed in Bosnia-Herzegovina
ISBN 978-3-8365-3427-7